MOVERS
& SHAKERS

Also by Terry Coleman

Fiction
A Girl for the Afternoons
Southern Cross
Thanksgiving

Non-fiction
The Railway Navvies
Providence and Mr Hardy (with Lois Deacon)
The Only True History
Passage to America
The Liners
The Scented Brawl

MOVERS
& SHAKERS

CONVERSATIONS
WITH
UNCOMMON MEN

TERRY COLEMAN

Introduction by
ALISTAIR COOKE

ANDRE DEUTSCH

For Eliza and Jack

First published in Great Britain 1987 by
André Deutsch Limited
105-106 Great Russell Street London WC1B 3LJ

British Library Cataloguing in Publication Data

Coleman, Terry
  Movers & shakers : conversations with
  uncommon men.
  1. Interviews
  I. Title
  920'.009'048   CT105

  ISBN 0 233 98166 7

Set by Action Typesetting Ltd., Gloucester
Printed and bound in Great Britain by
Ebenezer Baylis Ltd, Worcester

Acknowledgements

These interviews were written for the *Guardian*. I thank the editor, Peter Preston, and the features editor, Richard Gott, on whose pages they first appeared. I owe a particular debt to David McKie, a man with the deepest knowledge and gentlest judgment of politicians, whose advice I have often sought. Then there are four men whose kindnesses in early days I have never forgotten – John Anderson, Gerard Fay, Philip Hope-Wallace, and John Rosselli, all of the *Manchester Guardian*, who by their example and their spirit helped to civilise those who had the good fortune to know them.

Also, together with the publisher, I should like to thank the Estate of Richard Church for permission to quote from his *Collected Poems*, Faber and Faber Ltd for permission to quote from *High Windows* by Philip Larkin, and the Rt. Hon. Enoch Powell for his kind permission to quote from 'The Wedding Gift'.

—T.F.C.

Contents

Introduction

The Art of Interviewing
by Alistair Cooke

This introduction must be unique, in that it was not solicited by the author or the publisher. It was solicited by me.

For years now, whenever a Terry Coleman interview appeared in the *Guardian*, it was the first thing I turned to. Since this is an instinctive act, not performed after due consideration of everything else in the paper, it is the most genuine compliment a reader can pay a writer. It implies not just that the man is – as patronising critics say – 'highly readable' but that there is nobody like him. Only lately, after reading the marvellously sustained character sketch of Roy Hattersley, a piece penetrating, racy, mischievous but devoid of meanness, did I first wonder why there has never been a Coleman collection of interviews and then dare to demand one. The man has been at it for years, and he has made an art form out of a literary convention by now so humdrum that we take it for granted as we take for granted accountants, carpenters, civil servants – artisans of necessary crafts requiring diligence and some training, to be sure, but not calling for noticeable originality.

The celebrity interview is, in fact, fairly new. I may be wrong about the time it developed from a question tossed at a politican into a private audience but I am not aware that there was ever a published interview with Gladstone or W.G. Grace or, coming nearer our time, even with Lloyd George or Jack Hobbs. The only ones I remember from boyhood were reverential sessions with touring actor managers like Sir Frank Benson or Martin Harvey; Noël Coward at home, with everything in its anticipated place – the grand piano, the dressing gown, the simmering cigarette in its mother-of-pearl holder. And I recall gabby monologues by Bernard Shaw, with the interviewer playing monosyllabic straight man. But these were only intermittently, when at all, interviews, rather acts of obeisance, eager confirmations of the fan's stereotype.

In the mid-twenties, however, there appeared a collection of interviews by, of all improbable pioneers, Beverley Nichols. I remember the ones he did with George Gershwin and Al Capone in which, for the first time in my experience, anyway, an attempt was made to recognise the double image of the private and the public man, or to watch them merge into focus. The aim was implicit in the title: 'Are They The Same At Home?' Looked over sixty years later, I doubt they'd be any great shakes as psychographs, but they broke new ground. The interviewer emerged as a connoisseur of character as well as respectful admirer.

We have come so far that now we have television interviews with the royals, in which we expect to hear, and them to disclose, the worrisome details of their 'jobs'. (The mere suggestion of an interview, in any medium, with George V would have sent the mind reeling backwards and the monarch himself discharging a salvo of quarterdeck obscenities.) The interview has become a standard journalistic chore almost as peremptory as a subpoena, expecting the cooperation, however huffy, of everyone from prime ministers to rock stars. And in the past thirty years or so the job has been greatly eased by the invention of the tape recorder. Yet, there are still interviewers, and gifted ones, who forego this blessing. A mistake. I myself have been the victim of many interviews by intelligent and amiable journalists who, knowing no shorthand, scribble notes and what they take to be 'meaningful phrases' – rarely, I noticed, when they were amused. (Jokes are never meaningful except from professional comedians.) They then return to the office and exercise what they like to fancy as total recall, and you come out sounding like the Pentagon or an inter-office memo. In print, the dates, places and sequence of events can come out wrong, and the anecdotes scrambled.

But Mr Coleman's tape recorder is not only a reference check. Through watchful editing of the raw material, it becomes a delineator of how one man's conversational style differs from another's. A fairly obvious differentiation, but without a taped record it tends to be obliterated in direct proportion to the literary talents of the interviewer. I can think of one American, all of whose subjects – whether novelists or jazz drummers – wind up in print talking in the interviewer's own graceful, highly literary style. Furthermore, Mr Coleman has a gift which I don't think can be acquired, because it is born in natural mimics and is the one gift essential to literary parodists: it is the gift of adjusting his own talking and writing style to accommodate – at least not to embarrass – the natural conversational style of the subject. It is a talent, which, in his best pieces, fixes the character in an opening paragraph, so that the reader immediately spots an original, and what follows is by way of expansion and nuance. It is certainly quite a feat to distill the separate characters – two cultures wide apart – of Ted Heath and Mayor

Koch, and leave the impression that the pieces were written by two different journalists:

> When Mr Heath is passionate it is over great matters, and even then he rarely lets himself go, because he distrusts passion. He is a proud man, but that is not a deadly sin. He can be bitter, but he has cause for that. His pride shows itself in silences, and his bitterness mostly in shrugs.

> Ed Koch, Mayor of New York, the ultimate politician, had been mentioning his vitality, energy, leadership and intellectual honesty, and was about to launch into an anecdote about bubonic plague, when he broke off and said, 'Look, I don't want to sound arrogant, so if you'll leave the arrogance out when you write this I'd appreciate it.'

> So, OK. I'll play fair by stating that in private Ed Koch is not arrogant. He just believes what he says. The man has been nominated by both the Democratic and Republican Parties for a second term as mayor. There's no way, God willing, that he can lose the mayoral election, and Koch believes and says that God is great.

But these talented qualifications, though considerable and to be envied, don't explain the most striking characteristic of a Coleman interview: the victim doesn't talk like someone being interviewed but like an old friend having a set-to on serious matters of faith, conscience, political history and tactics, ambition, human frailty. It would be gallant, and might be correct, to ascribe this to charm on Mr Coleman's part. But charm, however infectious, is unlikely to work on a pack of characters as wildly different as Enoch Powell and Frankie Howerd, Michael Caine and Lord Carrington, Norman Mailer and the Kaiser's daughter. In each exchange, I sense that there is on both sides an assumption of equality, or rather a relieved discovery on the subject's side that the interviewer has an equal command of the facts and foibles of the character he is probing, a surprisingly researched knowledge of the subject's life and career, and a nice judgment of how much digging – with respect – the subject can take. (To be truthful, neither charm nor respectful equality seems to have worked all that well with Germaine Greer, and the Duke of Edinburgh must be cited as leader of the resistance to the charm or equal status of Mr Coleman, or – perhaps – of any other journalist.)

Most of all, though, and certainly most welcome to the older subjects is what we used to call a shared 'frame of reference'. This is rare and remarkable in any reflective conversation between an old man and a young man. 'Daddy, *what's* Hitler?' was the first jolt to my assumption that in our family there was no such thing as a generation gap. Another, more wrenching one still, was the shock of a discovery I made when, in the early seventies, I was conducting a seminar of bright undergraduates at Yale in the history of American presidential nominating conventions. While mention of the part played by the president of the Pennsylvania Railroad in contriving Lincoln's nomination was acceptably enlightening news, and while the mechanics of Kennedy's nomination, guaranteed by his brother's preliminary canvassing of the Democratic polls in about three thousand American counties, received sage nods of recognition, the very names of the men who steered Truman and Eisenhower into the White House provoked blank stares. These names were snoozing in the historical twilight zone through which we all stumble – names too late for the history books, too early for personal recognition. I was startled into the knowledge that these boys were in their nappies when Truman left the White House and Eisenhower entered it.

But Mr Coleman has read the poems of Enoch Powell and can bandy with him thoughts about Herodotus. He can recall to Joan Sutherland an old argument between her and a conductor over tempi, and can wonder how Tony Benn's present political stance was conditioned by the Levellers, the Chartists and 'the betrayals of Ramsay MacDonald and David Owen'. He must have ingratiated himself at once with Clint Eastwood by asking him about the point of a small, odd gesture he had used in an early movie, *The Outlaw Josey Wales*. With the Princess Viktoria Luise, he is quite at home with the ramifications of the old German kingdoms, and the Kaiser's hopes for the restoration of the monarchy. Whenever he seems about to verge on cheekiness, he is seen to be relevant. When he is sceptical, it is because he wants to have a puzzle explained. He stands quite outside the London intellectual wolf pack and the highbrow predators of Rome and New York: in short, he is not in the business of cutting people down to size. His whole approach to a distinguished stranger – and, I should guess, to the chance acquaintance in the local – is that of a man who, with malice toward none, is curious to know what makes another human being tick.

So, it has been a pleasure to suggest to his fans some of the reasons why he is a master of a familiar form. It is an excitement to introduce him to pe ople who, from carelessness or stark insensibility, have unaccountably overlooked him.

New York, 1987

THE
PRESENT PLAYERS

DENIS HEALEY
'A Bit of a Thug'

'I plan,' said Denis Healey, 'to be the Gromyko of the Labour Party, for the next thirty years.'

Ha! How old was Gromyko? 'I'm sixty-six. I guess he's seventy-six, and he's had a harder life than me. He's been foreign minister the whole time, and I've been luxuriating in Opposition. He's a bloody good foreign minister, and he's still there. He's outlived Brezhnev, Khrushchev, Kosygin.'

And did Mr Healey intend to outlive his leaders? 'I don't *intend* to, but I think probably my genes condemn me to it.' Mr Healey's genes may indeed condemn him. The above passage came about two thirds the way through a long conversation with him, a conversation into which he introduced Victor Hugo, John F. Kennedy, Pitt the Younger, Churchill, and Pericles, a conversation which began with his telling me that his father died at the age of ninety-two, and that his mother was still thriving at ninety-five, having recently read the whole of Turgenev.

We met at Mr Healey's London house in a Georgian square near the Elephant and Castle. If this one meeting was a fair example, he has developed the preliminaries of conversation to an art form, taking a spectacularly long time to pour drinks and place them on British Airways Concorde table mats, and keeping up a running commentary all the time on where is the whisky, where is the soda, where is the gin, and throwing in the information that these houses were originally built for the doctors who worked at Bedlam (the mad-house, now the Imperial War Museum, nearby) and that George Brown went to school on the corner, though that, he said, was something he didn't cherish.

He also said he had recently done a television programme on photography, had liked Don McCullin but thought Patrick Lichfield a bit of a pseud. His (Mr Healey's) paternal grandfather had been a working tailor and a Fenian, and Auntie Maggie had been a mill-hand all her life. Perhaps his first memory was of his father opening a tin of sardines.

3

Mr Healey's youth is well documented. He won a scholarship to Bradford Grammar School, where Delius went before him, and Hockney after. He got a first at Balliol. During the war he was a beachmaster at Anzio.

He fought the 1945 election, his poster showing a young Major Healey, in uniform, and with the inscription 'BA (Oxon.)' after his name. He said that of course he hadn't put the degree there, and that as to the use of his army rank – and he never used it again afterwards – well, it was a safe Tory seat and his Conservative opponent was a brigadier, an RAMC pox-doctor, and the Liberal was another brigadier, a heavyweight boxer and the nearest thing to Neanderthal man.

When I remarked that he must be one of the few remaining politicians to have had a humane, classical education, he said there were a few around: he'd met one the other day, much to his surprise.

That was why he was sometimes called Renaissance Man? 'Oh no, that's because I'm so brilliant at everything outside politics. Nothing to do with my education. I like philosophy, paint a little bit, very keen on music. Winston, you know, was like that. He was a Renaissance man. He painted very well indeed, and he wrote well, and he liked building walls.'

Wasn't his own second name Winston? 'My father believed in lost causes, and I was born when Winston was in the doghouse over Gallipoli.'

So he was named after a lost cause? 'That's right. But it [Churchill] turned out to be a winning cause. You never know, you know, you never know.'

After 1945 Mr Healey became international secretary of the Labour Party, publishing pamphlets like 'Cards on the Table', and 'Feet on the Ground', and 'The Curtain Falls' (in Eastern Europe, that is). He said then, and still believes now, that the curtain will eventually rise. He had gone into politics because he was a chap who only thought and worked well under pressure, and would go to seed otherwise. That was why he did not return to Oxford, as he was invited to do, even though he wanted to write 'the world's great book on aesthetics'.

It came out here that, just before the war at Oxford, he had organised an exhibition of Picassos, at a time when you could buy a good etching, of the Minotaur period, for five pounds.

Had he? 'No, I didn't have five pounds. Don't be silly.'

What would his advice be now to someone in such a situation, Borrow? 'Yes. Borrow, save, steal, anything.'

4

But to borrow was unsocialist advice? 'Yes, and I personally, like most people from my background, you know, I've never borrowed myself except for a house. I actually paid off my first mortgage early, which was financially insane.'

In the mid-fifties Mr Healey wrote a pamphlet on neutralism, a concept he carefully distinguishes from neutrality. Neutrality is the policy of such a state as Switzerland or Sweden. Neutralism, as I understand the idea, is the attitude of an individual who, disliking the facts of the world as they are, opts out. I asked Mr Healey how far his concept of neutralism described the state of mind of CND members. 'Well, I think the weakness of the CND approach is basically trying to isolate one element in the total international situation, namely nuclear weapons, from the rest. It's sort of single issue politics; in that sense, it's rather like giving up the whole of your life to saving the whale, or stopping seal culling.' Mr Healey said he was at the moment obsessed with the nuclear winter, in which the world might starve in a continuous arctic night. 'But,' he said, 'you can't opt out of the thing by being neutral, or even getting rid of your own nuclear weapons, because the other buggers can start the war. So somehow or other you've got to concern yourself about this appalling problem. You can't contract out of that, because you're on the same planet. And you can't step off.'

We touched on Austria, whose domestic policies Mr Healey admires. Now Austria, he said, had started off as the head of one of the greatest empires the world had ever seen, and in some ways one of the most benign. The Austro-Hungarian empire was still yearned for by people living in Yugoslavia.

As the British empire was still yearned for? 'Oh, yes it is.'

To jump from the Austrian to the British empire was permissible. To jump from social democrat Austria to the SDP was not: when I did so, Mr Healey asked me for heaven's sake to keep the conversation clean. In that spirit, therefore, I went instead to a speech of his made some months after the defeat of 1979, in which he mentioned the brotherhood of the Labour Party.

'I know,' he said. 'We don't make a good shift of it.'

Knives out? 'Yes I know, but, you know, we have a turbulent love life actually. We bash one another about, but there's a great deal of underlying respect.'

Quite simply, the public manners of the Conservative Party were better, then? 'That's right. I'm glad to say, though, that democracy is invading them and they're becoming much the same.'

I took a second point from the brotherhood speech. How, he had asked himself, could Labour ensure it did not lose the next election, and had answered that it was not by lurching to the opposite extreme of policy from the Conservatives and jumping into the trenches of the class war.

'As you jolly well know,' he replied, 'I had some miserable years trying to oppose this tendency.'

I said I was not convinced he *had* fought against it, at which he looked at me and laughed. Very well, I said, and shifted to Labour's policy of unilateral nuclear disarmament. Here his answer was too subtle to report briefly, but he ended by saying: 'I've always thought the question whether we have our own nuclear weapons is a question in the end of cost benefit. What does it cost? What do we get?'

So it was not a moral issue? 'Oh no. Of course it isn't. Because if I thought it was a moral issue I'd think the Germans had to have one too.'

What about the Falklands; what about his having said Mrs Thatcher gloried in slaughter?

'A bad mistake.'

Senseless, I suggested.

'It was a very bad mistake.'

Here Mrs Healey, who had been sitting at the other end of the room throughout the interview, interjected with some heat: 'If you were followed around . . .'

Mr Healey: 'Oh well, never mind. The plain fact is that the television recorded every word, and they didn't find a word they could use against me until that. But still, I don't claim to be perfect, and this was a bad mistake. Although funnily enough my own supporters said my mistake was withdrawing the word. But I thought it unfair [to Mrs Thatcher].'

But my question remained. How, with the Falklands a crucial issue, and very much to the Conservatives' advantage, could Mr Healey, with thirty years' experience in politics, make such a mistake? He said that Mr Wilson, with even more experience, had made the mistake of saying the pound in your pocket would not be devalued. And Mr Kinnock, for whom he had the greatest regard, had had to apologise twice during the campaign, over the Falklands. 'I only had to apologise once. It was a very bad mistake, and I was not so much ashamed of it as very worried about all the damage it would do the party.'

And Mrs Thatcher, next morning, had called him a political thug? 'With great respect, the real trouble is that the only politician who doesn't make that sort of mistake is the sort who tries never to say anything, and my great weakness as a politician is I always say too much. I dare say I am a bit of a thug. On the other hand, you know, every party needs some people who will rough it up from time to time, don't you think?'

When had the realisation come to him that he would never be leader of the Labour Party? 'Never's a big word. We don't know that even now.'

I just looked at him. He then said he supposed his chance came and went in the leadership election of 1980, when Mr Foot narrowly beat him. But that was life. That was showbusiness. It was a disappointment.

Just a disappointment? 'You will exaggerate it. I certainly would have been glad to be prime minister and leader of the party if that had come my way, but it's never been in a sense the focus of my ambition. What I like is doing a job well, and I think I was a bloody good secretary of state for defence, and a bloody good chancellor too. The first is generally recognised, the second not.'

He then repeated that he was not saying he had had it as prime minister, and it was at this point that he said he planned to be the Labour Party's Gromyko for the next thirty years.

Well, after the election of 1983, when the party needed a new leader, he had supported Hattersley, but it had turned out Kinnock. 'I like him a lot. Edna and I both like each of them [Mr and Mrs Kinnock].' People, he said, had needed a break with the past and a new face, and besides, Mr Kinnock had shine.

Shine? 'Yes, something glamorous and exciting.'

Now glamorous Mr Kinnock simply is not. And as for exciting, what was exciting? 'That's why they chose him. What they've got is something more than that. I think Neil is very influenced by the Kennedy example.'

Kennedy? Kennedy had been a Yankee aristocrat, surely? 'His role in American politics was to excite a generation of young people with politics, after Eisenhower and Truman. He excited young people not only in America but all over the world.'

He was comparing Kinnock with Kennedy? 'In that sense yes.'

But a successful leader of the Labour Party over the next five years would have to be a most talented trimmer? 'Oh no, that is not the right way to put it. Moving forward in politics, it's like being carried down a river; you can't suddenly start swinging across to the bank. You have to wait until the river divides and then decide which way you go.'

That, I said – thinking that a moment before he had been

describing Mr Kinnock as exciting – was just anodyne. 'It may be anodyne, but it has the unfortunate demerit of being true, and so it's terribly dull, *terribly* dull. But it's awfully true, and it's been true right through history, from Pericles on. He [Kinnock, not Pericles] is going to be a very good leader.'

I mentioned lack of experience. 'You know, William Pitt was very inexperienced when he was prime minister, very much younger than Neil.'

Well, Pitt had been twenty-four, but he had, I said, been the son of his father. 'I don't think Neil's illegitimate, you know.'

At this point, what with J.F. Kennedy and Pitt the Younger, it seemed to me we were drifting down rivers of political fantasy. 'You sound baffled,' said Mr Healey. 'But have another go; or have another drink.'

I said I'd have another go, and asked about the idea, which I'd heard put about, that Mr Healey, now he was no longer deputy leader, felt born again. '*They* say I'm born again. The Return of the Heli, they call it.'

I mentioned a book of Mr Healey's own photographs, called *Healey's Eye*, which was published in 1980, saying that in it he had described as a rictus of hypocrisy the false smile that some people put on when they pose for the camera. (Here my memory was inaccurate: what he wrote was rictus of stupefying dishonesty, but the sense is much the same.) 'Yes, yes,' he said, 'rictus is a word I adore', and did I know these lines of Victor Hugo, one man addressing another:

> —*Pourquoi ris-tu?*
> —*Je ne ris pas.*
> —*Alors, tu es terrible.*

Ah, Yes, but hadn't he just told me, earlier, that he didn't think Labour had a chance in the 1983 election? 'Nobody did.'

But there he had been sitting on the platform smiling, for God's sake? 'Yes.'

Was that a rictus of hypocrisy? 'There's an element of rictus in it, certainly, but, equally, I think your only chance of winning was to convey confidence and aggressiveness against the government. Let me tell you about rictuses. Edna and I were sitting in my room, which is like a cell block in a lunatic asylum, where the shadow chaps live (this was during the 1980 party leadership election), and someone came up with the results of the poll. And I was told I'd lost by eight votes, whatever it was.

8

'Now, so I felt, well, I'll put a brave face on – that's not a rictus, a brave face – and I walked smiling down the corridor into the room where they announced the results a couple of minutes later, and everybody thought I'd won. Michael shambled in looking desperately unhappy; everybody thought he'd lost. That's a comparison which I wish I hadn't made, but there you are.'

—January 1984

DOUGLAS HURD
The Tyranny of the Elect

Mr Douglas Hurd, Her Majesty's Secretary of State for the Home Department, looks the sort of Tory who is likely to have ancestors and, since I had come across an eighteenth century Bishop Hurd, who was a friend of George III, I asked if there was any connection. 'Yes. He preached rather long. Boswell complained . . . He was a bit of a scholar and was offered archbishop of Canterbury, and he said, "Sire, my next parish will be in heaven", which seems to me a bit . . .'

Just so, Mr Hurd is a very big man of amiable speech and appearance, but he is also rapid of mind, which is something neither his opponents nor his colleagues should forget. Sometimes he shows this rapidity by not completing a sentence when he thinks his interlocutor has already got the point. He is also the kind of man who would think such an answer, even by an ancestor, to be a bit much.

As a boy he was brought up with his brothers at Rainscombe farm, 488 acres of downland near Marlborough. Not a vast acreage for Wiltshire, he says, and some of it was vertical. Very little was ploughed. He remembers herds of dark red, rangy cows, sheep, and chickens. In one period of twelve years his father made a total profit of five hundred pounds. Both his father and grandfather were Tory MPs for many years, and both were journalists. His father was agricultural correspondent of *The Times*. Then there was his great uncle Sir Archibald, who wrote innumerable books on the Royal Navy and the merchant marine. His grandfather had several brothers and these old gentlemen mocked each other. He says his grandfather and uncle Archie were on speaking terms in order to mock each other. It sounds very much a men's world for a boy to grow up in.

'They were all men in my family,' he says, 'until three months ago.' Mr Hurd, who had three sons by his first marriage, remarried in 1982 and had by his second wife 'two tiddlers', the first another boy and the second, three months ago, a girl at last.

Mr Hurd's early career is familiar – Eton scholar and head of school, a first at Cambridge and president of the Union, and then fourteen years as a diplomat in Peking, New York, and Rome. But he first became publicly known as Mr Heath's political secretary, a position he held during the election of 1970 and until he entered parliament in 1974. How had he got that job with Mr Heath? Well, he said, he was sitting in Rome, having decided the time had come to leave the foreign service, and he wrote to Ted, whom he had met and whom his father had known. He also wrote to Warburg's and others. Ted sent a telegram saying come at once. No one else sent a telegram.

Mr Hurd was sitting, as we spoke, on a vast and modern sofa in his room at the vast and modern pile of the new home office, which is decent, and air conditioned, but has no grandeur whatever. So I asked if he felt a sense of awe when he walked through Westminster Hall.

'The one place where I do. I think Westminster Hall is the one awesome place in the Palace of Westminster. I think on a winter's day it is a very numinous place. I don't feel that about the Chamber [of the Commons] or anything else. Those dark beams. You need a winter's afternoon. You get that sort of London feel.'

I said I had asked that because Mr Hurd has written novels and the principal character of one, a junior minister, had expressed exactly that feeling. 'Oh dear.'

Well, I said, men who wrote novels, and then held high office, had left hostages to reporters. He said he knew it. And people always assumed that views expressed by his characters were his own, which they weren't, but, sure, he agreed that his general cast of mind would show itself.

Mr Hurd has written seven novels, political thrillers, five with collaborators and two on his own. They are pretty acute. I recommend them to anyone who wants to know how recent British governments have worked – taking out the obvious excesses like coups and assassination attempts. It all rings dreadfully true. Bits of the general elections of 1970 and of February 1974, which I remember vividly, reappear in the novels. Other familiar scenes are exactly caught – the awful American business lunch of rye bread sandwich and a milk shake, and the awful approach to a conference in an African city, 'filth and squalor, dust and decay, and a huge triumphal arch of metal, plastic, cloth, and tinsel'.

What about the moment in an earlier novel, one written by himself alone, where the prime minister's son, surveying politicians and their attendants, remarked that they are all mice; some rats, but mostly mice?

11

'Yes,' said Mr Hurd, and sent his private secretary, a young woman, for coffee. Secretaries figure prominently in his novels. 'This is the trouble about writing novels. You want to entertain, and the easiest way to entertain – it may even be a temptation for journalists, I don't know – is to send people up, and they mightn't exactly deserve it. Each time I've really sweated before a novel's published, not really because people would think it's them, but because the tone is a bit too sharp.'

Well, his novels certainly were entertaining. 'Hugh Trevor-Roper said to me, "How wise of you to write books. One must have something to reread in one's old age." ' (Laughter)

I went to an early novel of his called *Vote to Kill*, which has as its epigraph some lines by Philip Larkin. Now, I said, the author of that novel hadn't been playing when he chose that epigraph, had he? 'No he wasn't,' said Mr Hurd, and repeated aloud some of the lines, which I quote here:

> *Next year we are to bring the soldiers home*
> *For lack of money, and it is all right . . .*
> *We want the money for ourselves at home*
> *Instead of working. And this is all right . . .*
>
> *The statues will be standing in the same*
> *Tree-muffled squares, and look nearly the same.*
> *Our children will not know it's a different country.*
> *All we can hope to leave them now is money.*

No, said Mr Hurd, he had not been playing with that epigraph. If a slightly romantic view of politics came through there, it was what he felt.

I said I would get away from the books in a moment, but first there were a couple of points which were irresistible. 'Sure, sure.' In *Vote to Kill*, the prime minister, having just won an election, is at Number 10 wondering what to do with an awkward colleague, who must nevertheless be offered something. What about Ireland? 'It'd get him out of the way.' Or perhaps not Ireland, perhaps trade and industry – 'to keep him bogged down'. Mr Hurd smiled. He said it had always struck him as surprising the way posts were filled. Not by the present prime minister, because he knew little of how she did it, but traditionally. It had to be done in one evening.

'I remember one night in '70 when I was involved in it, as Ted's political secretary, thinking what an amazingly haphazard thing it was. Those kinds of comments – again they're too cynical – but there is a sort of casualness about the way it's done which I must say I did find surprising. Particularly someone like Ted, who prided himself on having everything organised in his mind.'

He had written that in 1972, but had since himself been sent to Ireland as secretary of state? 'Yes, yes, yes. I wouldn't write that now.' And his immediate predecessor as home secretary (Mr Brittan) had gone to trade and industry? 'Yes.'

I felt this was all pretty unfair of me, because God help us all if we are to be held to account for words written years ago, so I then suggested to Mr Hurd that, though he might have described some of his own comments as cynical, he wasn't in fact cynical, was he? He said he was not, and that you couldn't go on with the grind and aggravation of politics if you were, because it would drive the enjoyment out of it. You could be a backbencher and cynical. He could think of examples. 'But the grind of actually being in government for six years, which most of us have been now, you can't combine that with cynicism really.'

But his most recent book, *The Palace of Enchantments*, was no less acute than the others, and must surely have been written while he was holding office? He said it was, but only junior office. By luck, it was finished a week or so before he was sent to Northern Ireland.

But if it was not cynical it was acerbic, and yet at the same time as he was writing it he was working as a minister of state, and putting his heart into it? Were these things compatible? He thought they were. Most people didn't write books, but he could think of a lot of people in the cabinet who were acute and acerbic in their conversation. 'I think the chancellor of the exchequer is certainly one, who gets a certain pleasure out of a certain sharpness in his views of life and people.'

I turned to what is, I think, the most striking passage in *Palace of Enchantments* where a London merchant banker, of German origins, is explaining to an innocent American that though English politics is no longer a gentleman's profession it is possible for a gentleman to persuade himself otherwise, and that an MP does what he does not for power, but for the more insidious pleasure of being elected to serve, which is like the dangerous pleasure of the priesthood.

Mr Hurd said he had written that passage himself. It was the only bit that he had written and rewritten several times.

In what sense did he mean this comparison with the priesthood to be taken? That an MP was chosen as a priest was chosen, though by another kind of election? 'Yes, but chosen by people. It's what David Butler calls the tyranny of the elected person.'

Here Mr Hurd sketched the sight he saw in the Commons half a dozen times a day – the visitor, however important, kept waiting in the lobby, until the Member eventually arrived, trailing clouds of glory from some inner sanctum: that flavour. 'I'm sure,' he said, 'it was exactly the same in the Roman senate. I don't think it's peculiarly British. I think you'd probably have found Horace and so on describing it. You certainly find it in the United States Congress, even more so – a way in which elected persons are set, or set themselves, apart. By being elected, they feel, you know, something has touched them, and that is why I make this maybe rather far-fetched comparison with the priesthood.'

Even though some might be unworthy priests? 'Absolutely. That is an entirely different point. Certainly.'

We talked for a while about Mr Heath who Mr Hurd says gave him a good time, and whom he had admired and respected. He recalled the Heath taste for champagne, particularly before those 'ghastly' morning press conferences at Central Office during the 1970 election, and Mr Heath's diplomacy, the way he got on with the subtle French and Chinese, and with the rulers of the Gulf states. Later, visiting those same Gulf rulers as minister of state, Mr Hurd had tried to remember how Mr Heath had dealt with these very special gentlemen. And yes, he had written a short history of the Heath administration (a fair and affectionate account) which Mr Heath had thought trivial. Perhaps Mr Heath would write his own, but it would be pretty tome-like.

It is Mr Hurd's opinion that the administrations of Mr Heath and Mrs Thatcher ought not to be seen as contrasting, but rather as efforts to climb the same mountain, to deal with real problems which had not previously been faced. Mr Heath was the precursor, though Mrs Thatcher's efforts were much more successful.

It is the received opinion of political commentators that having been Heath's man did Hurd no good at all, and that this is why Mrs Thatcher kept him so long in the middle ranks. But he has high office now, having come from Ireland to the home office only to find English cities rioting.

Now, when he was asked if the Handsworth riot had not been a cry for help, hadn't he replied that it was rather a cry for loot? 'Um. That was a pious lady. From the BBC I think, who had picked up this parrot cry, with which I was impatient. What was very striking, going to Birmingham, was that whoever you talked to – Labour MPs, Labour councillors, policemen, the bishop even, the Bishop of Birmingham – you got this feeling of revulsion against crime. At the same time Shirley Williams was sounding off at Torquay at the SDP conference, and Gerald Kaufman was in the studio, giving what one might call the social message, you know, neglect and deprivation. But when you're actually there, you had this very strong feeling that what had actually happened was a great deal of crime.'

And he had also spoken of a desire for excitement on the part of the rioters? 'Yes. I notice Kinnock used the phrase, ''Violence for kicks''. It's the same thought that informs football hooligans.'

Did he believe in evil? 'Yes I do. I do believe in evil.' In original sin? 'Yes I do.' Wasn't that a very unfashionable belief? 'I would have said increasingly fashionable. Because I think the idea, which was very common, that the tendency to commit wicked deeds could be as it were ironed out of somebody by either medical treatment or social improvement or education, I think that idea's had a fair run, and its inadequacies are increasingly clear.'

Many socialists and Utopists might put forward the idea of the noble savage and of the perfectibility of Man? 'I've never believed that. I think Burke is the best Tory philosopher. His *Reflections on the French Revolution*, and what he says about the tendency to commit wicked crimes, and the importance of institutions in containing that tendency, that even if those institutions are imperfect and in need of reform, nevertheless it is important to have them and to respect them, and to have a beautiful queen and all that – purple patch that – rather than knock them down because of some feeling about the noble savage. Go to some of these areas, not just the riot areas, and you see all the efforts which have been made, very substantial efforts, and the money which has been spent, and you can argue whether it's well directed – we are arguing about it – but it's very hard to argue, after that, that spending more, spending better, you're going to iron the tendency to violence out of people.'

He believed that if you took a dozen English cities you would find just a few hundred people who were evilly disposed? No, he said, not all evilly disposed. As a Tory he favoured a tough attitude to crime but a fairly adventurous social policy. There were villians who were villains, just as in Northern Ireland there were terrorists who were terrorists, and it was silly to think you were going to coax the evil out of them. What you had to do was minimise their number and prevent that number being replenished. It was not just a pool of wicked people. It was a pool of discouraged people who had been told there was nothing for them, who had slipped through the educational system, and had nothing. Many of their parents had come from Caribbean islands with strong feelings about traditional education, and what they'd seen their children put their toes into was something they didn't recognise as education at all.

And these would be among those hundreds he had described as alienated from society? 'That's right.'

I remarked that Mr Kaufman, shadow home secretary, had said, after Mr Hurd was stoned when he visited Handsworth, that he had been an alien entrant there. Mr Hurd replied that he had been very struck by that.

But if we had a situation where the home secretary was an alien intruder in any city, weren't we falling to bits? 'I didn't feel an alien, any more than I felt an alien when people threw eggs at me at King's College, London. And I don't think G. Kaufman, as it were, fits very naturally into the habitat of inner cities. We live in a society under strain, which tends to be centrifugal. The bits are pulling away from each other. And one sign of that is that there are people, whether at King's College or in Handsworth, whose instinct when they see someone whose policies they don't agree with, whose views they haven't heard but tend to dislike, is to start to throw things, eggs or stones.'

Then I asked about shabbiness and poverty, because it's now unusual to find a politician who does not see how tatty we are these days compared with all Western Europe, and it can't be said too often. Mr Hurd was emphatic. Not poverty, he said, but shabbiness and dirt beyond doubt, which was, however, quite compatible with thronged supermarkets, videos, telly, and all the rest of it.

'The amount of litter,' he exclaimed. 'I have to curb myself, particularly now I have policemen with me, of a foible which is actually to pick up bits of litter off the pavement and put them in a waste paper basket, in a municipal bin. That is my instinct, born of my mother, who used to go out into country lanes and make little bonfires of crisp packets because it offended her. It offends me. And driving in from Heathrow is a fearful experience, all those broken, rusty centre things in the motorway. It's fearful. It must have a generally depressing effect. People may not realise they live in . . .'

Now if we had just been talking about rust and bits of litter I wouldn't report it at such length. I may be fanciful, and I may be plain wrong, but I thought Mr Hurd was stating again, though in a smaller way, the theme of those lines by Larkin about wanting money for ourselves, instead of working, which was all right; and about the statutes looking nearly the same, and our children not knowing it was a different country.

—November 1985

ROY HATTERSLEY
Vice-Admiral of the Red

Many years ago Mr Roy Hattersley published a life of Lord Nelson, in which he wrote that Nelson's success was above all a triumph of his own certainty. Had I got that right?

'Yes,' said Mr Hattersley. 'Certainty of will, conviction that he had a duty, indeed a destiny. But that's not what I admire about him.'

What was that? He said that at the ministry of defence he had looked for two years (1969-70) at the Hoppner portrait of Nelson. At the battle of Copenhagen, 'as it's miscalled', Nelson had to sail through the Kronenborg deep, between the shoals and the shore batteries. There was no avoiding the risk. But the night before, he went out himself in a longboat and took soundings. Then, having minimised the risk, wishing to take no wanton risk, but knowing there was a risk to take, he resolutely sailed through, in the firm belief that he would succeed.

Now I too admire Nelson, and listened with interest to this account of naval affairs which Mr Hattersley was giving to me in the little room at the House of Commons which is allotted to the deputy leader of HM Opposition. 'I tell Fabian schools,' he said, 'that this is exactly the way the Labour Party ought to behave.'

Admirable certainty. But hadn't he written in another book, an account of his Yorkshire boyhood, that his father, who was a Roman Catholic priest, had hated certainty and had rarely been confident of the outcome of events over which he had no personal control? He said his father had been gentle and unnecessarily unsure of himself. It had been his mother who had guided the family ship through the Kronenborg deep.

Now his mother had become lord mayor of Sheffield. His own political force and personality came from her? 'Certainly, certainly.'

Mr Hattersley did not know until after his father's death that he had been a priest and that he left the church to marry. But, I asked, so far as he knew from others, had his father ever felt the force of the Catholic doctrine which says that once a man is a priest he is always a priest? He said he supposed his father had been excommunicated.

But he had himself been born in 1932, and his father was still listed in the Catholic Directory of 1935 as a priest, 'awaiting appointment'. He said he had not known this.

Well, he has described his own coming into the world as 'a noviciate', but he was early into politics. He calls the 1945 election seminal, says that during the 1950 election he fell in love with the canvass and with the means to power, and vividly remembers 1 January 1947, Vesting Day, the day the mines were nationalised. He went on his bike to Barnsley and looked at the new NCB sign outside a colliery.

And what had he felt as he looked? 'I'll tell you exactly. That our family had achieved that enormous objective.'

What? 'I was in the Labour Party in those days for reasons which have remained with me, which are essentially tribal. That was us. That was part of me. That was the Hattersleys. That was like Yorkshire. That was Sheffield Wednesday. The Labour Party is a tribal thing. And in '47 my tribe had had this great victory.'

He went to grammar school and university. He became a member of Sheffield council. In 1964 he came into the Commons at the same time as Shirley Williams and Brian Walden. Twenty years later he was deputy leader of the party. Indeed, if the office had been in the gift of *Guardian* leader writers, wouldn't he have been not just deputy leader but leader?

'And the *Observer* and the *Mirror*. The three radical papers, yes. All in the book of golden memories.'

Did he think these newspapers had been right? 'No.'

There is, after all, no other answer he could conceivably give, but I remarked hopefully that it must cost him blood to make it.

'I desperately wanted to be leader. But I think the party made the right choice. I'll tell you now. Telling you may cost me more than blood. It's nothing to do with the rival merits of Neil and me, about which it would be wrong and impertinent to comment. It's to do with the right man for the right time. Neil brought about changes which because of my reputation and character I could not have brought about.'

How was that, I asked, though in a way you can see by looking, since Mr Hattersley's tailor is a very good one, who, if he were shown some of Mr Kinnock's suits, would very likely hold them up gingerly between finger and thumb. Mr Hattersley said he was always taken to be on the right wing of the party: he could demand the nationalisation of the hundred biggest monopolies, if there were that many, and he would still be seen as Roy Hattersley, able, jogging, ambitious, and right-winger. And that wasn't the man that the party had wanted.

Barbara Castle had called him an able, unscrupulous Tyke? 'I like being a Tyke. I'm not so keen on unscrupulous.'

The tribal Mr Hattersley has now written a book called *Choose Freedom* (i.e. vote Labour), which as he says himself is not tribal at all, but which sets out the ideology of the party. I asked if it was wise to do this, and whether it didn't give too many hostages to fortune. Mr Hattersley did not disagree. His closest friend had told him he had nailed twenty or thirty flags to twenty or thirty masts. And there was a line he desperately wished he hadn't put in, at the beginning, saying that if the general public found out what the Labour Party stood for they wouldn't like it. He could see that bit quoted in the *Sun*. It was supposed to be a joke.

If, I said, you took a large view of his book, you could see it as one great cry against reality. He complained, for instance, that lions always took the lions' share: well, they always would, wouldn't they? 'What we can do is give the other animals a bit more and the lions a bit less. We can move towards equality, and worry about perfection in another 150 or 250 years' time.'

Here he mentioned Sweden, at which I said he had named about the only socialist state that had ever worked anywhere. He broadly agreed: the Scandinavian countries. But socialism had worked in Sweden for fifty years. Indeed he had gone there at a time when there was, briefly, a conservative government, which had still been to the left of the Labour Party.

That was because some things were difficult to reverse? 'The socialist ratchet. Well, I'd like to give the ratchet a few twists!'

But Mrs Thatcher was busy knocking its teeth out, wasn't she? This is one of the reasons why I wanted to write the book. I don't believe we can succeed – indeed I think I use again, dangerously, the phrase, perhaps we can't *survive* – unless we match our ideology against hers.'

In his exposition of socialist ideology Mr Hattersley again and again sets up capitalist objections in order to refute them. The only trouble is that some of the examples he set up to knock down are so shiningly true that they evidently survive his refutation. Take his citing of Schumpeter's statement that it was capitalism which had brought silk stockings, once the possession of queens, within the reach of every shop girl. But that was devastatingly true, wasn't it?

He said he thought his refutation self-evidently true. He supposed we were swapping rival certainties. I protested that I was certain about very little. 'Well, I'm not as certain as you're going to make me out to be. It is extraordinary, again going back to my blessed plot [his constituency, Sparkbrook], to think that there are so many double garages and sunken bathrooms in Solihull, and so many houses without lavatories four miles down the road. It's a fantasy to think a few drops haven't trickled down. Of course they have. But so little.'

But I gathered that silk stockings, or say nylon tights, were still virtually unobtainable in Russia. He asked if he had written a word to suggest that he was sympathetic to Russia, to which my answer had to be that he had written not a word.

'Good. I'm against tyranny.'

But it did happen to be a socialist tyranny? 'That seems to me pre-posterous. You cannot be a socialist country if you are so organised as to frustrate and prevent basic freedoms.'

Mr Hattersley quotes many authorities – six political philosophers in one paragraph, eighteen in one chapter. Schumpeter of the stockings was a German later active in America. I rather took to Helvetius, an eighteenth century Frenchman, not a Labour voter, who said it was no lack of freedom for a man not to be able to soar like an eagle or swim like a whale.

Mr Hattersley apologised for some of his more extraordinary examples, saying he had chosen them to refute because they were classics. As to Helvetius and the eagle, he accepted that, but would go on to say that it would be a lack of freedom for an eagle if it were caged or if a society was created in which it was difficult for eagles to fly.

Very well, from eagles to an élite. Arguing for equality, he had said that progress did not require the presence of an élite; what it did require was the best education of the generality of men and women. But surely almost everything we had, from the wheel on, had been discovered by the few, by those who were better than we were? 'What about the rest of the ''we's'' who might have discovered the wheel earlier if they hadn't been held back on behalf of the self diagnosed élite?'

I said I was positing the existence of genius and high talent: wouldn't he accept that? 'Genius is going to continue to be genius. To give an example which doesn't give me very much pleasure, there are always going to be grocers' daughters from Grantham who become prime minister. It's a very great achievement.'

The dominant theme of Mr Hattersley's book is freedom, which he believes to be the purpose and true object of socialism. He adopts the late Tony Crosland's definition of socialism, as formulated by him in Mr Hattersley's presence at the foreign secretary's country residence at Dorney Wood. This declares, in part, that 'until we are truly equal we will not be truly free'.

My God, I said, what an impossible definition. If he was so set on equality, wasn't he working against the grain all the time, since people were, evidently and observably, not equal? Some could run faster. Some were more intelligent. He said he was sorry to hear that boring old running analogy again. Then, after a bit of Tawney, he quoted from a sermon by one of the great Victorians, Matthew Arnold. He had said that inequality was wrong not only because it damaged the weak but also because it pampered the rich: both things were debilitating to society.

I had remarked that Mr Hattersley's political philosophy took no account of Chance, which is a great and disinterested determiner of event and policy, but he then told me a story that plainly showed he knew the place of Chance in his own career. He had gone to grammar school in Sheffield, where there were many places, and had no doubt he would not have got in had he lived in Buckingham-shire or Hertfordshire, where there were few. He had gone to university at a time when the new universities were opening. And then Sheffield council. He said he did not know what my politics were, but in the 1960s I would have been writing about Sheffield's new tower blocks. True, they were now pulling some of them down, but in building them Sheffield had at least cleared the slums. And who, he asked, had been chairman of the housing committee at the time? It was him.

Then again, in 1964, when he was thirty-one, Labour won seventy seats in the election. 'Marginal seats were looking for people just like me. Now, God almighty, if I was thirty-one now and looking for a marginal seat to win: you know?'

Just so. What Mr Hattersley is now doing is devoutly promising to increase taxes. The last man I heard promise that was poor Mondale at the 1984 Democratic convention, and look what happened to him. Now it was Mr Hattersley's turn. He was promising higher taxes to anyone earning over twenty-five thousand pounds a year. He had also promised to be explicit, but I couldn't see that he had been explicit at all, so just what income tax rates did he propose? He said he would be daft to answer that.

Well, what was his strategy? Wouldn't he lose the professional classes? He thought many were lost to Labour anyway, but that others among them had values, and would see that decent health care and housing for the country were worth paying for.

'Again, they've got a vested interest in the lads from Brixton not turning up in East Cheam and breaking the place up because they're overcome with despair and frustration.'

The lads? I looked sharply at him and told him he could enforce the criminal law. 'No you couldn't. No you couldn't.'

But a few months ago, hadn't Mr Kinnock produced a brochure about crime which could have come straight from Conservative Central Office? Ah. Mr Hattersley said Labour would take a tough line. 'But if you have a situation like you had in Brixton or Bristol, which is the product of social unrest – I don't think Handsworth was incidentally; I have got into terrible trouble for drawing distinctions between Handsworth and Bristol and Brixton – but where it is the product of deprivation, the police cannot themselves deal with it.'

Never mind the lost professional vote then, what about the plumbers and electricians earning twenty-five thousand pounds a year: why should they stand for higher taxes? He doubted whether plumbers earned that much. (Later that day I paid one £181 for four hours' work.) But, he said, if there were, they didn't have BUPA or send their children to private schools, and so would want greater spending on hospitals and schools. Besides, all the polls suggested that where Labour needed the votes, people preferred better services to lower taxes.

But, I said, in a year's time the *highest* rate of tax in America would be twenty-eight per cent, which was less than the *lowest* rate here, and people were beginning to notice this: what if they asked, why should they pay more tax than Rockefeller? That, he said, was a different society, where you could die if you couldn't pay for medical treatment.

But everybody bought insurance, surely? 'Not very much in Watts [a run-down, formerly riotous, largely black part of Los Angeles]. All over the United States, in the inner cities; and, God help us, similar problems are beginning to develop in England.'

I said I was glad to hear a Labour politician make such an assertion.

We chatted about Mr Hattersley's wish to abolish private medicine and private schools in the name of the greater liberty. He cheerfully conceded this would abbreviate his liberty and mine. 'It's when everybody's somebody that nobody's anybody, and that's a loss of power for you and me.' Throughout the conversation he spoke of my interests and his together, until I began to think I had almost as much chance of getting to Number 11 as he had.

Herbert Morrison and pragmatism having been touched on and dismissed, and Mr Hattersley having told me that, God bless me, sir, I was enunciating the ideology of my own class and education (which don't as it happens differ that much from his), I asked for entertainment's sake why it was that he had got on quite as badly as he had with Harold Wilson.

'That's a change of gear. Well, Harold foolishly ...' and off we went into a tale of Wilson in his fantasy world being convinced that the young Hattersley was plotting against him. And of George Wigg telling Hattersley that he, Hattersley, had to this end attended a meeting at Lucy Fleming's house.

Lucy Who?

'Mrs 007, as it were.'

Plotting what? 'The overthrow of Harold.' But he hadn't been at Lucy Fleming's.

So what had he said in reply? 'I impertinently, and impossibly, and rashly, and idiotically, and shamefully, and indefensibly, accosted the prime minister of the United Kingdom going through the lobby and told him I didn't like the way his satraps behaved.'

Then he had been lucky to survive? 'It was a silly thing to do.'

Now Mr Kinnock loathes Mrs Thatcher and cannot bring himself to say a half-civil word about her. Mr Hattersley didn't share that feeling, did he? He mentioned his belief in her lack of concern and obsession with success. Then he said, 'Her character – it's what Proust called the certainty of the second-rate.'

How could he call Mrs Thatcher second-rate? He said I wouldn't want to spend an evening with her except for my interest in the office of prime minister, and that she was not interested in books, painting, poetry, or architecture.

'The other thing about Mrs Thatcher, which is an enormous strength, is almost a wicked quality. I have never known anyone who concentrated so much on her immediate objective.'

Yes? Mr Hattersley said take the example of a question at a public meeting. Himself, he would say he had to give an answer which approximated to the truth because there would be ten people in the audience who knew what the truth was, and who, if he didn't, would think him either a liar or an idiot. '[But] Mrs Thatcher has no concern with those ten people. She is concerned with the other ninety who may be encouraged to support her.'

He meant she would lie? 'Look at the statistics she produces in the Commons. Of course, of course.'

But lie? 'Well, lie is a big word, but she would invent the answer.

She would give the wrong figures. [Here he gave an example of mixed statistics.] Now that is a great strength, but it's not a virtue. It's not going to get her through the pearly gates.'

In the forthcoming electoral engagement Roy Hattersley – like Horatio Nelson, Vice-Admiral of the Blue, at Copenhagen – will be second in command. But there are one or two details of strategy which Hattersley, Vice-Admiral of the Red, ought to watch. And one question he ought to ask himself: is Labour's naval intelligence up to the mark? Because, in spite of his confident assertions to the contrary – and he might be thought to have some grasp of this, having written a life of Nelson – the battle of Copenhagen, as he says it's miscalled, really did take place right in front of that city. The fort of Kronenborg, which is well to the north, at Elsinore, had already been passed unscathed, three days before. If Hattersley, Vice-Admiral of the Red, turns a blind eye to his c-in-c's signals and insists on waiting there, his fleet will be twenty miles from the battle, and he will not become a national hero but will be court-martialled and shot to encourage the others.

But suppose he gets there, then he will know that Nelson's battle was a close run thing. Nelson's flagship and three other ships ran aground. His losses were terrible. A Danish general of anything like Nelson's nerve would have gained the day. And the enemy commander this time is one he has himself described as being of a wicked quality.

—January 1987

KENNETH BAKER
'Letting the Birds Fly Free'

How well, I asked the Secretary of State for Education, had his grandfather known Keir Hardie?

Laughter from Mr Kenneth Baker. Well, he said, his grandfather had been a delightful man, very short, who left school at twelve or thirteen, knew all the music hall jokes, and was a docker at Newport coaling port. He was in the early union movements in the 1900s, and, because he could write, was union secretary. He certainly knew Keir Hardie, and was asked to stand as a Labour MP but couldn't afford to.

So the Secretary of State was in the direct aristocratic line of the Labour Party? Mr Baker felt he ought to tell me that his grandfather had ended up as a docks supervisor, and practically a conservative, with a small c.

And Mr Baker's father? He had been a middle ranking civil servant all his life, concerned about public access to river walks on the Thames, a sort of Fabian socialist; but, said Mr Baker, really apolitical.

Mr Baker himself, after St Paul's School, did his National Service as an artillery officer, showing the Libyan army how to fire 4.2 mortars. This was long before Gadafy, still in the Italian post-colonial period. 'The chap running the finances of the whole country,' said Mr Baker, 'was an Englishman, who had inherited the mistress of one of the Italian marshals. It's funny what you remember.'

Was she a handsome woman? 'Oh yes, and a very handsome daughter too. The Italians had done well. He sort of inherited her as part of the bag and baggage, I suppose. Would have been a borough treasurer in a northern English town.'

After the army, Mr Baker read history at Oxford, where one of his teachers was A.J.P. Taylor. Ah, he said, he could see the socialist thread again, but he had to say he had been most influenced by another man, a great medievalist. He still enjoys history, and considers that those politicians who lack a sense of history lack also a sense of the tide on which they are trying to guide their ships.

At various times and in various capacities Mr Baker has worked for

Shell, Aquascutum, and Avon, but knows little about oil, mackintoshes, or cosmetics. What he learned was how to manage companies. He entered politics in 1964, at the age of twenty-nine, when he fought the hopeless seat of Poplar. 'Enjoyed that. First go. The year Alec lost. Used to be Lansbury's seat.'

In 1968 he did win Acton, a seat which disappeared from under him in the redistribution, but in 1970, when Lord Hailsham was re-ennobled, got his seat at St Marylebone, perhaps with a little help from Iain Macleod. He was chosen from a list of 437 applicants, one of whom was Douglas Hurd. He then held junior office under Mr Heath, and later helped run his campaign to retain the leadership. We shall come to this in more detail later. Enough to state now that this association with Mr Heath was to keep Mr Baker on the backbenches for some years.

I reminded him that in 1979, the year Mrs Thatcher became prime minister, he had seconded the Queen's Speech, and taken the opportunity to remark that backbenchers trod 'a fine line between sycophancy and rebellion'.

'Well, it's true.'

It might be true, but to say so would do him no good, so why say it? He said he had also likened the Tory Party to a bird, with a left wing, a right wing, and its brains in the middle. But what he said about the fine line was true: for ten years he had observed sycophants and rebels. 'I am,' he said 'a great devotee of the House of Commons. That's not true of many ministers of any party.'

So he would admire Mr Powell as a parliamentarian? 'Very much so, and Michael Foot – as a parliamentarian, not as a party leader. They both love the place, and that is special.'

Mr Baker was back in government in 1981, and is best known for having carried through the bills that sold off British Telecom and abolished the Greater London Council. Had he learned anything from Ken Livingstone?

He had learned, he said, not to be afraid of him. Mr Livingstone was an astute politician, a fine operator, and in 1981 to 1983 he'd had a good run, and got the reputation of being Mr Magic, at a time when the Tories, on that issue, were pretty much in disarray and in retreat. Mr Baker had enjoyed outmanoeuvring Mr Livingstone. Did he think Mr Livingstone was honest? 'Um. He's pretty slippery. I have a high regard for him, but he has this habit of betraying people he's used to climb up the ladder, and I think the Labour Party will never forgive him for what he's done.'

Mr Baker has not, like Mr Powell and Lord Hailsham, written and published poetry. Nor, like Mr Hurd, has he written novels. But he has done the next best thing. He has edited two anthologies, one of poems about London and one of satirical verse. Better still, he has provided each with an introduction and notes, which one reads most carefully.

'Ah,' he says, 'my character comes out.'

The anthology of satire is called *I Have No Gun but I Can Spit*, and takes this title from some lines by Auden in which he warns the stranger not to cross 'the frontier of his Person' unless invited to do so, for, though he has no gun, he can spit. I suggested that this sense of a frontier, or barrier, of keeping or not keeping one's distance, occurred in several of the poems.

'The privacy of the public figure. I do very much try to protect the privacy of my family, for example. The family's very precious. It's the centre of life and society.'

Mr Baker then got up and walked across to his private office to see if he could find copies of the books for me. He found them, returned, and digressed for a moment to describe affectionately a state primary school he had attended as a boy – Victorian, with no playing fields and a yard. Then I asked him about a poem of Richard Church's that he had included.

In this poem, two strangers, a man and a woman, find themselves wedged together on the Tube. Here are three lines of it:

> *Why not make the best of this indignity?*
> *Let our blood rioting together,*
> *Murmur stories of our Life's adventures . . .*

'Isn't that good?' he said.

He did notice women, didn't he? He did choose poems that noticed women? Mr Baker leaned back and recited the first stanza of Betjeman's affectionate and lonely lines about a thousand business girls having baths in Camden Town. He had it by heart.

In his introduction to the volume of satirical verse he had stated that hate was as powerful as love. Was it? 'It can be.'

No, he had said it was. 'All right. As a means of moving people to change, or to do things. Satire can be a force for good in that it can make people hate something which is so hateable that it has to change.'

He then quoted Milton: 'Strike high and adventure dangerously, at the most eminent vices among the greatest people, and not creep into every blind taphouse that fears a constable.' At the end he was practically declaiming the words, and laughed to hear himself doing so.

What did he hate then? He said indifference, bigotry, and fanatics of the Left and Right. But it was easier to say what he loved. He loved England and the landscape and language of England. 'And I think there's a yearning out there for all that to come back in a funny sort of inchoate way.'

He believed that England had suffered from the enormous changes and dislocations of the last fifty years, in a way which had undermined confidence. We had been enormously inventive in mid-Victorian England. Chesterton had a good phrase: he had said he preferred the fighting of Cobbett to the feasting of Pater. 'The trouble was, it became too much of a feast, late-Victorian England, wonderful weekend parties with ptarmigan for breakfast and all the rest of it, and all this while Germany was getting stronger. We've reaped a bitter harvest for all that. But I'm optimistic now. There's a lot happening. There's creativity . . .'

We were talking in Mr Baker's office at Waterloo, in what must be the meanest government building in London, and I asked, in the middle of this eloquent flow of his, if he didn't feel depressed in such a bloody awful place. 'Poulson,' he said 'designed this building, and if for nothing else he should have gone to gaol for six months.'

Now, to democracy. Mr Baker's satirical anthology has a poem by William Plomer which includes a line, written in bitter parody of Marlowe, which goes: 'To entertain divine Democracy.' He also includes an anti-Jacobin verse by George Canning, later to become prime minister, who derides the 'Sov'reign People.' Did Mr Baker ever have doubts about democracy?

This is a question at which honest politicians pause. Mr Baker paused, and then said, 'No, I don't,' and then said, evidently quoting, 'The real people, who have not spoken yet.'

Ah, but shouldn't we distinguish between parliamentary democracy; and what were known as people's democracies; and what amounted to pure mob rule? 'Yes. Mob rule is the collapse of all order. What democracy has to do is to ensure that civilisation does not break down, and civilisation is under threat, more and more. I think democracy in certain parts of this country is under pressure. What I saw in Liverpool, the manipulation of the democratic process by the Militants, is a very great worry. I think it's going to be a bigger issue in the 1990s. The thing is that a group of people are quite determined to manipulate the democratic process and democratic freedom of expression in order to undermine democracy, and I saw it working.'

What other places was he thinking of? Brent, he said. Haringey, Hackney, Islington, Manchester; and other cities.

28

Well, I said, Brent did seem concerned that its employees should think in the right way? 'Absolutely. This is thought police. It is all of that. "If your face doesn't fit, you've had it." It's wrong. It's wrong, fundamentally wrong.'

Well, Mr Baker had a mandate, it might be an inchoate mandate, to sort out the schools? He agreed he had.

So why not strike high and adventure dangerously, and bring back the grammar schools? He said that, plainly, in the next parliament there had to be a major reform bill. Rab Butler, if he were alive today, would barely recognise the system he tried to set up in 1944. Standards were low. There was far too much experiment. Central government, at the hub, had to take greater control of the curriculum. At the same time, at the rim of the wheel, the schools and the parents (not the local authorities) had to have a greater say in administration. But what about the grammar schools? He hoped his twenty city colleges would be a start. 'I've got to start somewhere. It's a great Leviathan out there, which is churning on . . .'

What about teachers? Could we agree that they were underpaid? He said we could.

And yet wasn't part of the trouble a loss of status, perhaps a loss which the teachers had in part brought upon themselves? 'It is sometimes said to me, you know, "Can't you give us back our dignity?" And I've said I can only help. People who have dignity, it comes from within as well. A teacher at the turn of the century had a higher status in society. My grandmother was a teacher. She went to Wandsworth training college, the Irish grandmother who married the docker. That was the thing to do. They came from a poor background. She improved herself, and she taught in schools. That side of my family were all teachers.

'Now, when teachers walk out on their classes, there is no justification, in my view, at all. Children see people whom they should respect betraying their position of trust and honour . . . Teachers should be sort of landmarks on how to behave and what to do. And that tradition and vocation I want to build back into the profession.'

Mr Baker then remarked that a lot of people had come into teaching in the 1950s and '60s who ought not to have done. I asked how far they were literate. Mr Baker brought his hand down on a large English grammar standing on a table next to his chair. 'I'm not suggesting they should all know the difference between synecdoche, and meiosis, and oxymoron, and all those lovely things. I'm not suggesting that quite. But I've got to improve the quality of the teacher training colleges.'

Would it be true to say that the main difference between him and the teachers was that he wished to reward merit, while they preferred an egalitarianism? 'That's right.'

Why did he think they had this preference? 'I think the best case they could put forward would be based on the collegiate principle – that if you have a community you should not try to distinguish the good, the bad and the indifferent, but assume that you all have to work towards a common end, and you all have to pull your weight.'

All priests together? 'All priests together. And somehow you have to shuffle the whisky priest off. If you can't shuffle him off in a sort of Graham Greene way, shuffle him off somewhere.'

I reminded Mr Baker that he had been accused of ambition. 'I have followed my star.'

All right, but in a newspaper column he wrote for the *Guardian* once upon a time, he had quoted Halifax writing in 1695 on how to choose a member of parliament. To paraphrase, Halifax had been saying that one should not choose men whose outward blaze only was for liberty and religion, but whose lasting flame was for 'somewhat for themselves'.

'Good advice, isn't it?'

But suppose someone were to quote those words back at Mr Baker; what would be his defence?

'I would say that I've never tried to calculate, in the way that some of my colleagues do. If I had I wouldn't have joined up with Ted in 1974. I wasn't actually particularly close to him. That is one of the ironies, but there we are. But if I'd been calculating – and some of my friends said, "You must never do this; you'll be washed up; he's a goner; a sinking ship" – I'd have trimmed and found a way of not going. I was proud I did it, and glad I did it. And I was excluded, what, for seven or eight years.

'I think it made me a better politician, that period. It made me my own man. I think it's very important for politicians to be their own men. Margaret's her own man. One likes and respects and admires her enormously for that.

'She's been a bit lucky too. The tide was beginning to turn against the corporate state. She realised the tide was there. It was turning against the belief that the state should have the answer to everything. Ted still rather believes that. She is an important prime minister. The most important since Attlee. He put up the architecture of socialism. Margaret is really the one prime minister who has rearranged the Attlee architecture.'

And her greatest asset was Will? 'Yes, determination.'

But earlier in our conversation Mr Baker had praised tolerance. Weren't there those who said that, with all her Will, Mrs Thatcher lacked tolerance? 'Well, in practice she doesn't. She has included in her government the likes of Douglas Hurd and myself, who were not gung-ho in the middle of the 'seventies, let's face it.'

On the way out Mr Baker showed me the framed political cartoons which hang on the far wall of his office. Mrs Thatcher as portrayed on the cover of *Crossbow*; a Gilray cartoon of Opposition rats, among them Fox and Sheridan; Pitt drunk; and a savage Searle showing a naked and bound politician pierced by spears tipped with pen nibs.

By the way, I asked Mr Baker, how had he managed to get twice as much for teachers' pay as Sir Keith Joseph? 'I argued the case.' (Laughter.)

There was a tide? 'There is a tide.'

—December 1986

31

TONY BENN
Put Not Your Faith in Leaders

Anyone who thinks Tony Benn is a ranter should listen to his quiet persuadings. Anyone who thinks he is a loony should listen to his lucidities. But, for all that, he does appear to be a man convinced that if you are not for him you are against him, and probably want to blacken him into the bargain.

The other day at his house in Holland Park we had been talking about Divinity, the Levellers, the Declaration of Independence, the Chartists, and the betrayals of Ramsay MacDonald and David Owen. We talked about Mr Benn's father, who was forty-seven years in parliament, and was once secretary of state for India. We talked about Mr Benn's uncle, Sir Ernest Benn, who was as convinced and active a capitalist as Mr Benn is a socialist, and once wrote, in one of his many polemical books, that he had failed to discover any material benefit which had ever reached mankind except through the agency of individual enterprise.

We talked – he a bit edgily – about Mr Benn's diminishing and then vanishing *Who's Who* entry. He told me, though I did not inquire the exact amount, that his private income amounted, after tax, to only five thousand pounds a year. We had of course talked about the sinful rewriting of political history, and about the 'bland fascism' of Mrs Thatcher's government. It was all most amiable.

Then, after about an hour, Mr Benn said that his constituency surgeries in Bristol, which used to be quiet chats, were now tragic. He told me the story of a man who had telephoned him saying he was out of work, that his wife and one of his children were ill, and that the Electricity Board had told him that unless he paid his bill of seventy-eight pounds he would be cut off and it would take three hundred pounds to reconnect him. He did not have seventy-eight pounds. Mr Benn phoned the Electricity Board, got through by accident to the chairman, whom he happened to have appointed, and all was well.

I said, 'Three cheers for a good constituency MP.' It was a remark very much in the tone of our previous conversation, but Mr Benn changed at that moment.

'No,' he said, 'No, don't say that.'

We looked at each other, and he then began to speak passionately. I give the passage in full:

'People,' he said, 'are absolutely *desperate*. And unless somehow – this is an appeal I shouldn't perhaps make to you – but unless these issues are dealt with in the public media and in parliament in a way that shows people are *concerned*, and not just about what happens in the sort of personality conflicts that are so beloved, then this country is going to descend into a major tragedy. Now I can't persuade you, and I musn't try like Mr Gladstone to address you as if you were a public meeting, but what do you think if you stop for a moment? Because you've asked me a lot of deep questions about *Who's Who*, and my father, but what do you think I am? Why do you think I've changed in my life? Do you think I suddenly read a book? Don't you think it's probably because I've been round the country, and seen people whose lives are being destroyed?'

This was a question which expected no reply. Mr Benn continued, headlong:

'And yet, having said that, I did try for many years as a minister to make the old system work. I was a very *conscientious* minister of technology. I was trying to make the SDP's current policy work. I had doubts about whether it would work, but that was the consensus – that we'd help, we'd assist, we'd protect. And it failed. And I'm fifty-eight. I'm getting on now. What do you think in the middle of life makes me change? It's that I've seen people's lives being destroyed, and it burns me up. Now if I say this, if you really want to understand me, look at what I've been in my life – that I've tried and I've failed. You've picked in this very clinical way round me, like a post-mortem, but what do you think chewed me up, what do you think made me what I am? What do you think makes a guy in middle life become a socialist, much to his surprise? It's the *circumstances*. I've seen the motor industry destroyed. I've seen the motorbike industry destroyed. I've seen Merseyside destroyed. I've seen Clydeside destroyed. I've seen South Wales destroyed. I'm seeing in Bristol a growing cancer of unemployment and hopelessness in a prosperous city. I was at a meeting the other day where a black family was present. The police had kicked their door in at four in the morning, got them out of bed, stripped them, made them stand against the wall. . . .'

Where? 'In London. It happens all the time. When they rang the local police station the next morning they'd never heard of it. It turned out that the police [of the night before] had got the wrong address. I mean, there are bookshops being burned. This isn't reported. And what's going on in the black community? I don't know whether any synagogues are being burned, but I mean ...'

This broke the spell. I asked if he knew of a single synagogue being burned. 'Well I don't know. There have been attacks. I was saying I don't know ... But attacks on left-wing bookshops are going on all the time, and the police are harassing people in West London, Asians; it's a serious problem.'

This was not Mr Benn's public meeting style, which is pretty cool. Nor was there a shred of acting about it. He was angry, and I thought he was close to tears of anger.

Now, to put this in context, back to what had gone before. On meeting, small talk about his American clock in the hall, a nineteenth century, factory-made clock, very pretty, sent here, he said, at a dumping price. The first clocks to be dumped. The clockwork had failed and he had replaced it with a battery. Then we talked about his grandfather, the publishing Benn who was made a baronet and served eighteen years in the Commons, and then about Mr Benn's father, William Wedgwood Benn, a younger son who therefore did not inherit the baronetcy but went into politics and in 1942 was created Viscount Stansgate.

He sat first as a Liberal, was whip in the great Liberal government of 1910 in which Churchill was home secretary, then in 1927 joined the Labour Party and resigned his seat the same day. Between 1928 and 1931 he was back in the Commons and became secretary of state for India, which is arguably a higher office than his son has ever held. The young Benn, then aged five or six, met Gandhi, expecting magic but finding only a kindly man sitting on an hotel floor. He met a Maharajah, a cruel man, who talked to him about tiger hunting and was later assassinated.

William Wedgwood Benn lost his seat in the landslide of 1931, and set off with his wife to travel to America, Japan, China, Russia, and round the world. Anthony was left alone in London, perhaps for a year, perhaps only for a few months. He cannot remember, but it seemed a long time. He and his brothers were looked after by a Norland nurse, who is still alive and whom he visited the other day. She is now eighty-three. She was born on 1 January 1900, so it's easy to remember.

Then to his relatives, Margaret Rutherford was his father's cousin. His father's elder brother, Ernest, the second baronet and a publishing magnate, was a Manchester school Liberal who would have been very pleased with what was happening now. In spite of the deep political breach between his father and uncle, the family used to go to Sir Ernest's at Christmas. The young Tony Benn played chess with the arch-capitalist.

Just before the war William Wedgwood Benn was elected equal first to the Labour shadow cabinet. In the war he and his eldest son, Michael, joined the RAF. In 1943 Michael was killed, and his father, though by then aged sixty-six, was so moved by this that he used his rank of air commodore to get himself on several flying missions, before the RAF caught up with him.

Tony Benn trained as a bomber pilot in Rhodesia, but the war ended before he could see action, and he returned to England where he went up to Oxford and became president of the Union. He also went across America as one of the Union debating team. Hadn't he said he always felt very much at home there?

'America did recreate in its own foundation some of the principles which were blanked out here. If you look at the Agreement of the People in 1649, of course it reappeared in the Declaration of Independence, and had some influence in creating a society which an English radical would find agreeable.'

With the Agreement of the People we were back to the English Levellers, who, with the Chartists, are Mr Benn's favourite people in history. He believes that, as you go back, you find men facing the same problems as you do now, and they are your roots. At times, reading about a man long dead, it is like recognising a relative. He says the Levellers saw the earth as common treasury, an idea that recurs in the ecology movement, and which came originally from St Francis of Assisi.

When I said the Levellers weren't much known these days, Mr Benn replied: 'It's the privilege of the victors to extinguish the memory of the vanquished, and yet they don't succeed. I suppose you could say that the New Testament story ended with failure, that Che Guevara was interred with his bones, that Trotsky, having been murdered in Mexico, was a figure of total failure. But you can't suppress ideas.'

It seemed to me that the pickaxe through Trotsky's skull had been the instrument of his apotheosis just as surely as the Cross had been Jesus's, but, not wanting to turn to Divinity I asked instead why the ideas of the Levellers had taken so long, 125 years, to find expression, as Mr Benn believes they did, in the American Declaration of Independence.

'It depends,' he said, 'whether you accept the Wilson view that a week is a long time in politics. I very often like to quote what Mao said when he was asked to assess the influence of the French Revolution on world history, and he replied "It's a bit early to say." '

Did Mr Benn believe that: 'Of course I do. Much too early to say.'

And Mr Benn believed, in spite of manifest evidence to the contrary, that all men were created equal?

'I believe there's an inherent right to equality, which you don't have to earn by your own effort: it's inherent. And I think that is the moral basis of socialism.'

A right to life, liberty, and the pursuit of happiness? 'Let's say peace and jobs and freedom. You can interpret it in different ways, but a right to a full life: and that right is where equality lies.'

We then came to the various forms of Mr Benn's name. His unwilling inheritance of the Stansgate viscountcy and his eventual disclaiming of it by means of an act which incidentally changed the course of political history by allowing Lord Home to become prime minister, are well known, and shall be left aside here.

But what about his entries in *Who's Who*? For years these had been routine. He was the Hon. Anthony Neil Wedgwood Benn; the Rt Hon. when he became a privy counsellor. His places of education were given as Westminster and New College, Oxford. Then first his public school and then his college disappeared, and his education was stated to be 'still in progress'; then in 1976 his entry was reduced from thirty-eight lines to three, and in 1977 disappeared altogether. Now what was the point of all this, when anyone could look him up in other reference books, and, in most detail, in the current Debrett, under the Stansgate peerage, where even his honorary doctorates at Strathclyde, Aston, and Bradford were given?

He did not at first answer directly, but then said he supposed *Who's Who* was a symbol of the Establishment and he did not want to be in it.

So, I said, he was now Tony Benn. His old nurse, and friends at Oxford, had called him Anthony. Mr Crosland had called him Jimmy. His mother always called him James, and still did. But what was there in 1975 or 1976 that had suddenly determined him to cut his *Who's Who* entry?

He didn't answer this. He did say: 'May I put this to you? *Tony* Crosland. *Jim* Callaghan. Charles Anthony Raven Crosland. James Callaghan. The truth is there's nothing to it. These comments were not made about Charles Anthony Raven Crosland. I don't mind if you want to, and I dare say the article could centre round some deep psychological explanation of this. I sign myself Tony Benn. And, all

36

right, I did it at a particular time, progressively, but all my friends have called me Tony all my life. At the end of his life my father was made a peer like George Brown, or Joe Gormley. Even if I was the eighteenth duke and owned all Yorkshire it wouldn't make any difference. People would have to judge you on what you said and did. That's all.'

About here I used the word 'populist' purely descriptively, but Mr Benn objected, saying he was no demagogue. In his speeches he tried to analyse and explain, so that people should feel there was more they could do themselves, rather than putting their faith in political leaders.

Wasn't it strange for a man who had spent his life in politics to tell others not to put their faith in political leaders? 'Well, look at them. Just take them. Take Ramsay MacDonald, take George Brown, take David Owen. Take Roy Jenkins.'

Not a bad lot? 'They're people who climbed into power on the back of the movement and kicked the ladder away, and they betrayed the people who put faith in them. They didn't resign their seats. That's why I'm so proud of my father, who resigned his seat the day he changed his party.'

We touched on Bevan, of the Left, who, said Mr Benn, had been wrong to ask, in the matter of nuclear disarmament, whether he should go naked into the conference chamber; and on Gaitskell, of the Right, who had been wrong to say, on the same issue, that he would fight, and fight, and fight again. Mr Benn said he no more wanted American bases in England than he would want Russian bases.

Then we came to the bland fascism which Mr Benn believes is being introduced by Mrs Thatcher's government. First he defined fascism, which in the 1920s and 1930s had meant the creation of a corporate state, the suppression of parliament, democracy, trade unions, and socialism, and was, he said, anti-women and anti-homosexual. These ideas were still in circulation, and in a society in deep crisis would have an appeal.

'If you want,' he said, 'to preserve the present pattern of power and privilege, then you are driven to unemployment, and the Establishment has to have plastic bullets, and then CS gas, and then a police bill which now allows the police to enter any house.'

I asked where this fascism came from. Did he mean from Mrs Thatcher? From her government? From the petty bourgeoisie in the constituencies who were to the right of the government? I did not get an answer. It is my reading that Mr Benn is so thorough a collectivist that he will not recognise merely individual responsibility if he can help it. He says he advises people not to attack Thatcherism as such, because if Mrs Thatcher were to go tomorrow there would be some other -ism. He asked me to uncouple names from ideas.

He believes this is a cruel government. When I said cruelty implied malice, an intent to hurt, he would not accept that, and it was agreed that he meant there was an indifference to suffering. It was here that he called his constituency surgery a centre of tragedy, and, changing his tone to one of the greatest intensity, spoke the words reported at the beginning of this article.

The conversation couldn't be maintained at that intensity, but it did not become relaxed again. Mr Benn mentioned the women at Greenham Common, over whose bodies he said the police had trampled. 'How,' he asked, 'does it differ from what's happening in Poland?'

I began to answer, but Mr Benn must have seen that I hardly thought it worth an answer because he said, 'Gaoling the dissidents here wouldn't agitate you like gaoling Lech Walesa? I feel that actually when we do talk about these things we live in very different worlds.'

He thought people in this country were afraid, and fearful, and said: 'If you take the view I do, that you're bound to try and reverse government policies, when I do that the language is used, that I am hard-Left, that I am extreme. It's none of these things. I should like to see a society where people have a better deal, and it's so simple, so moderate, and so modest in its objective. To want people to have work, homes, and schools, health, and dignity in retirement – that's not extreme. And it is the achievement of the media to present these modest demands as destructive of society. Clearly a way has to be found for change, but change can be set back if those who advocate it are blackened and discredited, distorted, harassed, and abused.'

Could he name a single socialist society which had not become a tyranny; 'Yes, London, the London of Livingstone.'

But a nation? 'Why a nation? Where is socialism to be found? It is to be found in those little pockets of our life where we have protected decent human values from the ravages of violence or market forces. Every hospital in the National Health Service is a pocket of socialism, and every comprehensive school.'

Then, at the end, he said he believed it was not socialism but democracy that was controversial.

Democracy? 'Oh, of course. I mean, look at the Labour Party. What people are really afraid of, in power, is having to share it. The reason that the climate of Labour Party discussion in the years since 1979 has got so hot is not because socialist rhetoric changed. It is because people said, ''We want to share the power more widely.'' What we suffer from is not too much democracy but too little.'

And there speaks a leader who passionately exhorts people not to put their faith in leaders. There speaks a man who says he has tried, and failed, and now sees people as desperate. And it's the *circumstances*. And he was a very conscientious minister.

—February 1983

NIGEL LAWSON
Shakespeare the Good Tory

It is nothing remarkable that Nigel Lawson, Chancellor of the Exchequer, should be happy to talk about tea-tasting and trade unions, because after all he has some experience of both. It is, however, remarkable that he should happily discuss original sin and the Toryism of Shakespeare. Conservative cabinet ministers are not on the whole given to discussions of abstract political philosophy. Mr Lawson is unusual.

We met at Number 11 Downing Street, in a room overlooking the gardens, and when, at tea time, he offered coffee, I asked about his father, who is well known to have been a tea merchant in the City. Mr Lawson recalled a long room in Plantation House, with spittoons, and different teas in little piles. 'My father tried to teach me to taste tea. I never acquired a palate for it. He could take a sip of any tea, blind, and tell you, exactly, almost which garden it came from. I couldn't.'

His father's father was born in Latvia, and came to England at the end of the last century. He was an easy-going, not very successful fellow, a mason, and a great gambler. At this I asked Mr Lawson whether, after the idea of a career in tea had been abandoned and he went up to Oxford, he had not been a bit of a poker-player himself. 'This poker thing,' he said, 'has been greatly exaggerated. One of my lesser interests.'

Or bridge, then? Had he been in the Harold Lever class at bridge? 'Oh good Lord, no. I always find that bridge leads to a lot of ill-temper.'

After getting a first in PPE, he went off to do his National Service in the Navy, starting as an ordinary seaman. It took an awful lot to make him seasick, so he was often able to have an extra helping of food because some other poor devil was too sick to eat anything. He was commissioned as a sub-lieutenant and ended up with his own command, which is what he wanted. She was a motor torpedo boat.

Then followed journalism with the *Financial Times*, and then with the *Sunday Telegraph* where again he had his own command, of the

City pages. In 1963 he was asked to go as speech writer to Macmillan, but before he could take up this job, Macmillan was succeeded by Home who took the young Lawson on in the same capacity, without even having seen him.

'Sight unseen,' he said.

That showed great faith?

'It showed great courtesy.' Mr Lawson was, and remains, an admirer of Lord Home as a politician and as a man.

Indeed, I said, he seemed to get on awfully well with prime ministers generally, with Macmillan, Home, Heath, and evidently Mrs Thatcher. He said he hadn't always got on with Heath, and had great rows, but nevertheless it was he who had drafted the manifesto for the election of October 1974.

Here I went back into the 1960s to ask the obligatory question about Mr Lawson's famous council mortgage of twenty thousand pounds on a house two doors away from Churchill's. This caused a great furore, and the amount would indeed be equal to about one hundred and twenty thousand pounds in present day money, but I decline to believe that a mortgage, however got, is a sin, and was merely curious about the interest rate. It was $6\frac{1}{2}\%$, which is known, but had that been a *fixed* rate.

No, he said: it had not been.

Pity. I believe that the more astute, and fortunate, a chancellor of the exchequer may be or may have been, the better. But, since you don't get an idea of the strength of a man's mind by watching him order fish and chips (and that turn of phrase is not mine but is lifted from one of Mr Lawson's books) I went on to ask about more fundamental things, like the concept of equality.

He had once quoted Oliver Wendell Holmes, of the US Supreme Court, as saying: 'I have no respect for the passion for equality, which seems to me to be merely idealising envy...' Did that express Mr Lawson's own opinion?

'Yes, pretty broadly it does. I'm in favour of equality of opportunity, but that's another thing. People are different, not equal. The appeal of egalitarianism is I think wholly destructive. It's an appeal to envy – one of the strongest emotions, one of the seven deadly sins too... It is I think something which is damaging in economic terms and in social terms too, because it can never be realised and so people feel permanently dissatisfied.'

And if a man believed what was stated in the American Declaration of Independence, that all men were created equal, and saw himself to have failed, he might therefore blame this failure upon

41

himself, which would be cruel? 'He should no more think it's his own fault than somebody who's less good as an athlete should feel somehow he's inadequate. Though he can train and improve his performance.'

Mr Lawson has occasionally quoted those lines from *Troilus* which say:

> *Take but degree away, untune that string,*
> *And hark what discord follows.*

Why did he like those lines?

'The fact of differences, and the need for some kind of hierarchy, both these facts, are expressed more powerfully there than anywhere else I know in literature.'

So Shakespeare was a good Tory? 'Shakespeare was a Tory, without any doubt.'

Could he give another example. 'I think that in *Coriolanus* the Tory virtues, the Roman virtues as mediated through Shakespeare, are ... it's written from a Tory point of view.'

So Mr Lawson felt that a social hierarchy was necessary and comfortable? 'Yes, within an open society, where people can move up and down.'

Wolsey the son of a butcher, and that sort of thing? 'Quite.'

Would he say that people had recently, over the last twenty years, been disorientated by too many changes? 'Right. The strength of the trade unions, I've often felt – it's all changed now but some years ago I felt that the strength of the trade union movement in the hearts and minds of people, working people, was the very thing that it was most criticised for, the fact that it didn't change. ... When every other institution in the country was going through a period of most turbulent change and nobody knew where they were, people did know where they were in the trade union movement, because it was very conservative, didn't change, and gave people a structure.'

The old carthorse? He nodded, but then, as I understood him, went on to say that resistance to change could be taken too far, and that the strength of the Conservative Party had been its ability to adapt without changing too greatly in essentials.

But, I objected, one of the changes of the last few years, this nonsense of changing county boundaries, of putting Bournemouth in Dorset when all the world knew it was in Hampshire, had surely been the work of his own party? 'Oh, yes, I think that modishness [he cast around for this word, and then spoke it with distaste] is something that can be very powerful. When there was a mood at the time that everything had to be changed, the Conservative Party, wrongly in my view, got seduced by that general vogue.'

Then we came back to the unions. I reminded Mr Lawson of his contribution to a book called *Confrontation*, published in 1978, in which he had quoted Robert Lowe, Gladstone's first chancellor of the exchequer, on the need for legal restraint of the trade unions. Lowe's view was that if this restraint were achieved, a threat to prosperity and industry would have been arrested and that a 'demoralisation which threatens to lower the character of the English operative to the level of the Thug of India' would have been stayed.

Did Mr Lowe's views reflect Mr Lawson's?

Mr Lawson said that they were Lowe's own colourful words. He had been a man of foresight, who had early seen the potential danger of the unions. The trade union problem was nothing new, and had come and gone.

Yes, but Mr Lawson had obviously been relating the argument to the present day? 'Oh, very much so, very much so.'

A thug was a highway robber? 'Lowe's picturesque language.'

Hadn't we had an example quite recently, with the *Financial Times* strike? 'Yes, I think there, that's right, it's a more sophisticated form of thuggery.'

Throughout Mr Lawson's contribution to *Confrontation* one could sense his feeling that time was running out pretty fast. Why did he feel that?

'It's very difficult to say when a country has passed a point of no return. Although there clearly comes a point when such a high proportion of the population is dependent on the state that it's very difficult to reverse the trend. I did feel that if we hadn't introduced a fundamental change of direction as a result of the 1979 election, then it might well have been too late. I can't say dogmatically, but one sensed that we were getting close to a point where a change of direction simply wouldn't be politically possible. I mean, short of revolution, which is the last thing I would want to see.'

I misquoted Nigel Birch as telling Macmillan, after the Profumo affair, that it would never be good confident morning again. Mr Lawson corrected me: '*Glad* confident morning.'

Then, given the difference in circumstances, did Mr Lawson believe that it would, now, ever be glad confident morning again? 'I don't know that it *ever* was glad confident morning.'

Ah.

'I am not a great believer in progress, in the sense of an inevitable upward movement.'

Progress was a nineteenth century idea?

'That's right. Man doesn't change. Or man's nature doesn't change. The same problems are there in different forms. Clearly there are parts of the world where there has been a very marked descent into darkness. But I don't think that is inevitable either, any more than I believe progress is inevitable. I don't believe in the inevitability of history.'

From history we went back to Mr Lawson's editorship of the *Spectator*, from 1966 to 1970. I said that one or two journalists, who were not ill-disposed to him, thought his editorship had been a shambles. He replied that he didn't think that was so, but that his own view could hardly be an impartial one. And, he said, the paper had always been readable, and there, though I didn't say so, he seemed to me to make a complete reply. Shambles don't matter if the result is good.

But, I suggested, the point was that if the *Spectator* had been a shambles, and he was now running a great department of state . . .

'You must judge the various things that I've done, that I've run at different times. This isn't the first department I've been in charge of. From running my little boat in the navy, to running the City side of the *Sunday Telegraph*, and the *Spectator*, you have to make your own judgment.'

Well, what about sin? Hadn't he said that your socialist believed in the perfectibility of man but that your Conservative didn't, because he believed men were born frail, and subject to original sin?

Mr Lawson assented.

Now this I baulked at a bit. If he was telling me men were sometimes subject to sin, very well. But why *original* sin?

'Because they are born into the world with it. It is not something that is (later) imposed upon them.'

Surely he didn't believe that?

'Having had several children,' said Mr Lawson, 'I am well aware that is the case, from my own observation.'

'Five children?' I asked.

'Six.' (Some laughter).

What? Sin in little children? 'It takes different forms. One develops in one's capacity for sin as one develops in one's capacity for other things as well. But the important thing is that it is there, innate, born. It is not something which is imposed.'

Ah.

'The Rousseau-ite socialist believes that man is really the noble savage, and that it is only society which deforms him and makes him wicked, and that naturally he is born good. This is a view which I don't share.'

So there he was insisting not just on sin, which I could well accept, but on original sin? He saw sin in little children? He asserted that? 'I believe it.'

I proceeded to negotiate with the chancellor. Would he accept that a child was not born into the world sinful, but that it was, rather, born with such frailties as might lead it into occasions of sin? Would he settle for that?

'I'm not sure that in practice it makes very much difference.'

Then, because it didn't make any difference he would accept it? 'Yes.'

It is of course a fundamental difference. But any chancellor who can apparently abandon a belief in original sin while still, plainly, having modified his views not one bit, will be able to negotiate easily not only with trade unions but even with his own spending ministers.

—September 1983

DAVID OWEN
The All or Nothing Man

'If they think that you just are all milk and water,' said David Owen, looking anything but milk and water, 'and there isn't any strength and substance behind you, then of course they won't vote for you . . . So the stance of the Alliance becomes utterly critical. And in that Alliance, I know that spending my whole time worrying whether David Steel or I are going to lead the bloody thing is absurd. Once I allow myself to be put in that box, I'll change. If I said, OK we'll have a leadership election between David and me, I know where the votes are, so to speak, and I'd do it, instinctively. I'm a politician. But I'm not prepared to put myself in that box. I'm not prepared to stand as Alliance leader against David Steel. Because I can sense that what would immediately happen is that I would start diluting the message, and then the Alliance won't then break through, because I would then trim on the miners. I mean, on the Falklands, lots of them wanted me to trim on that. Not many of the SDP MPs, I'm glad to say, but, I mean, lots of the Liberals.'

This was Dr Owen speaking at the end of a long day which started at Brighton, where he went to address a fringe meeting at the TUC. The fringe meeting was small, two hundred or so in a ballroom at the Metropole Hotel, but straight away Owen was demonstrating what he does best, answering hostile questions.

One question was a long, batty, rambling statement from a deeply aggrieved man. 'Question, question,' shouted Owen's supporters, but he let the man have his long say, then extracted what small bit of sense was in the tirade, and gave it a courteous answer. The man was amazed into silence.

Then Owen was out on to the sea front, being photographed in deckchairs with a tiny gathering of the SDP faithful; then he gave television and radio interviews; then, as if taxis did not exist, he set off on a brisk fifteen minute walk to the station, saying that the last radio interviewer had been wet and that he had splattered the man all round the studio.

Then, settled back in a compartment of the London train, he talked a bit about his own early days. When he was five or six, in the war, he lived with his uncle who was a blind rector in Wales. His study was lined with the huge volumes of the Bible in braille. The boy Owen used to read him leading articles from that morning's *Times*, having to spell out every other word.

As a young man, he first thought of becoming a lawyer, but in the end became a doctor like his father, and for a while was psychiatric registrar at St Thomas' Hospital. Sometimes he wishes he was back in medicine. The last time was after the 1979 general election when the decline was rapid and it didn't seem, in the shadow cabinet, as if Labour could ever make a coherent fight back. Sometimes, among his colleagues in the House, he would notice obsessives and paranoids, but then, he said, we were all slightly obsessive and paranoid.

Seeing we had just left Scargill country, at the TUC, I asked about him, and Dr Owen said there was a man who was not disturbed, but who was on the contrary deeply conscious of what he was up to, and very ably building a generation of people to think like him, in revolutionary terms.

Mr Scargill would rather like a red revolution? 'Yes.'

But nobody said that outright, surely? 'I do. I have no doubts about his political motivation, and I think it is not McCarthyism, not smearing, to remind people from time to time of his communist past; he makes no secret of it. He sees it as a class struggle.'

We then got early on to the Alliance. Dr Owen said that if the SDP and the Liberals had merged in July 1983, the SDP would now be only an excrescence on the Liberal Party. As it was, the Alliance was successful because he and Mr Steel worked closely together, and one reason they were able to do that was that they avoided too much character assassination of each other.

Dr Owen then engaged in a little bit of character assasination not of Mr Steel but of Liberals generally.

Dr Owen has published a book called *A Future That Will Work*, which is a collection of his speeches and his thoughts on practically everything. I had brought with me on the train a copy of another man's book, *The People's Rights*, a collection published in 1909, of the speeches of Winston Churchill when he was president of the board of trade in Asquith's Liberal government. I asked Dr Owen to read two paragraphs beginning with the words 'No man can be a collectivist alone or an individualist alone'.

Churchill wrote that man was at once a unique being and a

gregarious animal. Collectively, we had an army, a post office, a police, and a government. But man did not make love collectively or marry collectively, or eat collectively or die collectively, and it was not collectively that we faced the sorrows and hopes, the winnings and the losings, of this world of accident and storms. No view of society could possibly be complete which did not comprise within its scope both collective organisation and individual incentive.

'Agree with every word,' said Dr Owen. 'That's why toughness and tenderness have to be got together. That is classic liberalism. And it's ridiculous that I have to remind the Liberal Party about the market economy. That is what the lifeblood of liberalism is.'

Dr Owen's book and Churchill's lay side by side on the seat. The comparison was a hard one. Yes, said Dr Owen; well, he wished he could make words sing, but he couldn't. But those were the sorts of ringing phrases which even on a platform you wouldn't get away with these days. People would start laughing.

I thought that untrue, but remarked that Dr Owen's forte was questions.

'Debbie [his American wife, who is a literary agent] says I should only ever speak for five minutes and answer questions for an hour. I take questions seriously, and they've usually got a nub of truth in them, and I'll knock them down, but I'll concede they have a case, on some issues. I like being barracked in the House of Commons. I like being interrupted. I'm better on my feet thinking fast.'

There he was in the House, I said, a man certainly listened to and reported, but the leader of a party of only seven, and I wondered how many people could name the other six: did he know of any historical precedent for such a position?

Well, he said, nobody could name any other Liberal MPs except Cyril Smith, few could name even members of the government, and certainly not the shadow cabinet. This one-man-band thing was grossly overdone. Shirley Williams was instantly recognisable, there was Roy Jenkins, and Bill (Rodgers) was fairly well known; though after that he would agree there was a problem.

But did he know of any parliamentary precedent? He said he wished his history was better. He was trying to put it right. He had read Hugh Thomas's *History of the World*, and was starting to read about the 1920s and '30s. 'I've always been fascinated by Lloyd George, but I'm not very well up on Gladstone and all that sort of stuff, and I wish I was, because I think it helps. . . My wife is appalled at my illiteracy. You suffer from having had six years' solid science as a student.'

Dr Owen is for equality of opportunity but against egalitarianism. The message of one chapter of his book is that a just society is one in which the worst-off are as well off as they can be; the rich might indeed get richer so long as the prospects of the poor were thereby raised.

Yes, he said; if you wanted egalitarianism, then you should live it. It was all right for Tawney, who used to travel round the country second class and live a very modest, humble life. Dr Owen had a crack at those politicians who talk endlessly of egalitarianism while themselves leading lives of extreme affluence. For himself, he lived a reasonably well off life, and was not ashamed of it.

We came to the violence of the coal strike, and the failure of Her Majesty's government to use its own new civil legislation against mass pickets. 'It's a scandal. It's one of the decisions that they will regret most, in my view; and perhaps one that the country will regret.'

But to go back a bit, was it true that in 1972, when he was still in the Labour Party, he had put up some flying pickets at his own house in the East End? 'Right.'

He must have changed his mind since then? He said he had. In 1972 he and his wife put up twelve Nottingham miners for a fortnight. They were picketing Stepney power station. There were never more than six of them picketing at any one time; never more than four, because they did eight hours on, eight hours off, and eight hours sleeping. They were gentle men, and when they left they made a little speech to Debbie, and gave her a bunch of flowers.

But he changed his mind in 1979, when it became clear that in the unions' eyes it was OK to maintain picket lines but not OK to cross them. The essence was the choice. And after the ambulance men's strike of that year, when if you could not get to hospital on time it was just tough on you, he never wanted to see its like again. 'I am not prepared to see people die because of trade union action. If I'd been prime minister at that time I would undoubtedly have moved the troops in. If Jim [Callaghan] had done it he'd have had the whole country behind him, and it would have been a different story. We'd have won. He couldn't do it. He was haunted by being thought of as Ramsay MacDonald.'

We had arrived at Victoria.

Dr Owen is not a man whose animation easily fades away. As we went round Parliament Square in a taxi he noticed a statue of Viscount Palmerston and said he could never see any viscount without thinking of Willie Whitelaw and the shot gamekeeper. And as we went up the stairs to his office in the Norman Shaw building in old Scotland Yard, he told me how, after 1979, he never went near shadow cabinet offices in the Commons. 'Frightful horse boxes,' he said.

Squalor, I agreed. 'Pigstye,' he said.

His own office is quiet, carpeted, and civilised, and there we talked about patriotism, which is for Dr Owen one of the great virtues, and about the Falklands. 'What was at risk throughout that war was something much more than Mrs Thatcher's neck. What was at risk was Britain, our own country, and in a very real sense; had it gone wrong, the repercussions of seeing General Galtieri celebrating the first anniversary of the invasion would have been very marked.'

On our credibility? 'I think on ourselves. It would have had international repercussions too, but one can possibly live with that. But within the country – the Little Englanders, the people who believe that Britain should behave as if it's a small Scandinavian country . . . they would have been given an absolute shot in the arm, the neutralists, the unilateralists, the pull-out-of-NATO people. I think it would have been totally . . .'

Demoralising? 'Yes, demoralising.'

Then we got on to the idea of delusion, self-delusion, which he sees as one of the great English vices. 'I cannot get people to understand the facts. The facts are that Britain is, relatively, declining year by year by year, and it is obvious. At what stage do we realise we are at the cliff edge? Clearly we're not near enough yet.'

He says his underlying optimism leads him to believe that Britain will see the cliff edge in time, and recover, but what was in prospect was not a gentle slither. The gentle slither was now. Trying to convince people of this danger, he understood how frustrated the people must have been who fought appeasement in the 1930s, as they struggled against the cotton wool of indifference that was everywhere. The room for manoeuvre was now quite slight. Another fudge and nudge over the coal strike, another twist of delusion, would make it that much more difficult to pull back.

Surely a lot of people simply did not *know* that we were a scruffy, dirty, poor country? 'They won't face it,' he said, and went on to tell the story of Mitterand and Mrs Thatcher, after she refused the rebate offered at a Brussels summit. 'So poor old Mitterand had to explain this to the French people. He goes on television and says something like this: "My fellow Frenchmen, Frenchwomen, don't be too hard on the English. Of course they're behaving very badly, but their

standard of living is only about 75% of the average Frenchman's.''
Now, give or take a few percentage figures and he's right, and it
does irritate the bejesus out of me.'

Very well then. Since we were talking of delusion, wouldn't he be
deluding himself if he didn't admit that the chances of his ever holding office again were pretty damn slim?

'Um. That honestly is a degree of pessimism that I wouldn't
accept. I think there is a good chance that may be the case, yes. But
you've got to ask yourself something else too. It sounds a sort of vain
thing to say, but you are different if you've been foreign secretary
of this country for two and a bit years. You couldn't have responded
in any other way to the Falklands. You can't any longer act in terms
of a cautious, narrow, partisan politics. And I refuse to do so. I
could not have faced my electorate in '83 with a Labour Party
programme. How could I have done? I didn't believe it, on issues
which went to the heart of the security of this country. So you are
different.'

What followed from that? 'What follows is that you are not as
ambitious in the way people see politicians as ambitious. Of course
I still am ambitious. I want to be prime minister. But it isn't gnaw-
ing away at my vitals in the way it probably did when I was minister
of state at health and social security. You've seen over the hill.
There are no secrets left. You've seen the limitations of being prime
minister, as much as anything else. There's no job really, other than
chancellor of the exchequer, that tempts you. I'm not wildly keen
to go back to the foreign office, certainly not. What now is one's
ambition is to change the political system. I make no secret of it. I
believe it's vital if this country is to recover...'

Dr Owen then turned to the Alliance in what he sees as its most
likely role, that as holder of the balance between two parties, neither
with an absolute majority. He said it was not essential, as everyone
assumed, that, if the Alliance held the balance, Alliance members
should enter the government. It was not necessary to be 'tempted
by black Rovers and all that stuff'. The Alliance could instead
negotiate a deal, a substantial part of which would be a referendum
on proportional representation. All this, he said, was a new
proposal. He for one didn't want to be a minister. He'd had enough.
He didn't need it.

I looked at him. He said: 'I loathe the Establishment, and always
have done. They've never been able to envelop me.'

We walked down the corridor on the way out. He asked where all the moderates had gone, and where were they? Then he said, as a parting gift: 'I don't believe that either Thatcher or Kinnock is fit to govern on their own. I believe it is a crucial national interest that a third force should be there, to stop them behaving in a nonsensical way. And if we achieve that, achieve a change in the voting system, my ambitions would be more than satisfied. And I'd go back to psychiatry.'

—September 1984

MICHAEL HESELTINE
The Wild Blue Yonder

Michael Heseltine is the man who resigned by walking out of a cabinet meeting a year ago. It has been generally assumed he did this to give himself a chance of the Tory leadership. At any rate, it's mostly this that makes him interesting these days. He has now written a book in which he gives this resignation half a sentence.

Look, I suggested, he was a Tory and would be fighting the next election as a Tory? 'Absolutely.'

And would speak up and down the country to help the Tory cause? 'Absolutely.'

And if the Tories were returned with a working majority? 'Which I think they will be.'

Then the prime minister would still be Mrs Thatcher? 'Yes.'

Then, what was in it for him? 'Does there have to be a personal dividend?'

But he would not expect her to offer him anything? 'No, I resigned from the government. I knew what I was doing. But I had great regrets of the need to do so, and still have those regrets.'

Regrets but no doubts? 'Correct.'

Well, the last time we had talked at any length he had been secretary of state for defence, sitting behind Churchill's old octagonal desk, and showing me Churchill's old bookcase with its split panel from the admiralty, which he had in his room at defence? 'Yes, which he kicked in fury. That's the story.'

This time I had taken with me a little book called *The Tactics of Resignation*, which I held up. Mr Heseltine read the title. 'Nobody showed me that. This is where I retreat.'

Well, in it Churchill was quoted as saying 'Never resign', and as going on to say, 'Most men sink into insignificance when they quit office.' Churchill's father, after all, had resigned as chancellor of the exchequer at the age of thirty-seven, and never held office again. 'Correct. And that's the judgment you have to make. I did as I did.'

He said he knew the last time a minister had resigned by simply

53

walking out of cabinet, because David Butler had written to tell him. It was Joe Chamberlain (in 1903, because he was in favour of imperial preference). But, he insisted, everything had already been said about his own resignation. I said there were such mounds of cuttings that they obscured all understanding; it was as complex as the Schleswig-Holstein question. Could he just tell me what had been in his mind in the moment he got up and left? 'The suggestion was that I as secretary of state for defence should be silent on a matter which had never been the subject of collective decision, and no secretary of state could accept that.'

So he got up and said good afternoon? 'I'm not going to get drawn. People will misunderstand the issues.'

They would, so long as he declined to give plain . . . 'It's history. The chapter's written.'

Well, others had left Mrs Thatcher's governments. Francis Pym, having been dismissed, had written a book in which he had plainly reported her as saying, 'Francis, I want a new foreign secretary.' Mr Pym had then written a great deal about Mrs Thatcher. But Mr Heseltine, in his new book, *Where There's a Will*, scarcely mentioned her. He had served as secretary of state for six years, and now written a book of three hundred pages in which there were ten references to Mrs Thatcher, and only four of these by name.

'But it's not a book about Mrs Thatcher. It's a book about my experiences, my ideas.'

But he had served in her cabinet, and had written in great detail about it, and she must be the strongest prime minister for years? 'It's not a book about Mrs Thatcher.'

Quite soon after his resignation he had addressed a Young Conservative meeting – at which there were posters saying 'Let Tarzan Swing' and so on – and his speech had been widely interpreted as a bid for the leadership. He was stuck with that, wasn't he?

'Yes, I'm stuck with it. True. But I've never been for that sort of cant, that, when someone asks would you like to be leader of the party, you go a sort of blushing pink and say oh no no no no.' In the Commons, there were three hundred Conservatives who would love to be promoted, and then promoted further. They'd love to play on a bigger stage, and he was, he said, no exception to that rule.

Yes, but what was the wilderness like? 'I get more invitations, larger audiences, more coverage, than I ever had. If that's the wilderness, it's not so desert-like as perhaps one might have thought.'

Mr Heseltine here mentioned caring capitalism, a phrase he said he had invented last year. I said it sounded like David Owen. He said

Dr Owen might have copied it. To me, his most striking chapter is that on employment and unemployment. He commends the 'hidden heroism' of the many who work for low wages which give them very little more than they could get, in benefit, from doing nothing. And here he suggests a comparison between the rich, being taxed at 98% by a Labour government, and the badly paid, now gaining practically nothing by working. Some of the rich had gone on paying 98% but most found a way round it. In the same way, the lowest paid might stay in work, but they had every incentive to drop out. As to the already unemployed, he believes they ought properly to be regarded as a huge unused national resource. There must be hope. Men regarded in the 1930s as unemployable were found jobs in the war, and after the war continued working for the rest of their lives.

One of his proposals – his most extreme, he said, when I picked it out – is for a sort of Workfare. This is the American idea of working for welfare, or expecting the able-bodied to help look after the old or clear up filthy cities, and we have the filthiest in Europe, in return for their benefit.

My, wouldn't that raise a howl? He said if you tried it in the inner cities it would raise more than a howl, so he wouldn't recommend it there. First try less stressed areas. Do it where you could.

Say Winchester? 'So start there.'

Yes, but what about Brixton? What then? Mr Heseltine explained. If you took some bombed-out estate in say London, Manchester, Liverpool, or Glasgow, where there were 30, 40, 50% out of work, and said please would you turn up on Monday morning and we'll have things for you to do, well, he wouldn't recommend that. But if you said you were going to provide funds to renovate the estate, to 'give it a new destiny', and got this under way, then you could propose, later on, that the young should look after old people in those tower blocks, carry things for them, protect them, see to their gardens. This would not be too alien a proposition.

And, he said, the alternatives to doing nothing were horrific – disintegrating values, people moving in stirring up trouble, crime waves, a generation of hopelessness. He recalled a poll which showed that 40% of young people would welcome conscription, and what was that if not some form of community benefit?

But, I said, our big cities had been preceded in their predicament by those of North America. The Bronx, Southside Chicago, and so on; had any such place ever recovered? 'What about the East End of London? Recovering very fast, thanks to the Docklands Development Corporation.'

He was sanguine, wasn't he? Far from it, he said. But there was a sea-change sweeping across the world, in favour of an idea once brilliantly encapsulated as 'small is beautiful'. Momentum was gathering. The stock exchange had reopened in Shanghai. Mr Gorbachev was experimenting with openness. The idea that socialism was irreversible had been shown to be a hollow mockery in this country. Today nothing was impossible to privatise, but that was not to say that there was no role for the state. 'It was Margaret Thatcher, backed by me, who said we needed an urban development corporation to lift the inner cities.'

This was Heseltine in full party conference flow. I considered, and then objected that this was a minimalist government. 'It has said that it is.'

Yes. And hadn't John Nott, Mr Heseltine's predecessor at defence, said plainly that he was a nineteenth century liberal, that Mrs Thatcher was a nineteenth century liberal, and that this was what the present government was all about? 'And I'm a nineteenth century Tory.'

A paternalist? That, he said, was what caring capitalism was about. In a free society there would be privilege, which carried responsibility and obligation with it.

Now, Mr Heseltine has written that the Conservative Party, by its leadership in two successive parliaments, had implanted a new confidence in the British people. But the leadership had been that of Mrs Thatcher, hadn't it? 'I don't accept that political leadership is simply personalised in one person.'

But she was a dominant prime minister? 'A dominant politician, certainly.'

Then he had also said that a leader did not need to be loved, but to be respected? 'Yes. It isn't important that people should say, "Well he's a nice guy or she's a nice guy; I'd like to have tea with them", or "I'd like to have a holiday with them", or "They'd be nice to have to Sunday lunch", or, "We could take the dogs for a walk together." I don't think anybody thought that Montgomery was someone you loved . . . I don't think that's an essential element of leadership. Indeed I would guess it's a relatively rare quality.'

Was he saying that Mrs Thatcher was not loved? 'I'm not prepared to give any quotations to anybody which would enable me to see that sort of quotation in print.'

She was respected then? 'That is without question.'

He did choose to write and talk partly in code, didn't he? 'You're trying to put words into my mouth. It [his book] has been written to stop people who are trying to make certain points from finding easy quotations ... that is true. And that's a very wise thing for me to have done, otherwise people would have found endless quotations, if I'd been more careless, and goodness knows what suggestions wouldn't have been made about what I was trying to say.'

Mr Heseltine then having said it was a great danger for politicians to think they were more important than they were, and that he was, or rather had been, only one member of a government, and that there had been one dispute, one issue, I suggested that it really had been rather more than that, and that indeed there had been a con-catenation of disagreements between him and Mrs Thatcher.

'No, that's not true, not at all. I spent five weeks trying to avoid resigning.'

Well, a proper old wreck it had been: he resigned: Mr Brittan resigned ... 'I can't be expected to account for any of that. I account for what *I* did.'

Um. People might talk about acting for the good of the country, but surely no man could help thinking personally? 'One works on the assumption that all people think personally. That's realistic.'

So, the best election result for him would be a hung parliament? 'That's not got any consequence in it as a question. My endeavour will be to get the Tories to win, and you don't set out to do that by saying I want the Tories to get 13,643,000 votes, because that will produce a hung parliament. I'm out to find every darned vote I know how to garner. So you fight to win. It's a very uncomplicated process. If you start trying to make judgments about it all, it all looks too scheming, and too. It's just not me. I'm not like that.'

I asked about his political engagements for the next two days and he went through them from memory – six altogether, in places like Nottingham, Banbury, and Oxford, starting out at eight in the morning and ending in the small hours.

Who paid? 'I made a lot of money.'

I looked round his small office. It isn't defence. Churchill's book-case isn't there.

Wasn't it a hell of a comedown? A pause. 'You must do what you believe to be right. If you don't, you'll pay a price.'

We went into his outer office and there – to an audience of me, his very striking private secretary, and a newly arrived visitor – Mr Heseltine recalled one of his great days at defence. He had come to lunch at the *Guardian*. And the Greenham women assembled on the pavement outside, and then invaded the office and lay down in the editorial corridors. Now, said Mr Heseltine, the *Guardian* did a marvellous job, but had its political leanings like anybody else, and the Greenham women would have been a bit of a thing for quite a few *Guardian* journalists, so the *Guardian* didn't know what to do with them, and couldn't hustle them out as the *Express* would have done. 'Very funny,' said Heseltine, recalling happy days. (Merry laughter.)

—February 1987

JOHN BIFFEN
'A Deal of Ruin in a Nation'

John Biffen, Lord Privy Seal and Leader of the House, is often, in his utterances, about as straightforward as politicians come; and yet he can also be most complex and elusive. He will say, at one moment, that he is cynical of those men, of whatever party, who exercise power; and yet, at the next he will say that he does not doubt (as some Tories do doubt) that a Labour government, if there were to be one, would be perfectly proper custodians of power in the parliamentary tradition. He thinks of Mr Kinnock as Taffy in a Gannex mac. Mr Biffen is without doubt shy, and yet will say that he loved history, as he now loves Parliament, with a passion.

He will also state, with passion, that one of the political qualities he most admires is detachment. He is also a man who, at the Conservative conference at Blackpool, made a gesture of the greatest public magnanimity towards a colleague who had fallen on hard times, which was warming to see.

For this interview we met at his splendid office in Whitehall, whose windows overlook Horse Guards. It is a room which used to be part of a town house of the Sackvilles. Then, because he thought he might have unexpected business at the Commons, we made the short journey there in his ministerial Rover, and he showed me his office there, designed by Pugin down to the clock and the furniture. He was not, he said, a man who took much notice of his surroundings, and I believe him, in a way, and yet I can hardly help recording the evident pleasure with which he showed me these two lovely rooms.

Both sides of Mr Biffen's family have farmed for generations in Somerset. His father was a tenant farmer with about three hundred acres. The young Biffen won a scholarship to grammar school, where he loved history and made the discovery, very young, that the events of the Second World War, going on at the time, were part of a continuing history. That is a precocious connection to make and must have owed something to his history master, Jack Lawrence, to whom, as to others, he expresses great gratitude.

As a boy he bought and avidly read a Penguin book which was an abridged Hansard of 1939-40. He listened to 'The Week at West-minster', and remembers the voice of Emmanuel Shinwell. By the age of fifteen or sixteen he already wanted to be an MP. 'I could not,' he says, 'speak of this lightly, because it was something I felt with a real passion.' From grammar school he took an open scholarship to Cambridge.

Was it true that as a boy he had been so shy that, if he saw someone approaching, he would cross to the other side? Mr Biffen said it was. Knowing that Mr Biffen had written, in an article to do with farming, something about the blind hand of nature, which could be Hardy, and knowing that Thomas Hardy, man and boy, would also cross over to avoid meeting another human being, and feeling I was on to something, I confidently suggested that Mr Biffen was a reader of Hardy – blind hand and so on.

'Adam Smith,' he said. 'The unseen hand.' This was the agency which ensured that an economy, left to itself, came to a balance, which would be adversely affected by any interference.

After Cambridge, he went to work for Tube Investments in Birmingham. He was active in politics from the start. In Birmingham he met Enoch Powell, in 1959 he contested Coventry, and in 1961 he won the safe seat of Oswestry at a byelection.

When he arrived in the House he disliked what he calls the sham amateurism of Macmillan, and on Macmillan's retirement sup-ported Butler for leader.

He had thought Macmillan a decadent patrician? 'Yes.'

But surely Butler also had been very much a patrician? But, said Mr Biffen, he had not conveyed that in the same way as Macmillan, kinsman to the Duke of Devonshire. Butler was the man who encouraged and led the young meritocrats – Maudling, Macleod, Powell – who were taking the Tory Party away from the 1930s.

But surely Butler himself had been at the India Office in the 'thirties, and was a kinsman of the Courtaulds? 'That's right, but he was different in the perception, because he was identified with the more progressive wing of the party. I think it was a superficial judgment. Indeed I say that at once. I never knew Butler. Indeed I never knew Macmillan, but there seemed to be a degree of cynicism about his conduct of affairs that did not appeal to me.'

I asked Mr Biffen if – though wary of Macmillan's cynicism – he had not sometimes expressed himself as cynical of those who exercised power. 'That's a very deep feeling. The exercise of power is unavoidable. In no sense am I someone who is going back to the commune, wanting to see a withdrawal of political power in a rather idealistic fashion, but I do feel that it is the most aphrodisiac thing. There is much to be said for Acton's dictum about the corrosive influence of power . . . I'm not for going back to the nightwatchman state, and I'm not on the Adam Smith end of the Tory Party, but I've always wanted to see political power reasonably limited, and perhaps dissipated.'

When I asked for examples of such abuse he thought it might lie in tariffs which conferred too great a protection on domestic producers, in the near monopoly of some nationalised industries, and in the consequent power of trade unions in such industries.

And this, I asked, would fit in with what he had said in the mid-1970s, that Britain was then drifting towards a corporate state – with a government doing deals with the TUC and CBI to regulate prices, wages and dividends – which would be as corrosive of liberty as its fascist prototypes?

He replied that if you considered only the economic policies of fascism – leaving aside the fascist concepts of the need for the state to grow, and to strike back at external dangers – then there had been a fair analogy between what was happening here in the mid-'seventies and pre-war Italy, Spain, and Portugal.

We came to Mr Powell, who has been unarguably the greatest political influence on Mr Biffen, who admired the Powell language with its classical construction of sentences, and his reasoning which proceeded from premise to conclusion. So he was attracted by the intellectual force and rigour of the man? 'And also by his views, which I found most congenial.'

And they became friends? 'I'd got to know him very well before the Birmingham speech on immigration. I was abroad at the time, but when I returned I became more closely associated with him. At that point the whole thing was heightened, because once he'd been turned out of the shadow cabinet those who stayed with him were by definition determined to become foul-weather friends.'

When Mr Powell left the Conservative Party in 1974, and made a speech in which he cryptically urged Conservatives to vote Labour, on the issue of sovereignty and the Common Market, he sent an advance text of his speech to Mr Biffen. He knew that Mr Powell was going to kick over the traces, and act in a manner which he (Powell) hoped would be extremely damaging to the Heath government. Mr Biffen knew the press would ask him about it. So rather than read the speech and then lie between his teeth by saying he did not know what it said, he left the envelope unopened for two days, until after the speech was made.

Now it is accepted that on economics, and on Europe, Mr Biffen's views owe a great deal to Mr Powell's. The similarity between their views on immigration has not been so much noticed, but it seemed to me, having read Mr Biffen's speeches, that there was certainly a similarity.

Mr Biffen broadly assented, but made the points that his views were no carbon copy of Mr Powell's, that his language had been more moderate, that he had never spoken on the matter in the Commons and only three or four times outside, and that he had never made more than perfunctory references to repatriation, which was central to the Powell thesis. But he would in no sense try to disavow that he had spoken and voted with Mr Powell.

Yes, but Mr Biffen had in 1970, for instance, made a speech about the insidious opposition of silence which was averting public attention from the then, and the future, size of Britain's coloured population? 'The belief that, on the whole, this was a topic which was withheld from public debate and decision – there I agree with Powell.'

And hypocritically withheld? 'Yes, I think that's so. But there are some things which are proceeding more happily than I would have expected a few years back. We've come through a very, very sharp recession which many would have supposed would give rise to far more aggression than we've experienced, notwithstanding the Brixton riots . . . I've no doubt that tensions are sharp, and that there is a problem the potential of which I wouldn't presume to assess, but what I am saying is that you've come through the period to date without . . .'

With only bits of our cities burned down? 'That's right. What I am saying is, the debate you're having at your party conference, maybe there is a most fearfully dangerous disregard of these problems, but that was not a party conference that was preoccupied with these issues to the extent that I would have thought likely if in 1972 you had described to me what was lying in the future.'

I referred to a second speech of Mr Biffen's, made in 1976, in which he said that traditions of tolerance and of national cohesion could be torn down by a social transformation, brought about by immigration, which was as far-reaching in its impact . . .

'As the Industrial Revolution,' he said.

Yes. And I suggested that if one looked around here, one could see what was obvious in America, what the Mayor of New York called white flight, which was that from large parts of big cities the white population had gone, and been replaced by people whose culture was, one way or the other, alien. 'That's so. It seems to me it's undeniable.'

But it was just not done to talk about it? 'Well, I think that in the context of my association with Enoch, the speeches that I made were made, I think, conscious that the language that had been employed had been to a degree counter-productive, but I wouldn't contest the broad proposition that he was making. I wasn't clear how far you could argue about repatriation unless it was to be clearly a system of voluntary repatriation, because it seemed to me that here you were vulnerable to all the accusations that it would become something which would be intensely totalitarian, and which would lead to the encouraged harassment of the coloured community ...

'There was [Mr Biffen was here talking about his 1976 speech] this view that we would have in prospect areas that would become predominantly peopled by ethnic minorities; and it was in that context, being very sceptical about what you could do by social engineering to counter it, and, if you like, to disperse it. And of course it's something that Enoch Powell never observed, because his arguments led him inexorably and always to repatriation.'

He thought his speeches were bound to be seen in terms of relationship with Mr Powell. 'Because the test question is, "Did you ever make a speech on this before Mr Powell left the shadow front bench?" Answer, "No." These views were developed very much in the role of somebody who wanted to speak up when he (Mr Powell) was under attack.'

Did he see much of Mr Powell nowadays? Not so much, he said, as when they were in the same party and on the same committees, but he had chatted to him in a corridor the night before.

'I always find it highly exhilarating to talk with him, and I have an affection that political hazards and fortunes and misfortunes can never erase. I feel deeply distressed at some of the attitudes he's struck, and at some of the hostilities he bears to the Conservative Party and the government, but, that all said, politics are so much more about other factors, and loyalty is one of them. The same could be true in so many other instances. When I came into politics I had two heroes. One was Edward Heath. One was Enoch Powell. I would say that both are now pretty well as far apart from my present political patch as I could very well imagine, but whereas with one I can still enjoy a tremendous rapport, and a genuine respect, with the other it's a glacier.'

Another man for whom Mr Biffen has a regard, though he would fight him to the political death, is Tony Benn. At the mention of Mr

Benn I asked how far, in the mid-'seventies, Mr Biffen was afraid, as many Tories were, that the country was on the road to state socialism. He said it had not been a fear that haunted him. He had been concerned at the way some unions exercised power over the Labour Party, but these were the older, manual unions, which were losing members and would grow less important.

'However, as Johnson said, there's a deal of ruin in a nation, and you can wait a long time before the historical trends vindicate your patience. So I did have anxieties about the way the Labour government was proceeding in the late 'seventies, but I never remotely felt the kind of public schoolboy panic that seemed to have overtaken some of the City folk, who thought that Tony Benn and one or two other wild men were going to transform everything.'

Into a sort of Yugoslavia? 'Yes, something like that ... But, and I don't mean this in a pi sense, I am generally much more charitable towards the Labour Party than most Conservatives.'

Charitable? 'Well, first of all believing that they are as reasonably motivated as their opponents. Secondly, in believing that, in a plural society, Labour, as well as their opponents, have an expectation of governing. And in believing that actually they are reliable custodians of the traditions which have enabled society to pass from generation to generation, and from parliament to parliament.

'To some extent I am chained to that belief, because if I didn't believe that, if I really did believe that we were in a one-direction society, in which you had to make sure you were on the tram and driving in the direction which was congenial, then the whole of politics would become much sharper, inherently not of a character that I understand politics in this country to be.'

He had earlier quoted Acton. Did he ever fear that he might himself be corrupted?

'Well, first of all,' he said, and I never before heard any cabinet minister admit as much, 'first of all I enjoy the trappings. I'll be quite unashamed about this. I enjoy having a motor car to come and collect me. And since, during the many years I was a backbencher, I'd come to the House of Commons every day on a usually very crowded 159 bus, I'm totally shameless in the relish I get from having a car. I love the office in Whitehall. Also I love this office, because it is full of House of Commons history. I enjoy the work, and I do have a genuine affection for the House of Commons. It pleases me. I love being an MP. I love being in the Chamber, though because of my responsibilities as leader of the House I'm not so often in the Chamber now, ironically. But when I'm performing the job, from week to week, I don't have any great illusions about the importance of it.'

Then I came to the gesture I remember vividly. Throughout the Blackpool conference, Mr Biffen had not been the most ecstatic of applauders. When, on the last afternoon, a perfectly appalling appeal for money was made from the platform in an appalling way by an appalling man, he sat with his head resting in his hands and made no effort to hide his distaste. Then, that same afternoon, after a week which had been dominated by Mr Parkinson, and only a few hours after Mr Parkinson had resigned after the *Times*'s elegant scoop provided by his former mistress, Mrs Thatcher, in her keynote speech, made one brief reference to her former chairman. At which, Mr Biffen raised both hands over his head and clapped.

'That's right. All calculated. I'm so glad you noticed. I couldn't find any other way of saying that, although the resignation was inevitable once it was clear it wasn't going to be settled, well, I liked the man, worked with him in the trade department, and, damn it, I think you should stand by your friends.'

—November 1983

NEIL KINNOCK
'Sticks and Stones'

Keeping the Labour Party together is traditionally not easy, and the last few years must even have been a bit difficult. So I surveyed Neil Kinnock and asked if, with all those knives sticking into him from all sides, he didn't ever feel exhausted.

He gave this a thoughtful answer. 'No, but I think that's due to my age [he is still only forty-four], physical fitness, and the determination to see it through. And exhaustion? Well, anyone who gets exhausted needn't apply.'

Then he said, 'You see, it's not really as tough as my father's job was, or my mother's job. I mean that.'

His mother had been a nurse, and his father a miner? 'And then a steel worker. I don't think my children have ever seen me as physically drained as I've seen my father, and he was an immensely strong man. He was slightly shorter than I, and very wide, very broad. But he had a very, very tough job. I know there are other kinds of pressure, but there was a lemon-squeezing quality about the kind of work my father did.'

Mr Kinnock said he had done the same job himself for a few weeks. His father was a brickie's mate in a steel works. He stripped the old brick linings from steel ladles, which were as wide as a saloon car and about six feet deep, a kind of brick-lined bucket which had held molten steel, or molten iron, or molten slag. A man had to get inside and hack away at the lining with a drill held by two hands. It was still hot inside, 105 to 110°, and the moment you got in you sweated profusely.

'I could get through two and a half or three in an eight-hour day. He could get through four, and he was thirty-five years older than I was.'

I met Mr Kinnock in the leader of the Opposition's room at the Commons, which used to be Attlee's. He said they had done Labour's rooms up a bit. Where they now had their computer there used to be the old cells of the Palace of Westminster, where, during the time of the great Irish debates, they used to cool off those spectators who came and disrupted things.

Having in mind the Conservatives' recent embarrassments at the Brittan-Heseltine quagmire and at the bombing of Libya from US bases in Britain, and reflecting that the dangers revealed at Chernobyl cannot have made Labour's nuclear timidities seem less attractive, I asked Mr Kinnock how recently he had realised he really did have a chance of becoming prime minister.

He gave me, which is a pity, an answer which can only be described as full and frank – that this had been his belief since he first decided to run for the leadership. He went on to mention the depths of destruction of 1983, from which the party could only rise, and to quote his own remarks made last year about it being time to measure the curtains at Number 10.

But surely he had been reported as recently as this January as having said he would not be too disappointed if he narrowly failed to gain a majority at the next general election? He denied this. He said he had a friend who was a highly-placed churchman. Whenever they met, he would ask him, 'Say one for me.'

At Christmas this friend had proposed a special prayer, which went, 'The Tories have left such a mess, O Lord, let them have a majority of two at the next general election, so that eighteen months after that Labour can sweep to power with a huge majority.'

They had both laughed. Mr Kinnock then told the story at a press lunch and, such was the general mischief and incompetence of some who reported affairs in the newspapers, that the story appeared which I had seen. It was rubbish.

Well, I said, there's a lot of incompetence around, in journalists as in politicians. 'That wasn't incompetence. That was mischief.' He clearly does not like the press.

Wanting to reach more congenial ground, I remarked that John Biffen, leader of the House, was in trouble for suggesting a more balanced Tory leadership. He and Mr Biffen got on, didn't they?

'He's very straight. I like straight people.'

And Mr Biffen also accepted the good faith of Labour people, which some Conservatives did not? 'That's mutual.'

Well, Mr Biffen had for his pains been described as a semi-detached member of the cabinet. I had sometimes wondered, listening to the abuse hurled at Mr Kinnock by his followers, whether they did not regard him as a semi-detached member of the Labour Party. At the last party conference, at Bournemouth, he was called a Judas, a liar, and class traitor, and one woman said she would chew his balls off.

'You never saw anyone try it,' said Mr Kinnock affably. He is at

67

home with the repartee of his party. But he had been howled at from the floor? 'Sticks and stones.'

I said I guessed he had a bit of a temper, and asked if this abuse never got under his skin. Not personally, he said; but when people put the parading of their own egos above the advancement of the party cause, that was an extremely irritating habit, but a habit that had been reduced to a minor fringe abstraction.

After Mr Kinnock had dismissed the yelling of Mr Hatton, the Liverpool Militant, saying the man always kept his distance, didn't he, I asked if the words 'class traitor', though routine abuse, were not sincerely meant by some who uttered them. *If* they meant it, said Mr Kinnock, either they were hysterical, or they had a profound mis-understanding of British working people of all classes. Those who said, 'We must do for our class what Mrs Thatcher has done for her class', paid scant regard to the actual class structure of the electorate at the last two elections. In 1979 and 1983 some Conservative MPs could have claimed with justice to have secured a greater share than their Labour opponents of what by anybody's measurement could be described as the working class vote. Some people who were bold in their promises for 'our class' ignored the realities and aspirations of the working class, and did not know how best its interests could be defended.

So to that real working class he was no traitor? 'I'm nobody's traitor.' The only way to defend the interests of the poorest, and of the unemployed, was to secure power, and anything that impeded that was itself a treachery against those people who most needed help.

I had taken with me Labour's new package of promises, launched last month. The glossy cover shows a pretty girl raising a hopeful arm towards a blue sky. I suggested it could easily be mistaken for a Conservative pamphlet. 'Well,' said Mr Kinnock, 'other than shoot-ing it at sunset, it was difficult to have anything other than a blue sky, frankly.'

But what about the words inside? Anyone, of almost any political complexion could agree with them: put the word Conservative on the cover instead of Labour, and it would still be a credible document. 'Except that we mean it.'

But take the pamphlet on crime prevention. It looked like a Conservative law and order poster. On the front was a large lock. There was talk of making streets as safe as houses, and of more police on the beat. But how did this fit in with those Labour councils in London who had devoted a large part of their time to impugning the good faith of the police?

'Do you first of all think that they make Labour Party policy? And do you think that criticisms of the police are a basis on which to build a policy? I mean, I don't. I think that to make a profession of bashing away at the police without promoting any reasonable alternative for security on the streets is an entirely aimless activity.'

Thinking that the wild men would not like the sound of this at all, I mentioned the GLC police committee, and Mr Kinnock said a few kind words about its desire for police accountability, but then he deviated once more into unforgiving sense: 'Now I speak for myself,' he said, 'and I speak for the Labour Party, when I say that the people who have been most severely affected by the 40% rise in crime in the last seven years are people of the lower socio-economic groups . . .' He wanted better training for the police, and better means of crime prevention.

But surely, I said, here he was talking like the Mayor of New York, who said that it was the poor who mugged the poor, and the blacks that mugged the blacks? 'That's right. That's right. Yes, sure. That's been my view for a very, very long time. I consider that the fear which people feel – not just old people, young people too – about the kind of crimes now being performed, is the most intimidating and soul-destroying of all human emotions. And our business is to lift that fear. And one of the ways to do it of course is to have an improved policing policy. That's one of the ways. There are a lot of other things that have got to be done, as a lot of police officers acknowledge and as a lot of people in the rest of society understand. Mrs Thatcher of course is an exception to that rule. She doesn't comprehend it at all. She's been pretty hard on the country.'

I asked if he really had no belief in Mrs Thatcher's good faith. He paused, and then said: 'I judge on deeds. And it would be very difficult to have any acceptance of Mrs Thatcher, or admiration in any corner, other than the fact, to her credit, that she is the first woman prime minister of Britain. Outside that, I really wouldn't acknowledge much in the way of a better nature.'

But I was not asking him to approve of her, but to say she was honest. 'In her own terms, yes, she's an honest woman, but I'm not sure that she's honest in connecting up her motives with what she would think of as her accomplishments.'

'Well, Brahms,' I said, wanting to escape from this sad aridity. 'Brahms,' said Mr Kinnock, very lively.

Now, that snatch of Brahms's first symphony which has become the Labour Party's signature tune, had that been his own idea? 'Yes, and one day I'm going to have it played by the LSO on a party political broadcast.'

Picking up the glossy Labour policy package from the table in front of me, in order to put it to one side, I remarked that not only was there no red flag on it, but no red at all as far as I could see, except that the girl's scarf was pink. Mr Kinnock said no one had realised there was no red in it until it was finished, and that this was all an invented fuss.

'And,' he said, 'it may be necessary from time to time to remind ourselves of that. The Red Flag isn't gone in any shape or form.' Then he said that for him the colour of liberty was red; that of peace, light blue; and that of youth, yellow. A lot of people thought the new package was the best the party had ever produced, though the press might sneer.

Did he, incidentally, accept that I was not sneering at it? He did, but said he thought it extraordinary that someone of my experience, and he thought incision, should take the time to ask about that package.

I took the opportunity to ask an incisive question about the glass of champagne Mr Kinnock is supposed, in 1966, at an election party of Mr Callaghan's, to have poured back into the bottle, before going off to the pub. It soon appeared I had got it all wrong, and Mr Kinnock was as amiable as could be. How, he wondered, did you pour champagne back into a bottle? Anyway, what happened was that Jim had promised his election team champagne to celebrate and they had won, and they all packed in expectantly, and from a desk drawer Jim produced *one* bottle of champagne. At which they all collapsed with laughter and went off to the pub.

This had been the first of a chain of questions by which I had hoped to demonstrate that Mr Kinnock had over the years moved from the Left (disdainfully pouring back champagne) to Right, but we both agreed the chain had fallen apart. 'Superficial,' he suggested. 'Anecdotes,' I agreed. But then we got onto his maiden speech in the Commons, in 1970, and he said he stood by it absolutely.

But he had said the very existence of the Conservative Party was evidence of rapacity. Did he still believe that? 'Oh sure. The evidence for that could only be gained by very deliberate examination, let's say, in the Macmillan years and in the Heath years. It leaps at you in the Thatcher years. Organised rapaciousness.'

Now recently Mr Healey had said, and had later been reported in an Italian newspaper as having said, that the Labour Party still lacked the credibility to govern, and that Mr Kinnock was politically inexperienced. 'No,' said Mr Kinnock. 'He said, to be fair to Denis, that I hadn't had experience as a minister. Well, it's true, isn't it? He also then added that I had certain other qualities which he admired and gave him confidence. Fair enough?'

Fair enough; and I also wondered, as to experience, whether running the Labour Party wasn't more difficult than running a department of state. Mr Kinnock replied that those who had run departments, or had indeed been prime minister, had told him it was more difficult, or more challenging, let's put it that way, to lead the party. 'They are also,' he said, 'kind enough to say I do it rather well.'

If, I said, I had to think of liabilities to the Labour Party's chances of success [laughter from Mr Kinnock] then what about the Labour leader of Haringey council, Mr Bernie Grant. Now, Mr Kinnock had gone to see Mr Grant on 10 February, and they had a chat, and Mr Grant was reported to have called him Comrade Kinnock, and they were said to have got on. Did they?

'OK, yes.'

But Mr Grant was the man who, after the Tottenham riots in which a policeman was murdered, said they had given the police a good hiding? 'He did, and you know what my reaction was to that.'

Well, Mr Kinnock and Mr Grant met on 10 February. By the 21st of that month, Mr Grant was reported to have called Mr Hattersley a racist. 'And you also know what my reaction was to that.'

Yes, but weren't Mr Grant and his like a liability: he was a Labour candidate? 'I think some of his remarks have been exploited. And I think Bernie Grant is learning day by day how difficult he can make his life for himself. And I've confidence that the outcome of his experience . . .'

But he'd only got to say one or two things like that and there'd be a hell of a dent in the polls? Mr Kinnock thought one would need to examine the council elections in Haringey of the week before. I asked if he really connected the two, by which I meant Mr Grant's remarks and the election results. 'Well,' said Mr Kinnock, 'if there was ever going to be a chance to pinion Bernie Grant in the area where he is best known, then I think it might have occurred last week.'

I was objecting that the byelections were mid-term and that the council elections were only council elections, and Mr Kinnock was asking where else could you get an opinion poll of millions of people, and saying that if I didn't take it seriously he could tell me the Conservatives did. Then he said I was shifting the goalposts.

Shifting the goalposts?

'Well, that's what's happening, isn't it?' How had I shifted the goalposts? 'Well, the point is, you say, "I can think of a host of other liabilities", so we go to what you consider . . .'

But we hadn't got the time: I had to select. 'Haven't got the time? That's a fair way of putting it. I haven't got the time to knock off on every occasion that there are remarks reported or attitudes taken that have significance at the time but will not actually determine the attitudes of the people at the next general election. And I say that without any grandeur whatsoever. It is in the nature of politics. And anybody who expected to drive this particular wagon without any bumps in the road, should never have taken up wagon-driving.'

I mentioned the name of Richard Perle, US Assistant Secretary of State, at which Mr Kinnock brightened considerably. Now, back in 1982 the American embassy in London had concluded that Mr Kinnock would be educable in the matter of the restraints of office, which was generous of them, but earlier this year Mr Perle had said Labour's defence policies could have an almost uniquely destructive influence on the Atlantic Alliance.

Now here in Mr Perle was someone Mr Kinnock could have a go at, and in this mood he is fluent, and amusing, and in easy command of himself. This is not at all how he is when you ask him about Mrs Thatcher. His loathing of her is so sincere − and you might think so blinding to himself, which can't help him − that his flow almost dries up. Mr Perle is another matter. He is fair game to score points off. Mr Perle is himself, according to Mr Kinnock, the current holder of the transatlantic title for destructive influence − his claim to the title being recognised in Germany, France, Holland, Spain, Belgium, and Britain, as well as in the United States.

But what Mr Perle was talking about was the Labour Party's policy of unilateral disarmament. Wasn't that policy an electoral liability? Mr Kinnock thought not. He reiterated Labour's commitment to NATO and to conventional weapons, which would be more useful.

We talked about our children. Mr Kinnock's like pop music. I asked if he ever got any privacy. It appeared that he sometimes did, on a Sunday, in the kitchen with his wife Glenys, which was marvellous, like having a fortnight off. At home, he thought, there was this thin dividing line between democracy and anarchy, wasn't there? Step over the line, and life was miserable for everyone. At the age of fifteen his son had gone and joined the Labour Party without telling his mother or father, and, after a few weeks, began to remind his father, 'We've got rights, too, leader.'

On the way out I went to collect my coat in the passage next to the shadow cabinet room. Above the fireplace in that room is a banner, circa 1910, of The Workers' Union, Holloway Branch. It shows the workers of the world united – those of Africa, Asia, Australia, Europe, and America holding hands presided over by a statuesque woman carrying swathes labelled Fraternity and Equality. In its tones of idealism it goes splendidly with that Brahms signature tune. The election, however, cannot be more than two years away. The First Symphony took Brahms twenty years to write.

—March 1986

JOHN WAKEHAM
'A Unique Beast'

'You are a fixer?' I said to the honest politician sitting at the other end of the sofa.

'Yes, absolutely,' said the Parliamentary Secretary to the Treasury, otherwise the government Chief Whip. 'And proud of it. Absolutely. In that job that's what I have to do. Fix it, if I can.'

It is John Wakeham's job to keep Tory MPs voting the right way, in spite of the occasional most almighty hash. He also picks large numbers of ministers; it is then sometimes his duty to stop them from quarrelling too publicly. In spite of all this he is liked by almost everybody. He could have made a fortune in business, which, in fact, he did.

We met in his room at the Commons, whose walls are covered with Turner reproductions because he likes ships and the sea, and he talked first about his own early days. His mother's brother ran an ironmonger's shop in Godalming. His father – whose own father was killed in a car crash at the beginning of the century, one of the very first to die that way – trained as a civil engineer, served as an officer in the First World War, and then, in the ensuing slump, had to find work as a fitter at Vauxhall Motors. He became works manager, and then, in 1926 or 1927, left to set up his own motor business. He had associations with the old Brooklands track. He was one of the first Riley distributors, and one of the six or seven still left when that marque disappeared.

So there are no politics at all in Mr Wakeham's family. In that sense he is not at all like Francis Pym, one of his recent predecessors in the office of chief whip, whose lineage stretches back through centuries of parliamentary Pyms.

John Wakeham went to Charterhouse but then, not having won a scholarship to university, was given advice by his father on how best to earn a living. The best way, said his father, was to write, since that way you did what you liked and got paid for it. But there was just one thing; you needed the talent. The second best way was to become an accountant, and the third to become an engineer.

John Wakeham tried engineering for a few months, then saw the advantages of accountancy, and qualified at the age of twenty-three. Then, after two years' National Service as an artillery officer at Oswestry and on Salisbury Plain, he began to practise.

Was it true that it had been a speech by Gaitskell, in 1962, which had convinced Wakeham, who was then thirty, that he should take to politics? He said yes and no. Gaitskell had spoken against Britain's entry into Europe. Wakeham always took a broad view of a united Europe – the grand design, nothing to do with the price of butter – and was receptive to the advice of a friend who told him that the only way to achieve anything in politics was to join a party – it didn't matter which. The friend was Norman Hart, a Labour candidate. So, said Mr Wakeham, it was thus a lifelong socialist who persuaded him to join the Conservative Party.

In 1966 he fought the hopeless seat of Coventry East. In 1970 he came within three hundred votes of winning Putney. Now the Conservative Party handout on Wakeham in 1969, when he was adopted for Putney, is interesting. It describes a man who, apart from having written the usual joint memoranda on road haulage and other such essential matters, had travelled vastly, for years, all over the world. And yet he had been an accountant?

'Yes,' said Mr Wakeham. 'How come? Very easy.' He had worked for Arthur Young, accountants, of London, New York, and San Francisco, who employed teams of young men. They sent them everywhere. 'People who wouldn't cry for help. They'd find a solution, miles away from a boss.' He went to the Middle East and all over America, auditing the books of oil companies. And Australia. He'd be six weeks in Indonesia, and then they'd say drop off for two weeks in Karachi, and then hop over to Nairobi, or perhaps to Rome. When he set up his own business in 1960, he knew these places and still travelled.

So when by 1974 he finally got a seat – Maldon, the site of the famous Viking victory of AD 991 – he had sixty-one directorships. Now, what did a man *do* with sixty-one directorships? I must remember, he said, that a dozen or so would have been of companies he had formed and kept on the shelf against the time someone might want a company in a hurry.

What for? Oh, to keep certain transactions isolated. He gave an example concerning greengrocers. At any rate, as he agreed, when he joined the Commons in 1974 he was one of the few new Members with a chauffeured car and a telephone in it. He resigned fifty-seven of the sixty-one directorships.

For five years he was an Opposition backbencher. Then under Mrs Thatcher he became assistant whip, whip, under-secretary at trade and industry, and then minister of state at the treasury. When in 1983 he became chief whip he wasn't widely known. You looked him up in reference books.

But as chief whip he would, with the leader of the House, arrange the government's business? 'Absolutely.'

And he would probably see more of Mrs Thatcher than any of her ministers? 'Probably. Several times most days.'

And his second wife, Alison, whom he married last year, had once been Mrs Thatcher's constituency secretary for ten years, and then gone to Number 10 with her, and hadn't she been known to cook Mr Thatcher's breakfast? 'Denis Thatcher refers to her as a second daughter. And he proposed her health when we married. We had a reception at Number 10. She's very close to the Thatchers, as indeed, you know, I am; but I wasn't before. My relationship with the prime minister has grown since then.'

As chief whip, was his principal loyalty to the prime minister, to the government, or to the party? He said he was not conscious that these responsibilities diverged, but he would say his duty to the prime minister came first. She was entitled to a chief whip on whom she could totally rely to be frank with her, to tell her what he thought, and to support her.

Had he ever told what she didn't want to hear? 'Oh, many times. Oh, on appointments, over a lot of things. She's right most of the time, but my job is to try and give her the best advice I can. I think that she might not always give you the ready answer you want, but I think she listens much more than she admits, and, surprise next day, sometimes she thinks you're right.'

What, comes up and says so? 'Well, not quite, no. Just finding what you were proposing is being done.'

I quoted a passage from Bagehot's *English Constitution* (1872 edition) in which a chief whip is quoted as saying, 'This is a bad case, an indefensible case. We must apply our majority to this question.' Had Mr Wakeham ever found himself in such a spot?

Ah, he said, many times, government in bit of muddle, majority quite handy, take Top Salaries, good case in point. The government was right, but had made a most almighty hash of getting the message across – the prime minister, him, the private office – but as far as he was concerned it was heads down and get the thing through. (This was last year, when a lot of backbenchers were kicking at the large rises for judges and admirals and so on, and the government's eventual majority was only seventeen.)

'Seventeen,' he said; 'that required a bit of skilled whipping, because there were seventeen Opposition members who went home after ten o'clock, and might have stayed and voted us down. So I had the job of (a), persuading people to vote for us, and (b), not allowing it to get out quite what a mess we were in.'

So he had them all in, six at a time, the new intake? 'Not just the new intake. This is a canard that got about. I had all those in here whom the whips thought might be persuadable.'

What, lined up in front of him? 'I'm not that sort of a guy. I don't look that sort of a guy.' No, he said, they'd sat around as we were sitting round, and he'd smoked a cigar or had a drink in his hand, and laughed, and told forty or fifty of them the government might be defeated, and said that he was sure they wouldn't want to learn of this possibility only when it was too late. That's all.

Was it true that he had asked them if they really wanted to spend their holidays fighting an election? He replied that he had said that to one chap, with a majority of seven or something, that if he were him he wouldn't want to go paddling round the streets in August trying to get himself re-elected, but anyone could have seen he wasn't making a threat.

I think I had got the tone of that evening's jolly conversations, but objected that those he had in could have replied that his prospect of a dissolution and an election wasn't credible. 'Of course they could. I was just making the simple point, in a fairly relaxed way.' Well, someone must have taken him seriously? 'One did.' And he told the papers? 'That's right.'

So, it was all relaxed. He did remember on one other occasion telling an MP, who had let him down, that he was an absolute bloody disgrace. No, it had been stronger language than that; but he mustn't tell me what went on; in his office it was like the confessional.

Now, patronage. I had heard it said that, apart from the highest offices of state, the rest were in his gift. MPs would go round saying they wondered why Wakeham had wanted so-and-so as minister of this-or-that. Was this so?

Technically, he said, it was not true at all. The appointments were the prime minister's. 'But most are discussed, and she and I do most of the discussing. So I'm bound to have some influence, or I wouldn't be very good at the job. Now Willie [Whitelaw] has some influence; of course he does. And others have their say.'

I remarked that there were eighty-six ministers of one sort or another. He said, 'The very first thing a chief whip does on the day he's appointed – it was on a Saturday morning; I remember it very clearly. I arrived at Number 10. The prime minister gave me a scruffy piece of paper with her views as to who was going to get in the cabinet. And I went down into Number 12, and I got a large sheet of white paper, a great big piece, and I sat down with a pencil and paper and I drew up the rest of the government, the whole shooting match, including those she'd put in. I can't remember whether we shifted any or whether we didn't. It was the day the Trooping the Colour was going on outside, and I could hear all the bounce and all the bands playing, and here was I playing. Then I had lunch with her, and afterwards we sat down and she put her very considerable imprint on the places. But, I mean, I had to make the list of all those I thought should be asked to leave the government and all of those I thought were worthy of getting a chance.'

Yes? He said it was more than people to be considered; there was north and south, young and old, east and west, Right and Left, experience and inexperience, those who were good performers at the dispatch box, and those who were good thinkers. Then the civil service would see the list, and they might say, 'You realise, prime minister, that everyone on the home office list is a lawyer?', and you'd say, 'Oh my God, that's no good.'

How far up the ladder did his influence go? For instance, Mrs Thatcher had recently needed a new home secretary? Mr Wakeham said he would be very suprised if he weren't consulted on every appointment. Obviously Willie was a great source of strength. And he thought that if she wanted a new foreign secretary, she might well ask Peter Carrington: she might have a chat, even if it was oblique.

What about the chief whip's other, smaller bits of patronage, like invitations to go on fact-finding trips which were sometimes two-week holidays in the Caribbean. He controlled that? 'Um. A little bit.' Well, the awkward ones weren't going to get a fortnight's holiday, were they? 'Ah. They're the ones to send in some ways.' But obviously he was going to seek out and promote those backbenchers who were helpful.

What about someone of fierce intelligence and great eloquence? 'Yes, but if he doesn't support the government, isn't much use, is he? If the chap's opposed to what we're doing, why the hell should we . . .?'

Because he might be less trouble in than out? 'Oh that happens too.'

Heseltine? 'I can think of better examples than that.' Mr Wakeham said he couldn't remember the last man to resign by

walking out of a cabinet meeting, but in a sense he didn't believe Mr
Heseltine came to that meeting intending to resign. Something sort
of snapped. If he (Wakeham) had been able to take Heseltine into a
private room halfway through that cabinet, and talk, he would have
made a good attempt to persuade him that things were possible.

I said it was one thing for Mr Wakeham to bring backbenchers into
his room and sit them down in groups and tell them what was what,
but what happened when the people it might be thought necessary to
keep in line were Mr Biffen, who was leader of the House, and Mr
Rifkind, who was Scottish secretary?

A short pause. I had it in mind, and so must Mr Wakeham, that
Mr Biffen had the week before on television suggested a 'balanced'
leadership, and that Mr Rifkind in Scotland had made remarks
which could not have pleased the prime minister. Indeed, the next
day Mr Biffen had been described by Number 10 as a semi-detached
member of the cabinet? 'Not by me.'

No, but Mr Biffen was the man who, as leader of the House, would
arrange with Mr Wakeham the business to be got through? 'Yes. I
carried on as usual. I had the normal meetings with him. I didn't
discuss the television programme or anything of that sort. Business as
usual.'

What I was really asking was how far up the chief whip's authority
extended. 'Very good question. The truth of the matter is, it depends
on the personality of the chief whip and the prime minister. Nobody
knows whether I speak with my own authority or that of the prime
minister, and I certainly don't go round telling them.'

While I was considering this, Mr Wakeham said that his business
was as much within the government as with the backbenchers. Yes,
I said, but was it within the authority of the chief whip to rebuke a
secretary of state? 'Oh, not in any official way, but if I can persuade
a secretary of state that the show will go better if we do it this way . . .'

He could write a new and modern Bagehot, couldn't he? 'Yes, I
should think so. But I take the view that by and large one of the
essential qualities of a chief whip is probably not to write his own
memoirs, or, probably more important than that, to be someone
people don't *think* will write his own memoirs.'

Mr Wakeham then gave me a sketch of his advice to a spending
minister, named X, who was trying to get what he wanted through
the Star Chamber – which decides what shall be cut from whose
budgets and who shall spend what, and which is chaired by Lord
Whitelaw – and then through cabinet. The advice on how to fix it
went like this:

'X, in my view I should settle this with Willie before it comes to cabinet. Because, look how the cabinet is likely to go. Willie's going to be against you. He's on the Star Chamber. He, and he, and he will be against you. Now, here I speculate, but he will be against you, too, because what you get he won't get. Those two others have got in relatively low bids; my guess is Willie can buy those off. You're going to lose. So why not fix it now? Why not do a deal?'

So here he had spending ministers coming in to him and sort of shuffling cards? Well, he asked, who the hell else could they talk to? It wasn't routine, but at times, where there was a difficulty, it was possible to see a way out. 'Because,' he said, 'I'm part of the game, and yet I'm not *in* the game.'

Not in the cabinet, but present, and seeing more of the prime minister than anyone else? 'That's right.'

A strange beast? 'A unique beast.'

Mr Wakeham's first wife was one of those murdered in the Brighton bomb explosion of 1984, and he was himself badly hurt. I gathered that Mrs Thatcher would be going down to open the rebuilt hotel, and asked if he would be going too.

'Almost certainly, yes. Because, I think – the whole process was an agonising one – but the most important decision that I made in my own mind, afterwards, as soon as I could begin to get myself going, was, that I had to avoid bitterness. I had to rebuild my life, if only for the sake of my two small boys. I had somehow to keep the show on the road, and I fought very very hard to do so. Now I can get through most times. All right, there were ups and downs. There were a lot of downs, tears in bed at night. But that's what I did, and I think I consider myself to be as lucky as a human being can be, in these circumstances. And I've remarried, married someone whom my wife knew well, whom my children knew well, and I have just got to get through it all. And I mean, there are moments of anguish and anger, but by and large I think that's the way to go on.'

We came back to the Commons. He said I had called him a fixer, and he had agreed. He tried genuinely to be courteous, and helpful and cheerful. As he walked round the House he didn't walk past people on either side without saying, 'Hello Frank,' or 'Hello George.' It helped, apart from anything else, to stop him forgetting their names; and they all thought he was reasonably friendly, which he was.

Then he said he had tried to explain to the BBC why they had lost the vote on televising the Commons. The BBC, when anyone complained, always justified itself. What the BBC ought to do was say, 'Sorry, I can see your point of view'; and then some MPs would get invited on *Any Questions* – no connection between the two things; and then people would begin to say the BBC weren't a bad lot. But the BBC had made a terrible mistake. They needed a decent whip around the place, to fix things.

And as to MPs, he said, most of those he had to deal with had come into the House thinking they were going to end up as chancellor of the exchequer, or minister of transport, and they weren't. By those high standards they wouldn't quite make it. But he took the view that it was an honourable profession to be a back-bench MP, and they should be treated with the greatest courtesy. 'I ask them. I have them in here and ask them, "What do you think about so-and-so?" Now of course I'm trying to get over a message. I'm trying to get them to support the government...'

And he also had some knighthoods at his disposal? 'Well, yes. But those things, you know, you can't go round dishing those out totally. I mean, if I had my way, they'd be on a leasehold basis; take them back.' (Laughter.)

We had been talking for an hour and a quarter – about fixing, and about Biffen, and about the Brighton bomb, and about Bagehot, and about governments being constructed on large white sheets of paper. Someone else was waiting. Mr Wakeham said: 'I mean, we're all human. There's no limit to human weakness and frailty, and to human strength. You've just got to handle things.'

—May 1986

LORD CARRINGTON
On Not Sending Gunboats

Today is the two hundredth anniversary of the foundation of the foreign office and of the appointment by George III of Charles James Fox as the first foreign secretary. The present, and fifty-first, holder of the office of Her Majesty's Principal Secretary of State for Foreign Affairs is Lord Carrington, who counts his blessings and says he is doing exactly what he wants to do, and that, moreover, it is a job he always wanted.

Well, how long is always? Just how long had he wanted the job? When he was at Agriculture under Churchill, running the myxomatosis committee?

'The mixxy committee!' he exclaimed, delighted, as if at the mention of an old and dear friend. Now he could tell me a story about that one day.

But while he was consorting with rabbits the office of principal secretary of state for foreign affairs had been in his mind? 'Oh well, I didn't think I would get it. Make that clear. At the time I was doing mixxy I thought, and I still think, that I was exceedingly lucky to get *that* job. It was a rung up the ladder.'

But what had been the chances of his ever achieving that ambition? In 1959, when he was forty and first lord of the admiralty, which was the first time he could really have thought of the job, the previous six foreign secretaries had all been commoners. And today, before himself, fourteen of the previous fifteen foreign secretaries had been in the Commons. So what were his chances?

'Negligible. Negligible. I mean, the first time it even became a possibility was when Alec [Home] became foreign secretary. If I remember rightly, the outrage at that was almost not containable.'

He was called Caligula's horse? 'That sort of stuff,' said Lord Carrington, and mused a bit, and then remarked, as if by the way, that he had possessed his ambition before he was a peer.

But since he had succeeded his father at the age of eighteen, this must have been while he was still at Eton then? 'Oh yes, certainly . . . I had a lot of people interested in politics around me at school. Believe it or not, I sat next to Julian Amery for four years or whatever it was. One talked a lot of politics.'

I remarked that he had now served under six prime ministers. This didn't seem to have struck him. 'Count it up,' he said. But there it was – Churchill, Eden, Macmillan, Home, Heath, Thatcher.

Had anyone else done this, served under six? 'Quintin? There must be some Labour ones.'

I didn't know there had been six Labour prime ministers. 'That,' he said, 'is part of the luck of the draw, isn't it? We got through prime ministers quite quickly a couple of times.'

How, I wondered, had he got started in politics? Alec Douglas-Home sat in the Commons for years before he succeeded his father, but Carrington had been unable to do that. So how? He said he had got elected to his county council, and done agricultural things. 'I have,' he murmured, 'some agricultural property.' And then, after the war, there had been many young peers in the Lords, and it was quite exciting, with a new Labour government, but practically no Labour men in the Lords, and the Lords having to deal for the first time since 1911 with *political* things like town and country planning and nationalisation. 'And it was fascinating to see how Bobbity Salisbury dealt with it. He was superb at it. The way he manoeuvred his way through the shoals of Conservative opinion. I then became a whip, I think.'

How had he been offered his first real government job, at the ministry of agriculture and fisheries in 1951? By someone on behalf of Churchill, I supposed. 'By Churchill. I was out shooting [laughter], and somebody sort of bicycled up and said: "Mr Churchill wants you on the telephone." I said: "Don't be so ridiculous. Nonsense." But I went back and there he was on the telephone.'

He was appointed because of his farming interest? 'I doubt whether he knew who I was from Adam. I think he just got on the telephone, and said something nice, and banged it down. I was astonished.'

We went back two hundred years. When Fox was first appointed, I said, he had Richard Brinsley Sheridan, author of *The School for Scandal*, as his second in command.

'And fourteen other people,' said Lord Carrington. 'Including a housekeeper.'

Well, as to Sheridan, Carrington had Douglas Hurd as his minister of state, who has written novels. 'Yes I've got my Sheridan. A very good Sheridan incidentally. Very bright guy.'

Now Fox, I said, had his qualities: at fourteen he was gambling in

Paris, encouraged by his father, at nineteen he met Voltaire, and he once lost sixteen thousand pounds in a day on a horse. What could Lord Carrington offer to compare with all this? 'Absolutely nothing. A very conventional background.'

No wildness, I inquired hopefully, having it in mind that one of his recent ancestors, known as Champagne Charlie, drank with Edward VII. 'Well, you see, the wildness was slightly contained, because I was twenty when the war broke out. And so, I mean, life got quite serious. I had a lot of fun of course. Apart from the bits when we were frightened or bored, there was an immense amount of fun. It wasn't quite the same kind of thing as Charles James Fox had, of course. After the war there was a lot of austerity; and, you know, there were butterflies – you were a butterfly if you didn't work and people had to have their noses to the grindstone. We were really much worse off after the war than during the war. I don't think I was very wild.'

He thought the Second World War (in which, as it happens, he was a Guards officer and won an MC by taking a bridge in a tank) was not so terrible as the first, with those trenches. I said that evidently both Eden and Macmillan had been marked by that war; it was obvious when they talked. He said Harold Macmillan had sometimes talked to him about it, anecdotally, not about the horrors. But his own father, who died young, had been scarred by it.

Lord Carrington had earlier said the foreign office started with fourteen people. By 1914, just before the war, when England was perhaps at the height of her power, the number was 176. What was it now?

He thought five thousand.

Yes. What did that show?

He replied that there were now 151 countries in the world, whereas sixty years ago there were only a handful of any significance. The foreign office was now concerned not so much with war and diplomacy as with commerce and the law of the sea. To those who said that Britain was no longer a militarily powerful nation, and asked therefore what all those people were needed for, he replied that you needed more people if you weren't powerful.

'I mean, if you could send a gunboat and settle the thing, it's quite easy. If you have to use diplomacy to do it, you need more.'

Had he ever regretted not being able to send a gunboat? 'But I mean there's no good being nostalgic. Gunboats very often settled things in Victorian days, and that was admirable, but as I said it's no good sort of swimming about in nostalgia. What you've got to do is deal with the things and the problems that you're faced with now. And, alas, gunboats won't do.'

I said nostalgia had been his word, not mine, and he laughed. 'I think that Palmerston probably had a more straightforward job as foreign secretary than I've got, because he had the military power. After all, we were the top of the lot in those days.' As it happens, we were that morning sending the last of the gunboats, a gunboat indeed about to be scrapped, to South Georgia I didn't know until later, and I don't know whether Lord Carrington knew.

And now we also had 130 international organisations? At this, Lord Carrington turned his eyes to heaven.

Tedious? Too many? 'Of course. Of course it is. And some of them, it's difficult to see what some of them achieve. A lot of them are self-perpetuating.' But a lot, he said, were essential, and here he named the IMF and the World Bank. Then he continued, 'Even the least good of them . . .'

Such as the United Nations itself? He gallantly defended the UN as essential. One didn't applaud all it did, indeed one regretted a great deal it did, but one would rather it was there than not.

My mind running on papers and dispatch boxes, I mentioned that in the communications put before Lord Grey, colonial secretary about 1850, I'd seen his scribbled notes saying such things as 'Nonsense', and 'Tell him no, quickly'. What did Lord Carrington scribble on papers?

'I think you'd find out there [gesturing beyond the doors of his office] on most bits of paper, either a tick or no comment; or a thing which says, "Speak".'

Like a schoolmaster's 'See Me'?

'I'd rather see the guy who wrote it and talk to him. Much easier, you know, seeing people – certainly for me – than the written word, because the written word is very, very – particularly here – very carefully drafted. These guys are all absolute wizards with the written word.'

I showed sympathy, at which Lord Carrington added, in what I think a memorably acid phrase, that his people could 'distil something rather ably on a piece of paper'.

Then we came to the Atlantic Alliance, of which Lord Carrington said that as long as he could remember people had been saying it was in crisis, that things were worse than they'd ever known, and that they doubted whether it could last till Christmas. But one thing had struck him very much the other day, in the middle of a welter of talk about the Alliance falling to bits over Poland. There was a meeting of the NATO foreign ministers in Brussels. Now usually the communiqué took *hours* and *hours* and *hours*: he sometimes thought they took longer deciding what they had said than actually saying it. But at that meeting it was precisely the reverse. The meeting was over in two and a half hours, and the communiqué settled in fifteen minutes. His conclusion was that when the chips were down there was a feeling, shared by them all, that the Alliance was the most important thing there was, and that went for America as well as Europe.

But things, I said, had come to the pass where a US secretary of state, Alexander Haig, could call him a duplicitous bastard. I had thought he would pass this off lightly, with a well-chosen, though full and free, understatement. But he did not, at least at first.

He said, 'Well, I really. . .' and left me to reflect on the background to that piece of Haigspeak, which was that the Israelis, as usual, were in a terrible state, this time about America selling early warning planes to the Saudis, and because Sadat had just been murdered. The Israelis promptly turned round and bit Haig sharply on the calf, and Haig in turn was scared they would invade southern Lebanon or renege on the Sinai agreement. All very likely. Then Haig, feeling he had to do something to demonstrate brotherly love for Begin, turned round and bit Carrington, then president of the council of EEC ministers, whom the Israelis saw as running around the Arab countries promising that Europe would support a Palestinian state in Judea.

I returned to my question. Lord Carrington said, 'You know, "duplicitous bastard". . . I have said things in this room about people, which I should be less than happy to see reported in the newspapers. [Laughter.] And I don't necessarily mean them quite as they sound. I don't think he did either.' Hadn't Lord Carrington asked for the original of an *Evening Standard* cartoon that celebrated the occasion? 'Yes, and I got it. I mean, Al and I are perfectly good friends. Nobody believes that, but we are. We get on extremely well.'

Lord Carrington works, as every foreign secretary since 1868 has worked, in Gilbert Scott's magnificent Italianate pile in Whitehall. He has called it a mausoleum, though a splendid one. But apart from a few great rooms, the rest of it is in a state of unbelievable neglect, with barbaric bits tacked on here and there. I said that if I owned a listed building and treated it that badly, the GLC would probably do its best to see me in jail. Why was it such a mess? He said it was going to be done up in three years' time. His own room was mostly in its original state, with the original furniture.

Beautiful Queen Anne chairs, I said. 'Victorian walnut copies,' he said, 'I think you'll find.' As of course they are, since there's a set of twenty or so.

'Good old Westminster sofa,' he said, patting it; and he was going to have a new carpet; and the curtains were falling to bits. 'We're getting it all done, but if you do too much of it you become like Judith Hart. Don't you remember her bathroom? She was minister for overseas development, and she had a great suite made over there, with a bathroom and a changing room and one thing and another. Poor old lady never lived it down. Last thing I want to do is to be considered to have been extravagant. I think you've got to keep things up. After all, this is a room that represents Britain. I mean, people come in here.'

The pictures, he said, had changed. The portrait of George III over the mantelpiece had been taken down by George Brown. In its place there now hangs a picture of a Nepalese general, put up by David Owen. He himself had found a couple of Zoffanys in a waiting-room, and they now hang on an end wall. But he thought people really wanted to see Palmerston.

By now I could see anxious private secretaries hanging round in the background, wanting to get at Lord Carrington. British passports, I said, used to carry an adjuration beginning, 'We, Ernest Bevin, request and require . . .' but now they didn't say anything about 'We, Baron Carrington . . .'

'Do you feel deprived?' he asked.

I did a bit, and should feel a great deal more deprived when the present passport was replaced by the proposed paperback thing.

'No you won't. You won't see any difference. It'll be exactly the same.'

I protested that at the moment the British passport was the only one that was a hardback. Lord Carrington asked if the new one wasn't too, and was told by an aide that it had to be flexible, to go through a machine, at which I said it would look like a limp Japanese or American passport, and Lord Carrington said the mock-up he'd seen wasn't too bad.

Ah.

Then he said, 'I'm rather sad about the whole thing. But the point is that it's machine readable.'

Was that essential? 'Well, it's going to help you going through passport controls here, there, and everywhere.'

But in Europe there were hardly any passport controls left, except in Switzerland. 'Well, all the experts assure me that it's going to help like mad, and if it doesn't help like mad, I'm damned if we're going to change our passport.'

The Minister for Overseas Development and a whole gang of people were now practically clawing at the door and howling to get in, but Lord Carrington was talking about the numenism of the room in which he was sitting. He could feel the spirit of Harold Macmillan there, though he had only been secretary for six months or so, and the spirit of Alec Douglas-Home, and of Bevin.

Bevin? 'I see Bevin here very much, don't you? The sort of bulldoggy Bevin sitting round here, sort of going "Puff". [Here Lord Carrington blew out his cheeks and then exhaled.] You remember how he used to do that? I can see them all here, in their own way. Except the nonentities, whom I can't see at all.'

The incoming delegation had now established a bridgehead, but Lord Carrington was still standing urbanely in front of the great fireplace, to be photographed.

'Do you like Doris Day,' he asked.

What?

'Behind you.'

On a side table several colour photographs were displayed, one of a wholesome blonde.

Who was it?

'It's [much laughter] it's the president of Iceland. She was *charming*.'

What's her name? 'I don't know. What's the name of the president of Iceland?'

An aide told him, Vigdis Finbogadottir.

The minister and attendant delegates swarmed in. This is a room to which people come. Those eager to be in on overseas development, Vigdis Finbogadottir, and no doubt good old Al Haig, next time he's passing through London, England. The curtains may be falling to bits, but there's still a portrait of Queen Victoria at the foot of the grand staircase. So, as to good old Al, 'an aspersion on his parts of speech', as Richard Brinsley Sheridan said.

—March 1982

A week after this interview appeared, Argentina invaded the Falklands. Lord Carrington, who had so urbanely regretted that a foreign secretary could no longer send a gunboat, resigned, and a whole British fleet set sail for the South Atlantic.

JOHN NOTT
Inconceivable to Lose

'Nowadays,' said John Nott, Secretary of State for Defence, 'I would do anything to be a million miles from a foreign office telegram, but then I was fascinated by them.' He was talking about the time when, as a young Gurkha lieutenant, he went as aide de camp to the commander-in-chief Far East on a six week tour of India, and, seeing FO telegrams, got his first distant whiff of politics.

He entered politics. He learned that the House of Commons could be a mob. He told Mrs Thatcher he couldn't run defence like Marks and Spencer. His ships burned, but the Falklands war was won. He came, he saw, and he did remarkably well. Now, at the age of fifty, he is retiring. 'I have never, ever wanted,' he says, 'not for one daft moment, to be leader of the Conservative Party. I mean, I would make an appalling leader of the party, and an even worse prime minister. I hope I know my limitations.'

I had not asked him, or hinted at asking him, whether he had ever wanted to be prime minister. He volunteered this disclaimer. But one other thing ought to be said straight off, which is that television does him wrong, as it most notably wronged Lord Home before him. Television makes Mr Nott look like a mouse standing by Mrs Thatcher's side while she embarrasses everyone with breathy exhortations to rejoice. He is no mouse.

On his father's side, he comes from a family whose military traditions date back to 1770. One of his father's Christian names is Kandahar, which is because Mr Nott's great-great-great-grand-father, General Sir William Nott, led the famous march from Kabul to Kandahar in 1880, one of the few successes in a catastrophic Afghan war. Mr Nott has named his elder son Kandahar. On the maternal side, the family is deep Devon since the beginning of time – parsons, doctors, countrymen.

After school, John Nott went into the army and, his family happening to know the colonel of the regiment, took a commission in the Gurkhas. He spent eighteen months on patrol in the jungle, being shot at by communist guerrillas; not a proper war, he says, though they did have men killed and wounded. Then, going as aide de camp to the C-in-C, he got his distant whiff of politics, remembers sitting on a particular chair on a particular veranda in Singapore and telling himself that was for him, resigned his commission, and went up to Cambridge to prepare himself.

There he read law and economics, became president of the Union, and met his Yugoslavian wife Miloska. He is said to have told her at the first meeting that he intended to marry her. 'Well, no,' he says; 'she tells the story and it's for her to tell and not me.' What happened was that he had been travelling in the Canadian Rockies in the vacation, spending two or three months in near isolation. Later he showed his colour slides of this holiday, at Cambridge. She was there. When the lights went up she saw him, and was amused that the man she saw didn't fit with the voice she had heard.

'Then I was asked by her or by her friend, a very nice man, who's a schoolteacher, to a little party they were giving. And I was very much taken with her and in a joking way said. "I think I'm going to marry you." I don't think I could seriously have meant it at the first meeting; although perhaps I did a bit.'

What did she say? 'She laughed.'

They did marry. Mr Nott puts her full birthplace, Maribor, Yugoslavia, in his *Who's Who* entry. This is most unusual, and he says he can't think why, and finds it most interesting that he did.

Something to do with his often expressed feelings for roots, with his feeling that the rootless are the truly unfortunate of the twentieth century? He doesn't know, but says his wife left Yugoslavia when she was sixteen to look for her mother from whom she'd been separated in the German invasion, and then went to Italy, France, and Germany before she eventually came to England. She found her mother. Her father had been killed.

When he was about to come down from Cambridge he wrote to S.G. Warburg's, the merchant bankers, saying he admired what they had been doing in the City and asking for a job. Was it also true he had written that they needed a gentile? 'Quite untrue. I wouldn't have been that tactless; not seeking a job.'

Warburg's took him, although he admitted at the first interview that his ambitions lay in politics, and at twenty-eight he was general manager.

Then, after the 1964 election, when he was in New York where Warburg's was setting up a branch, he realised that if he was going into politics he had to do it quickly. The 1966 election came upon them rapidly, all the marginal seats had chosen candidates, and the

only seats left were the safe ones. For one of these, St Ives, he was
adopted. A matter, he says, of being in the right place at the right
time.

And at that time, so early, he was already clear that he was going
to spend fifteen years in politics, and then leave? 'Yes, I've always
known exactly what I was going to do with my life. My wife is right
when she says I told her about the fifteen years at Cambridge. And
at the last election my wife and I agreed it would be the last; though
that was not something that anyone knew but her. If you're in
politics, hoping to be in the cabinet, you don't say such a thing.'

In 1966 he became an MP. In 1970 he was disappointed not to be
given junior office by Mr Heath, who, he says, had always gone out
of his way to be kind. Therefore, he says, he knows what disappointment tastes like.

In the 1970s you could fairly say he was not politically notorious.
He was reported as having, on a parliamentary visit, caught a
Mongolian trout weighing twenty-five pounds; he made statements
to the House about the future of the sixpence; he introduced a bill on
historic wrecks; and at the Conservative Party conference of 1977,
when he was shadow spokesman for trade, a steward, not recognising
him, stopped him as he attempted to mount the platform.

He admits it all. 'I was,' he says, 'very much unknown.'

After Mrs Thatcher's victory in 1979 he was given trade – where
he was at the centre of government policy-making and in and out of
Number 10 four times a day – and then, last year, defence.

He had been given defence to cut spending, and found himself
fighting a war instead? 'The Falklands is of course the thing people
will remember me for.'

What about the famous debate, that Saturday, when he was
howled down, and loudly advised to resign, and to go? (Read in
Hansard now, his speech doesn't look too bad, but at the time it
sounded terrible.)

'Yes, I had a bad debate. Well, I knew what would happen before
I stood up. I think that the press comments are a little bit
exaggerated. The House of Commons, very occasionally, is in that
kind of mood. Mob rule prevails. I suppose in retrospect I had a
worse battering than I had expected. I don't believe that however
skilful my speech had been – and I agree it wasn't very skilful – the
result would have been any different. I haven't on the whole been
noted for making bad House of Commons speeches in my career, and
I do have a feel for the House. The truth of the matter is that it was
impossible for that speech to be anything but a disaster. And that's

why, if I may tell you so, it did not actually knock me up. I recovered very quickly, and the next day on the Brian Walden show on television I think I was in good form.'

Here was Mr Nott, very relaxed, in shirt sleeves, chatting affably in his vast office in Whitehall, and I very well believed him about the Falklands debate; but I was brought up short, for the first time in the conversation, by his mention of his television performance, and was about to suggest to him that any television show didn't matter a damn in the context, when he went back to the Commons again.

'That debate did not knock me up, although perhaps it should have done. It was the central part of the Falklands campaign which I found the most exhausting and difficult. It was the need to get our people there – with this Haigery going on, and the United Nations, and the clash of opinion among us as to whether we should accept this or not accept that. When we got ashore, and the United Nations was out of the way, we had a clear objective again, and it became much easier. I mean, I'm talking for myself.'

That Falklands debate must have sounded awful to people who'd never seen the Commons at work? 'It must have been horrendous. My parents heard it on the radio and they were absolutely appalled. It wasn't as bad if you were part of it, frankly. That's why the House of Commons, I think, shouldn't be recorded in that way.'

The sinking of the *Belgrano* had knocked him up, hadn't it? 'Yes it did, for a day or two I was upset about that, yes.'

But he must have been there when the decision was taken? 'I took the decision. Not wholly by myself but with two or three others. I took the decision to allow the submarine commander to sink the *Belgrano* if it was posing a threat to the task force. I was knocked up a bit, I confess to you. We were pretty sure the SSN [nuclear submarine] would get the *Belgrano*, and we thought maybe there would be some casualties, but we never conceived that survivors wouldn't be picked up. Indeed, the *Belgrano* was actually sunk by two World War II torpedoes. The Type 42s [her two escorting destroyers] pushed off and left the ship, which would never have happened in our case. They apparently had orders to do so. That is why so many lives were lost.'

I asked Mr Nott how he felt when the *Sheffield* went, but again he returned to the *Belgrano*, saying at one time he feared as many as a thousand had died, the whole ship.

But the *Sheffield*? 'You know, it was very difficult. We had the news coming back on an open press line, but we weren't getting the operational information back as fast on the operational line, because they were fighting a battle. So we had information that these things were happening, but no corroboration.'

But when he knew *Sheffield* was lost, the first ship of the Royal Navy to be lost since 1945? 'I expected to lose more ships than we lost.'

But the *Sheffield*, I said: for myself I had felt simple anger. 'Yes. It changed the mood of the country. It exorcised that wound of the *Belgrano*. People then felt angry. It was a terrible event, the *Sheffield*.'

Had he ever thought of just going and getting the Argentine aircraft carrier *25 May*? 'I was deeply concerned that if we held back, held back, held back, because of the negotiations that were going on first with the Peruvian proposals and then with the United Nations, then our people would get there and find themselves with a desperately worse battle on their hands. So we gave a great deal of consideration to the *25 May*, and we'd have sunk her if we found her.'

He didn't know where she was? 'We knew where she was, but she didn't come out into deep water.'

He never thought of going and getting her where she lay? 'Well, I was always against extending the conflict into the territorial waters. But we imposed the twelve mile limit, and if she'd come one mile out of that we'd have sunk her.'

Had he ever thought, when he saw ship after ship burning, what Beatty had thought at Jutland as he watched his battle cruisers blow up, that something was wrong with our bloody ships today? He said he knew ships had to be hazarded, and would be lost.

But burning like that? 'With the missiles it was the propellant [the missile's unused fuel] that was the problem. But these ships aren't like Admiral Beatty's. They are a mass of floating electronics. And it would be a mistake, whatever changes are made, to believe that the modern frigate is not going to create great fire problems if it's hit.'

For two days the *Canberra* had lain in San Carlos water, an almost unmissable target, a ship it would have been a disaster to lose. Had he slept at all during that time? 'I slept on the whole quite well.' The only trouble was that, with the change in time from the South Atlantic, he was sometimes woken up by the telephone.

Had he at any time thought we might lose and have to withdraw? 'Well, we couldn't have lost it. I mean, I knew that in the end we would win because we had to win. There was no way in which in the end we could afford to lose this. Once we'd set out, once the task force had set sail, it was inconceivable that it could turn back, and it was inconceivable we could lose. We never doubted that there'd be a victory, but I confess to you that I thought we'd lose more ships and men than we did.'

How many? 'Even if we'd lost double the number of ships we'd still have kept going forward.'

I said it had been reported that, before the Falklands war, Mrs Thatcher had told him he was being too soft with defence cuts, and that he had retorted she had given him an impossible job: was this true? Mr Nott said, waving his hand in the air as if to indicate the presence of a newspaper headline, that he was always hearing this quote, 'She asked me to do an impossible job', but he didn't think it could have come from him.

'I hope I've been one of the prime minister's closest supporters, and still am. That doesn't mean to say I haven't had any disagreements with her. I have. Because she's who she is, she encourages argument and disagreement.'

Yes? 'I will recall much of my time with Mrs T in argument and debate. [Whenever he mentioned her it was as Mrs T.] I was very angry, frankly, that having been through all the defence review here last year, and having got the full agreement of the whole cabinet to what I proposed, the treasury then started to chip it away. And this job is impossible if every time you settle a programme someone comes along and wants to chop this and that off.'

He had told Mrs Thatcher she couldn't run the ministry of defence like Marks and Spencer? 'I often tell her, yes, I often tell her. Yes, I think I've possibly gone a bit over the top with her, but, I mean, she's very decent about it. Mind you, you must understand that I was very much closer to all these things when I was at trade. We were closer politically in those days, because I was in and out of the place four times a day.'

Had these disagreements sometimes amounted to a shouting match? 'No, no. But she's a person who provokes argument and debate.'

Demands it? 'Almost demands it.'

In a way, he was a Gaullist figure, openly patriotic? 'I am a Gaullist, yes. I am a pseudo-Gaullist.'

He'd also said a few hard things about the French and their wretched wine, though? 'For God's sake, I made that as a joke in a speech. It was to do with sheep meat. They'd messed up my business on the farm. I remember it very well. I was in the early lamb business, and they wouldn't let my lambs in, and I said I'm not going to drink their beastly wine while they won't let my lambs be exported to France.'

As secretary of defence he saw as his first responsibility the defence of these islands? 'Yes.'

That was why he was buying Trident? 'Yes. I'm not buying it for NATO. In the last resort we must be able to stand alone. I'm greatly in favour of the Alliance, but you never can tell, and I can't be sure that the Alliance will be as healthy in twenty years' time as it is today.'

And with Trident, even though the Russians were much stronger, we would still be able to reduce Moscow to rubble, and that would be a sort of equality? 'Equality in the power to destroy?'

Yes; it wouldn't matter if they could destroy us one hundred times over if we could destroy them once. 'Well, yes, with Trident, and now with Polaris. The reason for Trident is that it is no use having a deterrent that is not credible to the enemy. You might as well have nothing. And within ten years, because of developments in anti-ballistic missiles, we need something like Trident, to be a credible deterrent.'

He was putting himself in the shoes of the Russians, taking their view? 'Deterrence is not how you see it, but it is how the other side sees you. That is wholly what it is about.'

We talked about the chancellorship of the exchequer. Mr Nott supposed he could have had it if he wanted it badly enough. But now it was too late, and he wouldn't take it if it were offered tomorrow. He would have done it differently from Geoffrey Howe, but doesn't think he would have been able to do more.

'I mean, I could have done the chancellorship. I didn't particularly, passionately, want it. I was very happy to have this job. One thing that I'd now like to say, and I haven't said this before, is that having been secretary of state for defence, I rather feel – I've been in the treasury and it holds no mystery for me – that the treasury would have rather little to offer, and I'll tell you why. Because I've served three years in the treasury. I've observed it from the cabinet and outside the cabinet. The chancellor's job today is three quarters presentation and one quarter substance. This is an open economy, and the capacity of the chancellor to actually change things is extremely limited. Now the thing about defence is that three quarters of what I do here is of real substance. Nobody bothers me. The chiefs of staff and I, and my permanent secretary, we have a huge budget, and of course we consult the prime minister on major strategic questions like whether we modernise the deterrent, but basically I have been able to take a whole raft of decisions which are real and which I know are important for the years 1990 to 2000. Vastly important for the defence of this country. I don't believe the chancellor of the exchequer any more has that kind of power, to make decisions that really count.'

Well, if the chancellor hadn't who had? 'What do we have to do? You see, I'm a Conservative and I don't think politics are frightfully important. I think that all politics can do is release the restrictions which stop people from creating wealth.'

So he wanted as little government as possible? 'I am a minimalist. It is the function of a government to remove specified causes of unhappiness. But governments cannot create happiness, and they cannot create wealth. That may not be the view of a socialist, but it is my view. Far and away the most important economic measures taken since we've come to office have been the abolition of exchange controls, and my abolition of price controls, when I got rid of the price commission. I don't know if you remember, but when we came into government the whole of the economy was regulated by Mr Hattersley from the price commission.'

He was talking, I said, like a nineteenth century liberal. 'I am a nineteenth century liberal. So is Mrs Thatcher. That's what this government is all about.'

Well, he was about to leave politics. He would not contest the next election. Politics was plainly not his be-all and end-all. Splendid. I recalled once asking Sir Alec Douglas-Home what he would do if his party lost the forthcoming election, and he replied that he would have other things to do. I took him to mean he would return to running his own large parts of Scotland, and much liked this disinterestedness.

'Yes, that's what I feel. My circumstances are entirely different from Alec's. I'm not a rich man; reasonably well off, but not a rich man. I want more time now to do some fishing, and I enjoy shooting, and I like my farming. I'm not going to kill myself in the next twenty years.'

Mr Nott is doing what Barber and Lennox-Boyd did before him. The first returned into business in 1974 after having been chancellor, the second in 1959 after being colonial secretary when there were still some colonies. Such men are generally compared to Cincinnatus, who, from being a great general, retired to his farm – and was found, incidentally, cultivating a small patch of land by a Senate delegation who begged him to accept the office of dictator, which he did for sixteen days, when, having defeated the enemies of Rome, he returned to his little plot.

No, no, said Mr Nott; he would spend some time on the farm but ...

Exactly. He was no Cincinnatus because Cincinnatus hadn't become chairman of the Standard Chartered Bank of Rome, whereas Mr Nott was likely to do something of the sort. But whatever bank he ran, wouldn't it seem a tiny business after defence?

'Yes, yes. But, you know, I had a letter yesterday from someone who's retiring, and he asked if I'd like to come in with him and start a restaurant chain, and would I put some money up, and we could build a chain of Wimpy bars in Bedford. And my secretary passed me this letter and said, "This man's a nut." And I said, "I don't think he's a nut", and, you know, I think I could almost be as enthusiastic about going in with this fellow building twenty Wimpy bars.'

And he had, he said, always wanted to be on his parish council. Yes? I said; at which he told me the *Guardian* was a bloody good newspaper but he never read it. He never read *The Times* either, or any paper.

Not even the cricket scores? 'I read *Farmer's Weekly*. I read *The Field*.'

And *Country Life*? 'Yes, and – not because Macmillan did it – I've discovered Trollope again. Every night during the Falklands I read Trollope for an hour before I went to sleep. I read the whole lot again – *The Eustace Diamonds, The Duke's Children, Phineas Finn, Phineas Redux*. I'm just about to start *The Prime Minister*. I've found them an enormous relaxation.'

Perhaps. But Mr Nott is reading not the pastoral, Barsetshire novels, but the political novels of a novelist who was obsessed by politics, and wanted all his life to be a politician.

I said so. Mr Nott said he had not thought of that.

—September 1982

THE TAKERS
OF LONGER VIEWS

ENOCH POWELL
'Laws, Councils, Monarchies'

Enoch Powell is seventy. It is almost nineteen years since Mr Powell last held office, as minister of health, in 1963. It is more than fourteen years ago, at Birmingham in 1968, that he made the speech in which he said he was filled with foreboding and seemed to see the Tiber foaming with much blood; and was in consequence expelled from Mr Heath's shadow cabinet. It is eight years since, in the first general election of 1974, he declined to stand again for the seat he had held since 1950, called the election itself essentially fraudulent, and advised Conservatives to vote against the Common Market and for Labour. From this attempt at political suicide he was rescued only by the unexpected offer of the Ulster Unionist candidature for South Down in the unexpected second general election of that year. He won that seat and has held it, and has remained one of the great parliamentarians of his day. He has never, in as many words, said 'I told you so.'

The other day we met in the central lobby of the House of Commons and Mr Powell led the way upstairs to the dismal, windowless office of one of his colleagues, where he said that if he appeared dilapidated I must remember that he had not slept for sixty hours because of two all-night sittings. This, after he had led the way through corridors at a pace I could hardly keep up with.

Throughout his public life, I said, he had talked of a sense of nation, and of national sovereignty.

'Carry on.'

We were in the middle of a Falklands war. Had that war either revealed a sense of national will, or augmented such a sense?

'I would prefer the alternative "revealed". While you made your own observation of my mode of thought and expression it passed through my mind that it was now more intelligible than it had seemed a few weeks ago, and much less indeed in need of explanation or defence.'

But was he a little dismayed by the humbug which still manifested

101

itself? We were fighting a war which we would not even call a war. 'Yes indeed. We find ourselves using the vocabulary deployed over the last thirty-five years to deny nationhood, sovereignty, and the rest; we are obliged to use a vocabulary which doesn't fit.'

We called it a 'conflict'. 'That's right. And we say it is in defence of liberty, or for the benefit of all nations which might find themselves aggressed. Well, quite plainly, nothing we do in the Falklands makes it more or less easy for any other nation, in any other circumstances, to resist an aggressor. So we've got the wrong terminology.'

Even the words had slipped? 'Well, the clothes that have been cut to the fashion of the last thirty-five years don't fit our present actions. Humbug is a very common ingredient in politics, particularly English politics.'

He appeared to have been kicking against it all his life? 'I've been drawing attention to it. Perhaps that was bad taste.'

Oh, it was. 'Yes. All right then, take out "perhaps".'

In something he had spoken or written he had begun, 'Herodotus relates', and what Herodotus had related was that the Greeks had an agora where they met to deceive each other and swear oaths. He had said that one such present day agora was the United Nations. 'Yes, it is the very capital and new Jerusalem of humbug – it is all humbug. The reality is naked power; what actually happens at the United Nations, the driving forces, belong to *Realpolitik*, but they are dressed up in this extraordinary garb. Now, dress is part of civilisation, and no one should complain if we have been accustomed to dress and cover the cruder aspects or emotions of mankind with myth, and with pretence, with poetry, *die dichtungszauberische Hülle*, and all the rest.'

What did those German words mean? 'Ah, that's Goethe, "The magic veil of poetry". But you can overdo it, and the danger of the United Nations is the way it has applied the democratic concept, transferring it from a context in which it has a meaning and a virtue, into a context in which it is a parody and a deception. You line up in the House of Commons 635 elected persons and they debate; you line up in the United Nations 160 nations and they debate; and you call the two things by the same name.'

And we had heard Mrs Thatcher constantly invoking Resolution 502 as if it were of any consequence, and at a time when the helplessness of the United Nations had been well illustrated in the Lebanon?

'Resolution 502,' said Mr Powell, 'is incompatible not merely with what we are doing in the Falklands but with anything we could do in the Falklands without total surrender.'

Long before he entered politics Mr Powell became, at the age of twenty-five, professor of Greek at Sydney. This was a disappointment since it meant he had lost by a year to Nietzsche, who had become professor of classics at Basle at twenty-four. As a younger man still, Powell had loved Nietzsche and the German romantics. To learn German, he used as texts the libretti of two Wagner operas, and his first published article, a scholarly analysis of a Greek text, was written in German. With all this in mind, I suggested to Mr Powell that any biographer of his would be under the disadvantage of having to be both a Greek and a German scholar to have any notion of what was passing through Powell's mind in his formative years.

'Curiously enough, it would be more important for him to be a German than a Greek scholar. I'm in danger of being misunderstood by saying that, but I'll try to explain why I feel so sure of it. I happened to use just then, in speaking to you, not a Greek quotation but a German quotation, and I used the German quotation because it conveyed to me a certain emotional association which would not readily find a Greek garb. Putting it another way, the qualities of Greek are extraordinarily close to those of English. Indeed, when I think Greek, I do not change. I am still myself . . .'

But when he spoke German? 'When I speak German I become a different person. I become a more emotional person. There is a band of expression, of temperament, what you will, for which German is a vehicle but for which Greek – though it may have been the educator of the English – is not. It is not a different medium, like the language of a viol, to which they [the English] must resort in order to sound emotions and to express feelings which English, even that of Shakespeare, could not arouse.'

Would it be true to say that throughout his life he had, in the sense Goethe might have used the phrase, lived dangerously? 'I understand what is meant by that. Danger, both physical and metaphorical, is to me a stimulus. And it's also a stimulus to the enjoyment of the other emotions. I was only reflecting, curiously, a day or two ago, how the romantic passions are, in my experience, heightened by danger and hardship. This has been observed before. A man come in from the hunting field is in a romantic frame of mind.'

This would fit in with his having said that he had totally abandoned himself, to love, to war, to politics? Hadn't he once said he had gone to war as a bridegroom to his bride? He replied that he had not said that, but written it about whole nations in a poem entitled 'Mobilization'. But it was true that abandonment was a characteristic of his.

Akin to this, he said, was a power of a sense of concentration, being able to cut himself off from what was around him. For example, he found the House of Commons library an ideal place for concentration. 'I would have less concentration if I was shut away in one of these horrid little rooms. But I can concentrate easily in the library because I have something to concentrate *against*. I am there, and yet I make myself a little private space at a table at which four other members are sitting, with members walking backwards and forwards, and division bells ringing. That's one sense of concentration. Another is that, to use a hunting expression, you must throw your heart over a fence in order to jump it. Your heart's got to be the other side for the horse to know that you mean to jump the fence.'

I think it difficult even to approach an understanding of Mr Powell without considering the passionate sensibility which, every bit as much as his strength of mind, determines the course of his actions. I said that his passion in politics should only have been expected by anyone who had read his verse, and particularly the poems in a volume called *The Wedding Gift*. There was one poem in which he wrote that the greatest thing a man could hope for was to know another soul.

'Laws, councils, monarchies . . .' he said, quoting the first line.

It should be said that *The Wedding Gift*, his fourth book of poems, published in 1951, contains a group of poems written by him to a woman he loved, and dedicated to her as a wedding present on her marriage to another man. Here is one of them, which was written not long after he had embarked on his political career.

> *Laws, councils, monarchies,*
> *On your hypocrisies*
> *I waste*
> *The only power,*
> *This hour,*
> *Which given is to me*
> *Of all eternity,*
> *In haste*
> *Before I go*
> *To know*
> *The thing alone*
> *Which known*
> *Is of reality*
> *The whole,*
> *Another soul.*

Mr Powell demurred at my saying he had at the time just embarked on his political career. He had never seen it as a career: he had chosen an occupation, way of life, profession, environment, whatever; he had 'taken up residence in a new college'.

All right. But at that time, entering politics, which was to be his life, he had still felt that, nevertheless, the greatest thing a man could have was the knowledge of another soul?

He agreed. 'Yes,' but then went on: ' "Laws, councils, monarchies, On your hypocrisies" ... I wasn't saying, "Honours, positions, gradations in a profession". I was living in the world of "laws, councils, monarchies", and I was living in the world of their "hypocrisies". And I like it. It's my world, and I'm happy there. Not only would I not require paying to be in it, but I would earn sufficient by the sweat of my brow to pay for it, if I had to pay for it.'

Twice, I said, in 1968 and 1974, he had gone over a precipice. He replied that there was a great contrast between the two occasions. 'In 1968 I didn't know there was a precipice. It was an elephant pit. But in 1974 I drove over the precipice knowing that the road I was on was bound to take me over a precipice, and telling everyone, and myself, "Look, there is the end of my public life." '

In 1974, when he had refused to stand again for Wolverhampton and urged electors to vote Labour, he had said he had 'descended into hell'. When I reminded Mr Powell of this he said I must remember the context. He had said he had 'descended into hell, and risen again'. 'So the expression, and I am open to criticism on this score, was a striking expression with two parts, and I chose it for the sake of the second part.' Torment no doubt was present, but it was not an inherent connotation of the phrase used for the purposes he chose it for. 'What I was saying was: "Look, here's a resurrection, chaps." I didn't expect it. Did you?'

I said I did not. 'No,' said Mr Powell.

But as to 1968? 'Sixty-eight was the biggest *surprise* of my life.' Sixty-eight has contributed, in its consequences, more than any deliberate act of mine that I can think of, to making me known and therefore unknown, understood and therefore misunderstood, by the great mass of my fellow countrymen. But that was pure accident.'

And if at the moment he was writing that speech someone had looked over his shoulder, and said: 'Mr Powell, if you deliver that speech you will be ejected from the shadow cabinet ...'?

'Yes, yes. I would have said: "Then I must alter the speech." '

Mr Powell then went into the circumstances of this extraordinary accident. He had believed, wrongly, that the decision of the shadow cabinet to vote against the second reading of the Race Relations Bill was a turning point in the internal policies of the Conservative leadership. He was writing a speech in support of that decision, a decision which he believed to be right, but which would need to be defended and explained. He remembered very clearly how the West Midlands agent, who saw the speech forty-eight hours beforehand, had said it would be invaluable in giving people such an explanation.

That was 1968. He does not see the Brixton riots of last year as a *proof* of what he said then. He thinks proof too strong a word.

Evidence, then? 'An illustration.'

Then what had he felt when he saw that terrible illustration last year? 'Supposing a man had been trying to persuade his fellows that a substance which they thought was harmless, or even beneficial, was in fact poison, and they had all said: "No, it's not poison, what a fool you are. You must be suffering from delusions if you think that is harmful." Then, if I saw a person actually poison himself with it, I wouldn't dance on his grave. I wouldn't say: "How absolutely splendid!" But I would say: "Well, it's evidently not I who was mistaken." '

He had felt sadness? 'Ah yes. Though sadness *not* devoid of an element – words are tricky, aren't they? – an element, I was going to say, of reassurance; but I only mean reassurance in the sense of knowing that you're not suffering from delusions yourself. You are reassured when you find that there is actually a wall over there. You go and touch it. That's a reassurance.'

I asked how well Mr Powell knew the United States. 'Very little, and the less for being unsympathetic towards what consciously impinges upon me of it.'

I explained that I had intended to ask whether he knew that whole parts of New York City had been taken over by Hispanics. 'I have seen that. I do not in fact believe that it made much impression upon me, or that it has affected my thinking, or my perception of the United Kingdom.'

Why not? 'For instance, the United States is a continent. For instance, you can ruin New York, and still the United States would be recognisable as the United States. The setting of the United States is to me devoid of analogy with Britain. I mean, I slightly bridle, for instance, when the word "democracy" is applied to the United Kingdom. Instead of that I say: "We are a parliamentary nation." If you, my dear friend, are going around with a collector's case, collecting beetles, and you put us into the jar labelled Democracy, I can't complain: I can only tell you that you have understood very little about the United Kingdom.'

How was that? 'We have institutions, which you can't separate from us and from who we are. I have often said of myself that I am an "institutional man". My perception of society, perhaps paradoxically for a person so ready to pursue his own ideas and his own thoughts wherever they may lead him, is wholly social; that is to say, about institutions.'

School, college, army, House of Commons? 'Yes. And moreover, I can't think about mankind except by starting with society. I can't think, in a way which is evidently congenial to many people, by starting with the individual. I don't start my train of thought with propositions about an individual. I start with propositions about a society.'

I had introduced the United States because there is now a body of opinion there which, alarmed by the huge and mostly illegal influx of Hispanics, foresees that the second great crisis to confront the United States, the first having been the Civil War, may be a conflict between the Anglo-Saxon and Hispanic language and cultures. If this were so, would it fit in with the theme of *The Decline of the West*?

'But,' said Mr Powell, 'I'm not a Spengler man. If you like, I'm too specific. I say to myself: "This around me is something which has never happened before – there is only one of this." I see certain biological analogies, admittedly. I assume that as it came into existence, so one day it will pass out of existence, but . . .'

But civilisations had, one after the other, declined?

Even that proposition, said Mr Powell, was one which, if he were speaking *ex cathedra*, from his professor's chair, he would be inviting his students to repudiate rather than to verify.

As an exercise? 'No, more than that. I would say: "Now, you are given to suppose that the age of Belisarius was a decline from the age of Cicero. My dear young men, I want you to understand that this idea is something which *you* have imported, something which is wholly you, as if you had placed an opaque substance between yourselves and what you think is the history you are reading and learning. I do beg of you to believe that the judgment you have made is a falsification." '

Not being able to make any comparison at all between Cicero's Rome and the Eastern Empire of six hundred years later, I asked if the Britain of the past twenty years was not in decline from the Britain of 1890. 'I can see some points of view which, if you accept them, will lead you to that conclusion, but I do not regard those points of view and categories as self-evidently, or even necessarily, normative. I happen to have made a speech yesterday – was it yesterday or the day before?: when you have all-night sittings you "forget all time", like Milton – in which I asked a question. It was a speech to the Institute of Directors. I have a paper on "What *is* a recession, after all?" And I suggested that this notion of a recession was an illusion which we had ourselves imported, to our own danger, into the observation of economic phenomena.'

I was about to remark that three million out of work was a recession, but by then we were really talking about the relationship of perception to reality, or the nature of reality, or something pertinent to that, and we were anyway running out of time.

As we left the office and walked rapidly along corridors back to the lobby, I asked Mr Powell if it was true that he no longer listened to music because he did not wish any longer to arouse expectations in himself which could not be fulfilled. Wasn't this terrible?

'It is rather. It's a disappointing experience. But it's not unnatural to think: "Well, there are only a certain number of things I can do, and if I'm to do them I must concentrate." If so, there must, alas, be a whole part of one's past experience, of one's emotional development and all the rest of it which must be renounced – just as if you found, being a devotee of the Italian Renaisance, that you could no longer spend a month every year in Italy. You must reconcile yourself to the fact, especially as you grow older, that of the "many mansions" there are some in which you won't be able to take up residence. You may not even be able to remain in residence in some of your most favoured.'

Mr Powell loves Wagner. I asked if he had seen the recent production of *Tristan und Isolde* at Covent Garden? 'Well, no – for simple reasons of inability to book ahead. In parliamentary life, I only occasionally, very, very rarely, see a Wagner opera. But I don't begrudge it. I say: "Well, if being a member of parliament means that for five days of the week I can't do anything else, so be it." But it doesn't frustrate me. What a lucky man I am.'

We were now back in the central lobby. In a biographical sketch of Joseph Chamberlain, Mr Powell once wrote that all political lives, unless they were cut off in midstream at a happy juncture, ended in failure, because that was the nature of politics. So I asked if he still believed political life ended in failure.

'Not only political life.'

Was that *necessarily* true?

'We must define failure in a particular way. There is a sense in which lives are built so as to fail.'

Had he failed? 'Only in that sense. I must bid you farewell.'

—June 1982

JAMES CALLAGHAN
An Instinct to Trim

'I don't know,' said James Callaghan, 'what the introduction to the British passport says now, but you remember the old days.'

Having discussed this same matter with Lord Carrington when he was foreign secretary, I do remember what the preamble to the British passport said and still says, and recited the words to Mr Callaghan: 'Her Britannic Majesty's Principal Secretary of State for Foreign Affairs requests and requires . . .'

'Requires!' exclaimed Mr Callaghan. (Laughter.) 'And I think, you know, in one's innocence, when one went abroad then, to be a citizen of the British Empire was a pretty considerable thing: and you were so regarded. There was so much about the empire that was a credit to us. There was a great deal that wasn't. But we seem constantly ready to emphasise all the things we've done which were discreditable.'

He recalled a visit he made as a young MP in 1946 to Sierra Leone, the Gambia, Nigeria, and the Gold Coast when he had seen young district officers, living in villages up country, working as hard as anyone could have done to improve the lot of their people. Of course, he said, it was all very patronising, and he had no doubt those countries now did better under self-government: it was better to be governed badly by oneself than to be governed by others.

When I said that earlier this year, also in West Africa, I had seen Englishmen no longer governing anything but still doing their utmost to avert famine, Mr Callaghan said that in a non-political way these people were the lineal descendants of empire, an extension of empire. We should not assume that everyone who had gone out had done so for the worst of motives. Take India, he said; we had carried to India a legal system, a constitution, and a language which was the only one they shared in common.

I asked if this feeling for empire was nostalgic on Mr Callaghan's part. He said it was. It was at this point that he asked about the preamble to the passport, and wondered who it was who had said that if we lost India we should descend to the level of a second-rate power.

Had it been Churchill?

'Probably. He said almost all these things. There was no doubt you could throw out your chest if you were British ... But we mustn't have all this conversation about the empire. [We had drifted that way because we had both seen a Granada TV programme on the end of that empire.]You'll turn me into an old blimp, and I'm not. I really wasn't a blimp in those days, I promise you, even if I am now.'

All right, but wasn't one of his earliest memories that of attending, as a boy of twelve, the Wembley Empire Exhibition of 1924? He said it was, and recalled the little train that took you from Australia to South Africa to Canada in two minutes flat. And then of course, he said, his father and grandfather had been in the Navy. His father had served on the West Africa station and been present at the sacking of Benin after the murder of the British consul, in 1897.

Hadn't his father, as chief petty officer, volunteered to go on Scott's last and fatal expedition of 1912? He said his father had volunteered both for that and for the Royal Yacht *Victoria and Albert*. Now his father's wife had already been widowed before she was twenty when her first husband, also a seaman, was cut down by a destroyer as he was coming ashore in Devonport harbour. So she said to her second husband when the choice came, that she would prefer the *Victoria and Albert*, since Queen Alexandra hated the sea, and the yacht would stay in harbour. Her will prevailed, she was also right about the queen, and CPO Callaghan used to go on board every morning at seven and return home every afternoon at four.

But if he had gone with Scott? 'I shouldn't be here. Just think what misery everyone might have been saved.' (Laughter.)

CPO Callaghan later became a coastguard, and died in 1921. The Admiralty at first gave his widow no pension, and then one of sixteen shillings a week to keep herself and the young James. They lived in two rooms. Mr Callaghan said he had been back the other day, invited by the captain of a frigate his wife had launched years ago. They had really wanted his wife, who had after all done the launching, and it was the first time he knew what it must be like to be Mr Thatcher. He went to Brixham and saw the old house, and the fish auction where, twice a week, a fish merchant used to give him a fish to take home for dinner. They were poor, and he was kind and a member of the same Baptist chapel. The rest of the week, it was bread and dripping and cocoa.

We had found some common ground – my grandfather, like Mr Callaghan's father, having been a naval petty officer, then a diver, then a coastguard – and Mr Callaghan was talking freely. But then

110

he said he really didn't want me to believe he spent his life thinking about all this. If I hadn't been there, these things would never have crossed his mind.

Then, I said, let's come on to later things. I wanted to ask what had been in his mind at two particular moments. The first was the moment he became prime minister.

Here he paused for a long time, and then explained that first of all he hadn't expected it ever to happen. He had thought Mr Wilson would call him in, thank him for long service, and say something about making way for a younger man. But Mr Wilson had retired, and he became prime minister.

What had he felt at that moment? Mr Callaghan said he felt then and felt now that the nation was one nation; and he scorned Mrs Thatcher when she spoke about the enemy within, and so on. Miners, whether they were on strike or at work, were all our fellow countrymen.

Yes, but at that moment? 'I think I had a vision; of course, certainly. I promise you, Mr Coleman, and you really mustn't make fun of this – my wife said I was wrong to give you this interview because she said you weren't a very kindly man: I said never mind, it's vanity that's making me give it to him. Anyway, I promise you, that when you stand by the prime minister's chair at Number 10 you know that you are a trustee of the past as well as someone who has to try and carry the nation forward into the future. And you do. I'm sure that Mrs Thatcher feels it. I'm sure that any prime minister with a spark of imagination must have felt that, the greatness of sitting in that chair.' Then, lowering his voice, 'There's so much of empire.'

Well, there was his sense of continuation? 'No, no, I said it for fun. I said it for fun.'

Mr Callaghan said that our former leaders of the colonies and dependencies were always impressed to sit in the cabinet room at Number 10. He particularly remembered Mr Begin – who was very glad to be received, because after all there was his terrorist background. Mr Begin sat opposite the prime minister's chair, spread his arms, and declared (a bit, it seemed to me, listening to the description, like an American tourist), oh what it was like to be in that historic room where so many of the great events in British history had unfolded themselves, and then he ran through some of them, ending up with the Balfour Declaration. And Mr Callaghan politely agreed, and didn't tell him the Balfour Declaration had actually been signed in the foreign office.

Now, for the second moment. What had been in Mr Callaghan's

mind when he went to the rostrum at the Labour Party conference in 1983 to speak against abandoning our nuclear armaments unilaterally, and had been booed, 'At the point of booing? Oh, just that I'd fight back. I've Irish blood in my veins. Booing never deters me. Oh, I was angry of course . . . It was Neil's debut. I didn't want to spoil it. But when I was accused as I was, I simply felt – and perhaps this was again, some would say, vanity on my part – but I felt that I could not go back on what I had done and said while I was prime minister.'

Had he felt any clash between conscience – speaking up for what he believed to be right – and loyalty, or what might appear to be loyalty, to the party? 'Ha [long pause]. I think I'd probably be a little hypocritical if I said this question of loyalty was very much in my mind, because the party seemed at that time to be departing so much from the principles that I had grown up with and lived with. I don't feel that now: I must emphasise that. I think Neil Kinnock is getting back on the road.'

But he felt then that the party had gone to the dogs? He said he didn't believe he ever said that. Nor would he ever use that phrase because he cared for the party too much. It was a part of his life. It had taken the place of the Chapel, as it were. He still had not changed his views, but those passions of 1983 had died down a lot.

I then inquired about David Owen, who after all was Mr Callaghan's protégé, whom he promoted to be foreign secretary. Here Mr Callaghan showed himself at his Byzantine best. He now possessed, he said amiably, the advantage of free speech for the first time in thirty-five years. This freedom was, he confided, like nectar. It was, he assured me, very savoury. By now he was so cordial that I knew for certain he was going to tell me nothing at all about David Owen, but he was still talking so persuasively that I expected him at any moment to declare, 'Behold, I show you a mystery.' He showed me instead, by way of consummate diversion, what he described as the only picture of the cabinet taken by a *Daily Mirror* photographer in two parts, the two parts then having been stuck together to make a whole. This miraculous picture was displayed on a wall, and showed, as Mr Callaghan explained, David Owen next to Shirley, and Shirley next to Benn, 'this lamb lying down with the lion'.

So I confined myself to saying Neil Kinnock seemed to have a good line in abuse where Dr Owen was concerned, at which Mr Callaghan said Neil had absorbed his parliamentary history, but that what he had said of Owen was nothing to what Lloyd George had said of Sir John Simon – that he had sat on the fence so long that the iron had entered his soul. I couldn't see any sort of fence on which Dr Owen could be said to have sat, but left that alone, and passed on to betrayal, which is always a congenial topic to any member of the Labour Party. I said the classic betrayer was Ramsay MacDonald, and there were always comparisons made.

'Comparisons with me?'

No, with David Owen.

'Oh, I see. But the people on the hard Left will tell you that I betrayed the Labour Party. But the ordinary voter doesn't.'

No. I changed tack from betrayal to *Realpolitik*, asking Mr Callaghan if it were either possible or wise for a man holding high office to be wholly honest.

He thought. 'Possible,' he said, 'in all things that really matter. I'm not sure that it's always wise. But on the whole I leaned – I suppose this is going to sound frightfully hypocritical – but I leaned towards being honest.' Internationally, he thought, it might be another matter. If you were dealing with people from countries which had other values, he doubted the wisdom of total honesty. He could think of two countries like that. Having established that he doubted the probity neither of Russia nor of the United States, I did not pursue the guessing game, as he half-invited me, into the other 140-odd sovereign nations of the world.

But, I said, taking a domestic instance, had he himself been wholly honest when . . .

'Go on. I knew that was coming. He's got an illustration.'

Had he been wholly honest when, coming back to Britain from Barbados in the December of 1978, at the beginning of the winter of discontent, he had said, 'Crisis? What crisis?' Had that been a piece of showmanship? If so, was that entirely honest?

'If I'd said it, it probably wouldn't have been. I'll tell you what happened.' He had returned to Heathrow to be met by a group of reporters, some of them hostile. One of them asked, 'What have you got to say about the chaos that surrounds you?' He had replied that he saw no evidence of chaos, which had appeared as 'Crisis? What crisis?' There was a transport strike and the refuse wasn't being collected, but if that were described as chaos it required a denial from him. The word crisis had not been used. If he had been asked if there was a crisis in the transport strike he hoped he would have replied yes.

So crisis for chaos. Did he think this was malicious or a mishearing? Well, he had said this at a time when the press was determined to get him. Every day the *Sun* carried an unflattering cartoon of him as Mr Micawber with a battered hat and baggy trousers. He didn't know whether it was a mishearing or not, although frankly he and the reporters were within six feet of each other.

Now, last year in the Commons, Mr Callaghan had given a warning that we might be drifting into a genteel and shabby poverty. How far had we already sunk? He thought very far. There was scandalous neglect. He remembered an old Italian priest from the south who had told him that socialism meant a job to go to, a house to live in, schools for children, hospitals when you were ill, and dignity in old age. We were neglecting two of those things – housing and jobs.

But not only socialism could offer these things; 'I know; but that was his definition.'

Did he think that people who did not travel realised how poor and shabby we already were, compared with the United States and almost all of Western Europe? '*All* of Western Europe. I don't think it is appreciated. Although more young people are travelling and are therefore becoming more discontented with this country.'

This was certainly something Dr Owen had gone on about, wasn't it. 'Yes, and I hope the Labour Party won't neglect it. The trouble, when you've had a Conservative government and Labour comes in, is that people's expectations are so high. And sometimes we add fuel to it by the undertakings we give, I think Neil Kinnock and the shadow cabinet are conscious of that. But even without their saying anything, people's expectations may be higher than they should be.'

I mentioned that there were a lot of former prime ministers around these days. How much did they see of each other? 'Harold and I, Macmillan, that is, we meet from time to time. And always enjoy each other's company. Harold Wilson and I don't meet socially. We hardly ever did. But we do meet and talk. Ted Heath and Alec Home, we all meet; we all talk to each other.'

Did he know whether there had ever previously been so many ex-prime ministers still living? He thought not. 'People used to last longer in office. That's the fault of the media. Now they consume us.'

Now Mr Callaghan has held all the great offices of state – home secretary, chancellor of the exchequer, foreign secretary, and prime minister. Yet he says that what he would really most like to have done is built St Paul's. Why? 'Yes, oh, I think, yes; I used to say a reservoir. Then gradually I got more bold and said St Paul's. I think it's vanity of course.'

I said he seemed to use that word frequently. 'Yes, I think it's true all politicians are rather vain. No, what I was going to say is, if you're prime minister you probably get a footnote in history. If you built St Paul's, or if you write a great poem, then your name lives on. Now why should I worry whether my name lives on? The answer is I don't. No, not now.'

Was this because he was pretty sure that it would anyway? 'I think it's because my values are now different. And I get my happiness now out of many other things. I suppose I get more happiness now out of seeing 234 tons of wheat in the barn.'

On his own farm? 'On my own farm. Or assisting at the lambing and saving a lamb, that's really something. And this is genuine. I'm not pulling the wool over your eyes. I hope I give the impression of being a very contented man. No one has any right to be too contented when there are still great evils. I therefore try to do what little I can about that, but personally I think I've never been so contented in my life.'

But? 'I walk round and I have this feeling that I have to guard against because I had a very Puritan upbringing, and I say to myself, "I'm so lucky; I must be careful".'

Here Mr Callaghan explained that as a boy he had believed the Second Coming was going to happen and that he was going to be left behind because he was too wicked. He was not one of the elect, one of the chosen. 'It was a real fear in those days. What a terrible religion it was, wasn't it? For a boy to feel that way when he was six or seven, or something. Yes, Calvinism. To come into the house, to hear no response when you called, and to say to yourself, "They've all gone to heaven. I've been left behind".'

When did he last have that feeling? 'When I was about nine, probably. But those early years leave a mark on you. I must always be doing something. The sense of guilt for leaving time idle is terrible.'

He asked me if I was like that and, when I replied that I supposed I was an Anglican agnostic, said that was a more civilised tradition. Perhaps, I said, but also less demanding, at which he remembered, and told me, that as a boy he had each Sunday gone to Sunday school at nine thirty, to Chapel at eleven, to Sunday school tea at four, and to Chapel again at six. And every morning of the week his mother read the Bible aloud at breakfast, the Authorised Version.

Then leaping on to much later days, he said, 'I must say I enjoyed being prime minister when I had to deal with the Church of England. The Queen takes it very seriously, oh yes. She cares about her position as Defender of the Faith and head of the Church of England. I don't know where the thing came from about Prince Charles not going to Mass [with the Pope], but I'm sure the Queen had a strong view that nothing should be done to compromise the position of the Crown as head of the Church of England.'

Then he said, 'I'll tell you a funny story about Number 10', and told me about the summit of the seven industrialised nations he insisted on holding in Downing Street. Of course, at the time he had an ecclesiastical adviser on the appointment of bishops and deans, and it was taken very seriously too. Well, he gave each of the summit delegations a room in Number 10. One of the American delegation went up to Mr Callaghan's private secretary and said, look, there's a map on our wall with pins in it, and we know it's not our nuclear bases, and we know it's not your defence bases, so what are the pins? The private secretary told him the pins marked the bishoprics of England.

'Isn't that rather nice? There's great fun in being prime minister, you know. Now see what's happened. She [Mrs Thatcher] has appointed Bishop Jenkins, ha ha ha ha ha.'

This was real, happy laughter. Mind you, said Mr Callaghan, Bishop Jenkins had make people think.

I said perhaps, but take away a belief in the resurrection of Christ and then who else could expect to be resurrected, and what was left of the Christian faith then? Mr Callaghan asked if that was fundamental. He said he had no expectation that his own body would be resurrected and thought a man lived on through the way he influenced those he lived and worked with. He found now that the younger members of the party in the House would come and sit at his table in the dining-room to hear his stories, to which he added a bit here and there, about the years after 'forty-five and what they were like. He passed on his recollections, as coloured by him, and thus influenced others.

Then he said, 'Oh Hell, where are we getting to?' (Laughter.)

To Heaven, I hoped, not Hell. Then, speaking aloud, Mr Callaghan wondered what we hadn't covered, consulted a list he had made, and said he had written down the lessons he had learned in his life.

'I will,' he said, 'add one personal word if I may. I think I was arrogant, ambitious, and was often accused of being devious. I don't think that was true. Arrogance and ambition I must confess to. Deviousness, not. First of all, I think I always had some desire to learn both sides of questions. I think in some ways I am a trimmer.'

This is something I have never heard anyone confess to before, let alone a former prime minister, and here was Mr Callaghan stating it off his own bat.

'That is to say, although I have certain principles, they're principles

I care about more than measures. I've always felt that to go to excess in measures was not the best way of governing this country. A sailing ship sails fastest when it's upright. And therefore, if it cants over to one side, I tended to throw my balance the other side, in order to bring it upright. I think I tried to ask myself, did I deserve the reputation for deviousness. Am I devious? I think that [I took him here to mean the instinct to trim] is the reason perhaps why I got that reputation, in early days. I don't think it's true now. I think now that I'm too blunt in what I say to people, and care too little. But now I have a responsibility not to dissipate any influence I might have by just being too blunt. I'm accused of just being an old man, you know, who ought to take a back seat now and then and let everybody else get on with it. They ought to get on with it. But I think one can still contribute something from one's experience, and I'm going to try to do so. [Pause.] I hope you don't mind that last bit.'

He rose, and we walked across the room to the wall on which are displayed photographs, among them one of the Labour cabinet he led and another of Mr Callaghan and Mrs Gandhi. He told me he had had an appointment to see her again on the afternoon of the day she was assassinated.

'My last story,' he said. 'I was in India, and I stayed for the funeral of course. Mrs Thatcher and Denis Thatcher came out. He's a nice old boy.'

This is a statement which always brings spontaneous agreement. Mr Thatcher is a natural. 'And Denis Thatcher and I were standing together and he said, "How did you come to be here?" And I said, "As a matter of fact I've been in Japan getting an honorary degree, then I came back via Thailand, and I happened to be here on the day. Wonderful thing, you know, to be a former prime minister. You go where you like. You have a wonderful time. Really good." He looked straight ahead and said, "Can't wait. Can't wait." Ha ha ha ha ha.'

As we left Mr Callaghan's room and walked into the outer office, his secretary told him that someone – I did not know the name but guessed from the tone of voice that he was an old acquaintance or friend – had died.

'How awful,' said Mr Callaghan. 'Oh I am sorry.' He enquired after the man's wife.

Then he insisted on showing me out, through the labyrinthine corridors of the Palace of Westminster, down to the ground floor. That, he said, meaning the news he had just heard, was one of the drawbacks of getting older. You wrote so many letters of condolence.

He had written two the day before, and already one that day.

We walked a bit. The twists and turns really are impossible, the place is vast, and I wondered whether Mr Callaghan, even after all these years, really knew his way around.

'I know the runs,' he said. 'I'm like a rabbit. I know the runs.'

—July 1985

TED HEATH
History Rewritten

When Mr Heath is passionate it is over great matters, and even then he rarely lets himself go, because he distrusts passion. He is a proud man, but that is not a deadly sin. He can be bitter, but he has cause for that. His pride shows itself in silences, and his bitterness mostly in shrugs.

I have seen him passionate on the ideal of One Nation, in which he believed with his heart, and still does. The other day, when we met at his house in London, he spoke with passion – though he will not thank me for using the word – about a greater thing than One Nation, about the snapping of a generous international tradition.

He said: 'Ever since Churchill and Roosevelt in 1941 agreed the Atlantic Charter, we knew what our objectives were, and one of them of course was the right to work.'

From then onwards, he said, men from both sides of the Atlantic had worked together. He went through a list of names – Jean Monnet, Paul-Henri Spaak, Averell Harriman, Oliver Franks. 'The tradition went on through governments, and now, suddenly, it's stopped. And there's nothing there, except a new generation who think the only thing is to look after yourself, and Devil take the hindmost.' The thirty-five years of joint effort after 1945 had ended.

He said this with great feeling, but only after an hour of conversation. He started, which is very rare for him, with small talk. He had seen the musical of *Forty-Second Street* on Broadway, and wondered how they could make a smash hit out of songs fifty years old. He had been in Los Angeles. I said when I was last there, there was an earthquake. He said that during his last visit there had been two.

Then he said, 'Well, what do you want to talk about? When is this coming out?' He settled down to business.

I said I had seen a Conservative Party political broadcast on Europe which had contained no mention of him. 'I suppose,' he said, 'it's all part of the attempt to rewrite history. They've attempted to rewrite the whole of the 1970-4 period and to blot it out as if it never existed. They omit me as leader of the party and as prime minister.'

119

This sounded like the *Great Soviet Encyclopedia* whose new editions omitted those who had fallen out of favour since the previous one. 'Yes, that's right.'

That was sinister? 'Yes, very. It hasn't happened in this country before, as far as I know. I think you have to show considerable ingenuity to write a television programme about Europe and not mention my having conducted the negotiations from 1960-2, and then as prime minister settled the negotiations with President Pompidou and Chancellor Brandt, and then signed the treaty.'

But, he said, he was going to Strasbourg on Wednesday to receive the gold medal of the European parliament. 'So not everybody has forgotten history.'

How did he feel now about the Heath-Brandt-Pompidou comminiqué of 1972 which foresaw economic and monetary union in Europe by 1980? We still hadn't got it. 'No. I was thinking about it this evening. I am afraid very little of it has come about. I think if we hadn't had the oil crisis of 1973, and if President Pompidou had lived, and if Chancellor Brandt and I, the three of us, had remained in positions where we could govern the development of the Community, it would certainly have gone along those lines.'

We returned to England. I said he must be the first prime minister publicly to oppose his successor, and he admitted that in his own party that must be so. But his recent speech at the conference should be seen in the context of others he had made.

'A year ago I warned the party that if it continued with its policies then it would once again become known as the party of unemployment, which is what happened in the inter-war years, when I was at school. And then in the immediate after-war years, when I was a candidate, this was what we had to fight against the whole time.'

He thought three million unemployed was immoral? He did; his mind had been considerably influenced by what he had seen in England and in Europe in the 'thirties. In Europe, unemployment was really what brought the dictators into power.

But that was a cataclysm: he didn't foresee anything like that, did he? Mr Heath said unemployment both here and in Europe was worse than in 1931. Mussolini had come in in the 'twenties and Hitler in the 'thirties, and that had led to the Second World War. Britain had preserved its social system, but the scars ran deep.

But we should be able to preserve the social system here? 'We've had riots on the streets. I've no doubt that these weren't racist. They were caused by frustration and fury at continuing unemployment, and there's no point in trying to disguise this. They will say

120

eventually, ''The system has failed us and therefore we must change the system.'' '

He was seeing riots in Parliament Square? 'I am not saying necessarily riots in Parliament Square. No. What I'm saying is that the pressure put on parties in opposition, and on the government can mount to a stage where the democratic system begins to cease to work.'

But a government with a majority could get anything through the Commons that it wanted to. 'No it can't. No, no. Not once an Opposition decides that it won't allow the process to work. And of course we can see innumerable ways of industrial action in which government can be prevented from achieving its purposes.'

I suggested that the classic example of that was his government of 1974 broken by the miners, but he said no, that was an election lost. 'That's quite different from the recent example we've had, of our being unable to use computers [because of the civil service strike], and the impact that's had on VAT, and the impact that's had on business.'

From computers to Mrs Thatcher. He had described his relationship with her as one of polite nihilism: what did he mean? 'It's a jolly good phrase.' He laughed. 'It means there's nothing there.'

But Mr Heath does admit the existence of the Liberal-SDP Alliance. When he was asked about it, he said we should have to wait and see, that he remained a member of the Conservative Party, and that if I was going to ask hypothetical questions, I couldn't expect answers.

All fair enough. But after the first election of 1974, which he so narrowly lost, he had tried to form a coalition with the Liberals, and had been bitterly disappointed to fail in this. And now he had seen the Alliance usurping the middle ground which might have been his. 'Yes. Obviously this is their purpose. What I want to see is the Conservative Party reoccupying the middle ground.'

That would mean getting rid of the present leader? 'It depends what the views of the present leader are.'

But we knew what Mrs Thatcher's views were: he would not expect a reform of mind on her part? 'Well, at least we can show the public that there are a considerable number of members who believe in what you have called the centre ground, and the traditions that we've passed on from Churchill, to Eden, to Macmillan, to Home, and to myself.'

Why, in 1975, during the Tory leadership election, had he retired after losing the first ballot when his opponent had not won an absolute majority, and he might very well have won the second? Some members might very well have voted not so much for Mrs Thatcher as against him, and then been very surprised at the result. That, he said, had not been his view at the time, and the advice of all his friends had been to withdraw.

The general view of Mr Heath was that he had very few friends? 'That is another of the myths that have been created; I can't bother about myths. Friends are part of one's private life. I've said again and again that the real problem in life is to have sufficient time to think. So many friends in music, so many friends in all the arts.'

But Mr Heath has an undoubted reserve which looks perilously like coldness. I remarked that in his books on music and travel he wrote words like hope, despair, and joy, even love, the like of which I had never heard in any political speech of his.

'How many of my speeches have you heard?'

Many, many, many.

'You say that as though in despair.'

But why was there no place for public political passion? 'I've always mistrusted rhetoric and I still do.'

That was his loss then. 'Maybe. But it's very dangerous. Perhaps this is also a legacy of the 'thirties.'

He was thinking of the rhetoric of Hitler and Mussolini? 'Yes. And so I think it's probably been natural to turn away from rhetoric. I used to use humour, and was then told that politicians ought not to be funny. I think it was bad advice, bad advice. I reread one of my conference speeches the other day, in which I referred to Mr Wilson trying to solve the industrial problems of the country by offering to sell to the developing world masses of little 1¼ hp motors, and the conference rolled up in laughter. I thought the other night that I'd really been rather unfair to Mr Wilson, and perhaps the developing world would be better off if we had given them lots of 1¼ hp motors.'

A little later on, when Mr Heath again mentioned the rewriting of history, I asked him if he was saying there was a conspiracy to suppress and rewrite.

After a long silence he said, 'Well, a conspiracy conjures up pictures of . . .'

Of people putting their heads together.

'No. But in general, as far as the party organisation is concerned, yes, this is quite true, of course.'

Then we came to catastrophe. What should we do to avert it? Catastrophe is a word Mr Heath has used of Mrs Thatcher's administration, but he took my question more broadly than that, and spoke about the whole world.

The present depression, first, was one from which no country on its own could rescue itself, not Britain, not the United States. Not Europe itself. Second, he said, this was a period of history like nothing before. 'Because oil,' he said, 'is in the hands of the most powerful cartel the world has ever seen. If a process of recovery begins, then the power of that cartel is increased, and will be used in a way which will cause a repetition of the problems we've had since the autumn of 1973.' Third, the United States was now following policies which were like our own, but which were showing bad results much more quickly. Before 1973 the United States could by its own prosperous and flourishing economy bring Europe out of depression, but this could no longer happen.

'Now this is obviously with a broad brush. But surely the astonishing thing is that world political leaders are doing absolutely nothing whatever about trying to influence these factors. They are just content to go on drifting into deeper and deeper depression, with the social consequences which are bound to follow.

'You were talking about the most extreme forms. Riots in Parliament Square. Let's say they're not going to happen. What is going to happen is what I saw for myself in the north-east when I was secretary of state for industry, trade, and development, where after long unemployment, when we finally got to the stage of providing jobs, they were incapable of holding jobs. Their whole psychology had gone. Their power of concentration had gone. They were willing to work, but they were no longer capable of concentrating even on machine jobs.'

As he spoke, Mr Heath was now stroking the arm of his chair. 'And so,' he continued, 'what I find so appalling is that there's been no attempt by the American president, by the British prime minister, or by the European prime ministers, to deal with OPEC.'

But how on earth did one set about getting OPEC to sell you oil cheaper, which was what it amounted to? 'I have my own private contacts with the powers in the Gulf, and I make a point of finding out what their views are the whole time. No attempt is being made by anybody to find solutions to these things, and really, when historians come to look back on it, they will say that there was paralysis everywhere.'

Mr Heath sat back, and said he must go, but I asked for one more question. If he never became leader of the Conservative Party again, but if people came to believe in their heart of hearts that he was right, would that console him? 'I'm in no need of consolation. I think the evidence is growing, very fast, that people do believe that what I'm saying is right.'

He gave instances – one meeting of 1200 who had come to listen to him at Cambridge, another of 1000 at Lancaster, and another of 750 at Glasgow, where another 600 were turned away. 'Well,' he said, 'they had to have tickets, and tickets were refused them.'

It was then that he spoke about the snapping of international tradition, and after that he said, 'There you are, that's enough.' But then he seemed to change his mind and offered me a drink. We were both standing.

The difficulty of dealing with OPEC, I supposed as he poured, was how to persuade a madman like Gadafy.

'You don't bother about him. How much soda?'

You got at him through the Saudis?

'And the Kuwaitis, and the Emirates. They're the people who really matter and the rest will go along – Venezuela, Nigeria. Mexico isn't OPEC but they will go along with what's arranged.'

Mr Heath poured himself a glass of whisky. 'They [OPEC] want to have a business deal' he said; 'and of course they realise the damage which they're doing to the West, which in its turn can be damaging to them as régimes; the ruling house can be damaged. We're having a Brandt reunion in Kuwait on January 7 and 8.'

We went down to the front door together, I carrying away Mr Heath's litany of Conservative prime ministers from Churchill down to himself, and the names of Roosevelt, of Monnet, of Spaak, and of Brandt with whom he had a rendezvous in Kuwait.

I should like to think that Mr Heath is wrong when he says, with passion, that something has snapped. As I left he was remarking to the young policeman on the door that it was getting chilly.

—November 1981

LORD SHINWELL
'I've Seen It All'

Lord Shinwell will be one hundred years old next Thursday. He contested his first parliamentary election in 1918. It was he who, in 1923, nominated Ramsay MacDonald as leader of the Labour Party. In the Attlee government, in 1947, he was the minister who nationalised coal. He was made a life peer in 1970, and still makes speeches in the House of Lords. No one alive has a longer political experience.

But, I asked, when I went to see him at his small flat in St John's Wood, would it also be true, did he think, that no other man had ever had such a length of political experience? And I began to recite the obvious comparisons – Churchill in the Commons more or less constantly from 1901 until 1964, sixty-three years; Gladstone in the Commons almost without break from 1832 until 1895, sixty-three years; Walpole, in parliament only forty-five years, nowhere in it; and so on.

'I know about that,' said Lord Shinwell, a bit sharply.

Yes, but he'd been in trade union politics long before he ever entered the Commons in 1922, and . . .

'Let's get the facts right,' he said. Lord Shinwell, at one hundred, may be slightly deaf but he is mighty brisk. 'I joined the ILP under Keir Hardie in 1903. I won't say that I became a socialist then. I knew nothing about it. I never studied Karl Marx. I knew nothing about dialectic materialism or the theory of social value, or any of these economic mysticisms. I took part in the election of 1906 when Bonar Law – this is a piece of history you may not be acquainted with – Bonar Law who later became prime minister, a Conservative, was MP for the Gorbals division of Glasgow, the most impoverished constituency in the Commons – a Conservative.

'I went to a meeting addressed by Bonar Law, at a boxing stadium which I knew well because, well, I knew boxing stadiums pretty well. The place was crowded out with the impoverished unemployed of the Gorbals, and they were applauding Bonar Law to the skies. I couldn't stand it, so I got up and shouted. "What about the workers", and they threw me out.'

Well then, if Emmanuel Shinwell's political career is to date from that interjection, or even from his subsequent work with the seamen's unions, his length of experience is approached by no one.

He was born in 1884, the year that Gordon was surrounded at Khartoum. He was born in Spitalfields, of Jewish, Polish, and Dutch descent. His father was a poor tailor. His mother sang, 'I dreamt I dwelt in marble halls', and had thirteen children.

Emmanuel, one of those children, has lived through the politics of all but a few years of this century. And hadn't he once written, I asked, that throughout all that time the country had been let down by its leaders? 'I've done more than that,' he replied. 'I've *condemned* most of the prime ministers.'

And so he has, with exceptions being made, in part, for Churchill, Macmillan, and Wilson.

What of the present leaders? What of Mrs Thatcher? 'Strangely enough I've never criticised Mrs Thatcher. On the verge of a recession to become prime minister, what a task, what a daunting challenge that is.'

Hadn't he called her a graceful woman? 'A capable woman. Quite a friendly woman. I'm not surprised she's having a bit of trouble now. Every prime minister that I've known this century, and I've known every one since Balfour [1902-5], and Baldwin, and Campbell Bannerman, and the rest – I've known them intimately – every one after three or four years faded away. Baldwin did, Eden did, MacDonald did, Churchill even, after four years in the war, faded away; even Lloyd George. I know from my own experience as a cabinet minister, not prime minister, that after four years you've had enough.'

But Mrs Thatcher seemed to have lasted. 'She's showing signs of strain.'

What about Neil Kinnock? 'I tell you what I told him myself. I said, "Boy", that's what I called him, "Boy", the only time I met him on the terraces of the House of Commons. He came along. "Boy," I said to him, "Take that smile off your face. You've got a serious job facing you. Leader of the Labour Party, after the decline of the last election. You've got a job on. You think you can exude charm".

'He said, "Can't I grin?" I say, "You can grin like a Cheshire cat, but it's not getting you anywhere".'

What had he thought of Mr Kinnock's speech to the Labour conference at Blackpool? 'I only watch television when I'm doing it myself. I read the speech. Listen, I don't miss anything.'

Then he devoted a few last words to Mr Kinnock – asking what experience did he have, never having been a junior minister, which was a good thing to be because you learned the rules, and saying besides that Kinnock tried to emulate Nye Bevan, which he couldn't do because there was only one Nye Bevan, though that was a good thing too because you couldn't stand more than one of them.

I asked about the miners' strike. Lord Shinwell did not have a good word to say for anyone – not Scargill, Thatcher, MacGregor, Walker, no one – but he said it would never have happened if the coal industry had taken his advice.

What was that? He said that when he was minister of fuel, and coal was nationalised, he had to appoint the Coal Board. 'I said to the miners' leader, the late Sir William Lawther, and ten others – who are all dead, every one of them – I said, "Look here, I want you to appoint three of your number as members of the Coal Board, and I want you to regard yourselves in future not as employees but as partners." They wouldn't do it. I'm going to tell you something. I'm going to say something to the country. Until the trade unions begin to understand that they've got a great opportunity to take part to some extent, in the management of the nationalised industries, unless we get that, there's no hope for this country.'

I asked about 1921, and some admonition of his to the miners in that year, but he wanted to go back further. At the beginning of the century, he said, a miner might earn six bob for an eight hour shift, sometimes working only three days a week, and three days on the dole. So what did it matter to a man if he lost such a job? But nowadays, miners had perhaps £150 a week, perhaps £180, perhaps up to £200, and they had cars and washing machines and colour television sets and some of them sent their children to private schools. Six bob a shift, you could afford to lose that, but not £180 a week; then you belonged to the lower middle class.

'And people,' he said 'don't seem to understand. I understand it. I've gone through it all.'

And in 1921, I asked, getting back to that, at the Labour conference, he had condemned Arthur Cook, then the miners' leader? 'Yes. And he was worse than Scargill. Because he was barmy. Scargill's not barmy. He knows what he's about.'

As early as 1924 under MacDonald in the first Labour government, Shinwell was parliamentary secretary at the department of mines, more than twenty years before he was minister of fuel under Attlee, and in our conversation he kept coming back to coal. He didn't give twopence for the Coal Board. It wasn't worth twopence and never had been. 'That's it,' he said. 'I sit here, knowing it all because I've been through it all, and I understand. I don't condemn or criticise anybody.'

Then I asked about Ramsay MacDonald, who is one of the legends of the Labour Party, of all its leaders the most plebeian in origin, having been born the son of a crofter; of all its leaders the most shining; and of all its leaders the most execrated, because he abandoned the party to lead the national government of 1931-5.

How had Shinwell first met him? He said he was often asked to chair meetings in Glasgow, because he knew how to handle such things. And how did he handle them? He would tell me. There was this meeting, during the First World War, which MacDonald came to address. And before the meeting there was a crowd outside, and terrible noise by the door from those who wished to break up the meeting.

The young Shinwell went to the door. 'Fellow with a terrible red face shoving with his shoulder, and the crowd behind him, so I ran down and hit him between the eyes and knocked him out.' The meeting took place. Shinwell was later charged with hitting the man with a length of lead pipe, but acquitted. MacDonald, though he disapproved of violence, was grateful, and that is how they became friendly.

Hadn't Lord Shinwell once called MacDonald princely? 'You've got to know him. Fine, wonderful voice. A handsome person. You know who telephoned me this morning?'

Lord Shinwell insisted that I should guess, so I guessed a grandson of MacDonald's. But it was MacDonald's only surviving daughter, Sheilah, from Swansea. She was asking about his hundredth birthday party, to be held at the Houses of Parliament.

It was Shinwell who in 1928 nominated MacDonald as leader. It was also Shinwell who, in 1935, ran against the apostate MacDonald who was standing as national prime minister in his own constituency of Seaham, and thus ended his career. How had he felt, standing against his old chief and old friend? 'Didn't like it at all. I swear that nobody could ever say that during the three weeks of that campaign did I ever criticise MacDonald once.'

But why, since Shinwell could have had another constituency, did he choose to fight MacDonald? 'Somebody had to do it. Who could have won it?' The old majority of twenty-nine thousand for MacDonald became one of twenty-one thousand for Shinwell.

And about that time, I said, wasn't Lansbury, another Labour leader, supporting the Peace Pledge and going round preaching what he called A Truce of God? 'Now listen, he was allowed to go and talk his pacifist rubbish, and I did the very opposite. I'd a respect for Lansbury, but he was an old idiot.'

Did Lord Shinwell see any comparison between this pacifism of the mid-1930s and the present unilateralism of the Labour Party? Lord Shinwell did not answer specifically about unilateralism, but said that if things were left to NATO the Russians would be in this country in three weeks. Without the American deterrent behind us we'd be finished, and don't let it be forgotten.

'And suppose,' he said, 'that the Americans insist on their missiles being placed in Germany or in this country. And we say, "Take them back." Suppose they say, "All right, we'll take our forces out." Do you think that would be wise? Wait a minute. Let's face it. Suppose we say, "Take your bloody missiles out" – that's the language of Blackpool. Then they say, "Right you are, then we'll recall all our soldiers, we'll take them all out. Thousands of them." Would that please the Russians?'

I thought the Russians would be delighted. 'Yes. What about us? And what would the Labour Party say then? They say to hell with the Americans and the Americans say to hell with them. And then where are we. If you're in this business you've got to know about this. You don't require to have gone to Eton. No disrespect to Eton.'

Did there seem, nowadays, to be more violence and unrest in this country than for years. 'I tell you. I say to the trade unions, "What the hell have you got out of these strikes and all the rest of it? What have you got out of defeating Heath? What will you get out of defeating Thatcher? You'll get bugger all." That's what I'm saying to them. But why didn't they adopt my policy? I'm going back to what I advocated when I was trying to nationalise the mines. I said to the miners, Partners not Employees. And you know what Will Lawther said to me. They said, "No minister. Now that we've got nationalisation, we want all the benefits. Otherwise you're not going to get the coal." Look up what I asked them to do. You'd have had no Scargill. And if people say Shinwell's a traitor I don't mind a bit. The more they've attacked me, the nastier they've got about me, I've gone up and up and up and up.'

In 1921 Shinwell was sent to prison for five months for inciting Glasgow workers to riot. This was at the time when ten thousand troops had been sent to Clydeside, along with six tanks. But hadn't he always said, then and now, that there would never be revolution in this country.

'You can't have a revolution by shouting your head off. Lenin didn't start a revolution. It was started for him by the war. Give us another war, and we'll have a revolution. When we were on the Clyde, and make this the last point, people talked about us being revolutionaries. What outrageous damned nonsense. There wasn't the slightest talk about it. There would occasionally be philosophic discussions, but the idea of revolution was never in our minds, never. Of course some of us used the language. They're using it now.'

He laughed. He was very amused, I think, at the idea of such talk. Of course, he said, some Tories wrote wild letters to him too, they used language, but they knew it was damned nonsense too.

We were getting to the end of the conversation, and somehow got on to trees. I recalled that towards the end of the last war he had written pamphlets about planting green trees by the side of avenues. It was really small talk, but he took it for more than that, as if I was deriding past visions, which I was not, and said, 'This goes on. If you're saying that we're stupid, as politicians, how right you are.'

He showed me the framed citation or commission, signed by the Queen, which created him a Companion of Honour, and said he had something to put round his neck too, but never wore it. We walked to the door, past his bookshelves. He said the books together with his papers, would go to the London School of Economics.

As we said goodbye, he looked behind him for a moment, as if reviewing what he had told me, and said, 'That's my story.'

—November 1984

BRUNO KREISKY
Franz Joseph to Ronald Reagan

Bruno Kreisky has been Chancellor of Austria since 1970, and is thus the longest-surviving leader of a Western European country – because Austria, though neutral, and far to the east, can only properly be described as Western European. Partly because of his long tenure, his friend Willy Brandt calls him Kaiser Kreisky. As a young man, in the Anschluss of 1938, he saw his country disappear. In 1955 he was one of the delegation which negotiated the State Treaty by which Russia conceded to an occupied and astonished Austria its independence.

He is a Jew who has received Yasser Arafat of the PLO and who now says that Israel, by its actions in Lebanon, has destroyed the moral basis of its existence. He holds the same high office as Metternich once did, and though that prince was chancellor of a very different Austria, there is a link.

It is this. The aged Metternich, having returned from the exile enforced on him by the revolutions of 1848, advised the new young emperor, Franz Joseph. That young emperor lived to reign even longer than Queen Victoria, and when he died in 1916, after sixty-eight years on the throne, the boy Kreisky saw his funeral in Vienna.

'I remember the funeral. I was five and a half. I have a very clear – no, unclear – memory of a long, dark, and black procession.'

What had he seen? 'Horses. Black uniforms.'

What had he understood? 'I understood from the people around me, and because my father was in the army, that there were feelings of something more than the death of an emperor. A lot more.'

Two years later the First World War was over, the Austro-Hungarian empire had collapsed, the line of Hapsburgs stretching back 640 years was at an end, and the tiny Austrian republic, stripped of its power and territories was established. It was a revolution, and yet the boy Kreisky knew it was no revolution. He saw that the same policemen who had previously watched the parks, and watched them playing football, still watched, and he told his friends. 'This is no revolution.' This he remembers clearly.

The Chancellor and I met at his villa on Majorca, where he was on holiday, and as he spoke of the end of the Hapsburgs he was looking out over the Mediterranean. I asked what he had meant when he said that his whole life had in a way been a bridge between the Hapsburgs and the years after. He said the collapse had been very real to his family. Some lived in Vienna, others in Moravia, which was then no longer in Austria. His uncles' textile factories were on a border which had not existed before. His mother was distressed when she went as usual to take her summer holiday on what had been the Austrian Riviera, which had become Italian.

'So,' he said, 'in all my life the empire has been present.' He had constantly asked himself whether the empire and the monarchy could not have been saved. If it had been, millions today would not be living under communism. Could the empire, he asked himself, have been changed into a kind of Swiss confederation, into a common-wealth of nations?

Even after the First World War? 'Not after. Not after. The first war had to be prevented. The monarchy did not prevent the war, because of the alliance with Germany.'

But we were talking about changing the history of Europe and therefore of the world? 'Maybe. If Austria had not been in the German alliance, things would have been totally different.' The whole experience of his life told him that nothing was inevitable. There was always a choice. The empire could have been preserved by reforms carried out in time; in 1934, their own, homemade Dollfuss dictatorship could have been avoided by a political coalition; the coming of Hitler in 1938 could have been avoided.

'We are responsible for our history. It was not others who destroyed Austria. We destroyed her. Our ancestors destroyed Austria.'

At the age of fourteen Kreisky took part in his first demonstration, against the Vienna school system after a pupil committed suicide. He says that, to be fair, many were not so much interested in school reform as in having a demonstration. By the age of nineteen he was a militant socialist, and remained so throughout the 'thirties, when it was dangerous, in Europe, to be a socialist. He organised meetings of a banned youth movement in the Vienna Woods, and in 1935 was arrested and charged with no less than high treason. As he was to tell me later, as we were parting, he has always been grateful to the *Manchester Guardian* for reporting his trial so fully. He was sentenced to one year.

The next arrest, after the Anschluss, was by the Gestapo, who released him on condition he left Europe. They said they did not want him around as a potential knife in the back. Could he, they inquired, go to South America? 'Bolivia?' he suggested. It was the first name that came into his head. He now says he might as well have named Mexico. In fact he went to Sweden, a country which profoundly affected him. Why?

Because, he says, for the first time in his life he saw a working democracy. In Austria there were only bloody demonstrations and near civil war. In Sweden in 1940 he met Brandt, who has remained his friend ever since. There was some longing for his native country, but on the whole he cannot say exile was a period of suffering for him. He returned to Austria after the war, but soon returned to Sweden as a diplomat, and in all spent ten years there.

When he returned to Austria for good it was as political adviser to the president and later as state secretary to the chancellor. In this capacity he went as one of the Austrian delegation to Moscow to negotiate the State Treaty in 1955. Now, Austria had been occupied by the four powers since the end of the war. Three hundred meetings of the Allied foreign ministers had failed to reach any agreement, and Austrian independence must have looked a remote prospect. So what did he expect from this summons to Moscow?

The Western Powers, said Kreisky, were pessimistic. The Austrian delegates were pessimistic. People said, 'They will put you up against a wall, and they will ask you to take communists into the government, and, if not, the iron curtain will come down in the middle of Austria.'

Partition? Yes, said the Chancellor. But at Moscow airport they were met by the entire diplomatic corps, fifty people. The Austrian national anthem was played. Molotov, Malenkov, Mikoyan, Bulganin were all there.

And then? 'When we arrived at the Austrian embassy in Moscow there was great nervousness. I tell you this because I don't know how long I shall remember. Old men forget. There was great nervousness because they had invited the whole Politburo. They always did this; but they never came, only one minor official. But that evening they all accepted.'

All the Politburo? 'Bulganin, Molotov, Malenkov ... only Khrushchev was not there because he was in Leningrad. There were not enough tables. So there we were and they made fantastic toasts, after every schnapps, every brandy. To friendship, and friendship; we didn't understand. Finally the last speaker, about midnight, was the prime minister, Bulganin. And he started by saying, and I will never forget this, that they had come to the conclusion that there was no chance of a peace treaty with Germany for a long time, so they had decided to work out a State Treaty for Austria. "We don't like to keep you waiting," he said. This was for me – it still is – the biggest event of my life.'

Then Kreisky, who felt a strong fellow sympathy with Mikoyan, asked him. 'What about Germany?'

'I will tell you something,' replied Mikoyan. 'I will tell you one thing. Austria's neutrality can be founded on a piece of paper. You will always respect it. But this cannot be done for a country of eighty millions. If the Germans accepted neutrality, one day they could change their minds. There would again be a tendency to have a hundred million Germans in an empire, and could we then go to war just because Germany gave up neutrality?' The Russians, said Kreisky, understood that there would never be a strong communist party in a greater Germany, so they decided to keep a part of Germany and make it into a communist country, and to keep it as a cornerstone of the Soviet empire.

I supposed the Russians were very happy to have Germany in three bits – West, East, and Austria. 'They told me *four* pieces – Western Germany; what they call central Germany, which is the DDR; the Germany that belongs now to Poland; and Austria. I once told one of them, "But Austria doesn't belong to Germany", and he said, "For you, not; but for the Germans, always".'

I asked the Chancellor if he would agree with Mr Heath that the leaders of the western world nowadays lacked experience, and he said he would have to agree. Experience was almost all. There was always genius of course, but how to find it? President Ford had once told him Kissinger was a genius, and he certainly wrote big books. But experience was most important. Why, asked Kreisky, had *he* been among the first to see the real nature of the Middle East problem? Then he answered his own question. 'I will give you the reason. Because I found out that the Palestinians are not only living in Israel; they are living all over the Arab world. They are nearly half the population in Kuwait. They have a decisive position in many other countries, in the Emirates for example. They have as decisive a position in the Arab world as the Jews did in Europe.'

Another Diaspora? 'There *is* a Palestinian Diaspora, which is more important, and more influential, than the Palestinians inside Israel. If we recognise the importance of the Arab world, we have to know who is important there – the Palestinians.'

That was why he had met Arafat? 'Yes, I am an old man. I am a

Jew. I am anti-Zionist. I don't believe in this nationalism. I can do
the job. If Ted Heath were to do the job, people would say he was at
heart anti-semitic because he was a Christian, or something. A man
like Mitterand would be accused of being anti-semitic. The Jews are
always finding anti-semites. But nobody can accuse me. I lost my
closest relatives to Hitler. They were liquidated. I am not religious,
but I have never converted. I am an agnostic. I accept Israel as a
political solution, as a consequence of Hitler. But I tell you frankly,
without Hitler and Mussolini and their anti-semitism, Israel today
would be a little colony. It would never be a state. A feeling of guilt
towards Jews created the state, and that is what I tell my Israeli
friends.'

And was this European feeling of guilt as strong as it used to be?
'No. This is what I say to them. "You have destroyed the moral basis
of the existence of Israel by your policy of war".'

What did the Chancellor think of the events of the last months in
Lebanon? 'It's a catastrophe. The State of Israel has definitely,
believe me definitely, lost its moral reputation. Why? How can a
state built up by some of the finest men and women of Europe, and
of the world, lose its moral prestige?'

Because of Menachem Begin? 'Begin, yes. How can a man like
Begin be in power? I'll tell you why. The State of Israel of today is not
the State of Israel of thirty years ago. It was a state founded by
refugees from Russia, Poland, Germany, Italy, South Africa,
Britain. Then because of the enmities between Israel and the Arab
world, the Arab Jews were pressed to leave their countries. So today
Israel has a majority of Moroccan Jews, Iraqi Jews, Tunisian Jews,
Jews from the Arab world. That is the majority now. And these
people never lived in a democracy. They are full of sympathy for the
semi-fascist policies of Mr Begin and Mr Sharon. I am so pessimistic.
You cannot change the nature of people. They will always think of
war, and always elect men who are warriors.'

But surely if Israel continued to make war it would lose in the end
because it was so very much outnumbered? 'Finally they will lose. No
doubt about that. This is my conviction. Once you are on a tightrope
you have to continue, and they will continue. They made war against
Lebanon. They can displace the Palestinian leadership. But somewhere the Palestinian leadership will be re-established. And then
Israel will have to make war again, and again, and again.'

At this point the Chancellor went in to answer a telephone call and
Mrs Kreisky offered drinks. When he returned I asked about this
nickname of Kaiser Kreisky. He said it was the popular papers. First

they had called him the Sun King: he didn't know why. Then, when he had run the country for so long, they had taken to calling him Kaiser. Brandt had borrowed the expression.

We were now chatting, and I asked if, working in the same rooms as Metternich once had, he felt in any way the spirit of the prince. He dismissed this. No more, he said, than Mrs Thatcher felt the spirit of Disraeli. But then he went back to the time, in the middle of the nineteenth century, when the aged Metternich had been advising the new young emperor, and advising him never to make war. But the emperor had made war, and lost, forfeiting Lombardy and then Venice. Then, reflecting in his mind over many years, he said, 'And making war destroyed Austria, totally.'

He told me he was at present reading a history of Queen Victoria by a German journalist, who said she was a little bourgeoise. When he was in prison, in the 1930s, and been alone in his cell twenty-three hours a day, he read and read, studying the way in which great men had changed history – Napoleon, Disraeli, Kaiser Wilhelm. So, he said, he was probably, by accident, better educated than other politicians.

How much, I asked, had the 1956 rising in Hungary to do with the Austrian treaty of 1955. 'It was a consequence. Seeing fifty thousand Russian soldiers going home across Hungary, and the liberation. Then it takes at least ten years for a new generation to arise which has not had the experience of defeat. Ten years after Hungary – Czechoslovakia. Ten years after Czechoslovakia – Poland. In the next ten or twelve years you will see it again.'

What about the theory, fashionable in America and on the face of it harmless, that Russia would fall apart from its own weakness? 'One of the reasons I am opposed to American policy is that if this policy – which is not one of containment, like Truman's – goes beyond containment and has consequences inside the Soviet Union, this will create restlessness, and this restlessness will create a military dictatorship of twelve marshals within the Soviet Union. This will mean war, definitely war. Military dictatorships always end in war. The economy is bad, because the generals spend too much on the army. The political situation is a dictatorship and they have to make war. And in a time of cold war there is a danger of hot war. We are now preparing the ground for a cold war. What does a cold war mean? Mr Weinberger (US Secretary of Defence) is talking today about a limited nuclear war. The Europeans are asking, "Where?" A limited nuclear war? Where, on the moon? It's the lack of experience of the new American administration that is so dangerous. I told you experience meant so much.'

After 1945, said the Chancellor, the policies of Truman, Acheson, Marshall, and their contemporaries had succeeded in Greece, stopped the blockade of Berlin, hampered Russian interests in Yugoslavia, and concluded a peace treaty with Japan without the Russians. It was a policy of containment which had led to the Austrian State Treaty.

'But the present policy is weak. It's not based on a realistic analysis, it's based on a *feeling* "We have to show the world the strength of the United States." I remember an American oil boss who told me over lunch in Houston, Texas, "You diplomats are all very bad. Every day, every morning, people all over the world should realise the strength of the United States." . . . Now Reagan is acting in this spirit. "Every day show them our strength." How? You may have an overkill capacity, but today you can never believe that the others will be so weak that they cannot destroy you. That is the problem.'

—September 1982

LORD ECCLES
Flying Boats to Lisbon

I suggested to Lord Eccles that he had obviously at one point wanted to slap Wallis Simpson, Duchess of Windsor.

He said, 'She seduced me, very nearly, in a sense. I first thought she was an awful woman, but at the end of the time I really, well, I mean, she had a lot of experience in dealing with men.'

But he had written that she came so close, and just asked to be kissed, and that it was deceitful of her to take advantage of the fact that you couldn't smack her? 'You feel that about very, ah, smelly women, I mean scent and all that.'

David Eccles met the Windsors in Lisbon in the summer of 1940, when they were passing through on their way to the Bahamas, where the Duke was to become governor general. Eccles was there as HM representative for commerce and bribery. He thought the Windsors the arch beachcombers of the world, and describes the Duke as pretty fifth-column. Wasn't that a bit hard?

He said this was a difficult point. He had conducted many of the Lisbon negotiations with the Windsors. The foreign office had not kept copies of his telegrams, and he had agreed with Buckingham Palace not to say what happened: he said he ought not to have left in that bit about fifth-column, though in 1940 that didn't mean a man was pro-German, only that he would have been willing to negotiate with Germany.

'She was much more pro-German than he was – wounded vanity and all that, you know.'

Lord Eccles's opinions of the Windsors, and his accounts of his efforts to keep Franco's Spain neutral, and of his dealings with Salazar, Pétain, and Roosevelt, are set out in letters he wrote to his wife, Sybil, in the period from 1939 to 1942. His letters, and some of hers in reply, are published in a book entitled *By Safe Hand*. The safe hand was that of HM diplomatic bag from Lisbon, Madrid, and Washington. I met Lord Eccles the other day at his house at Westminster to talk about the book.

He is best known as the Sir David Eccles who was minister of education under Macmillan. He held other high offices, and ended as minister for the arts. He is now seventy-eight, and an elegant man. And his is an elegantly written book, which he calls part history, in so far as it deals with the war, and part novel.

Why novel? 'It's a story of love. It's not untrue. It's all true. On a very modest scale it's *Antony and Cleopatra*. It's someone saying, "Politics is OK, and I love power, but when it comes to the point I prefer the girl." You see what I mean?'

What he means is that he, Antony, when he was nominally only a counsellor in the diplomatic service but really, as he puts it, was a man who had a grip on Spain and Portugal, chose to cast all aside and come home when in 1942 he thought he was losing his wife, Cleopatra. He was certainly living a life of Bogart-style glamour at the time. As his wife wrote, he was having a lovely war, with flying boats to Lisbon, intrigue, lovers, rogues, jewels, and finery.

'That's right,' he said. But his main business in Madrid was to persuade Franco, by means of trade, that it was better to remain neutral than to join Hitler. I said that it now seemed obvious that, with Spain exhausted after the civil war, and with Franco anxious to stay where he was, at the top, neutrality was Spain's best policy. Yes, he said, but people didn't see it that way: Spain was Fascist and therefore an enemy. People like Churchill said we must take it into consideration that we needed Gibraltar, but half the government was against Eccles's efforts to treat with Spain. Dalton was hopeless because he disagreed with Eccles.

Lord Eccles now supposed that the greatest mistake we made in the conduct of the war was the failure of the military to work with the economic people to plan a war strategy. Mountbatten was the first of the general staff to see what total war meant. 'Total war meant that you could either send a division, or forty bombers, against someone, or you could bribe them to come on to your side. Roosevelt understood that the first time we talked to him.'

So Eccles was in the bribery business? 'Yes, it was my business. Yes. Yes. Because I saw we couldn't fight for Gibraltar. Nothing to fight with. So we bribed. I was an apostle of bribery.'

That wasn't put so bluntly in the book, was it? 'The book doesn't say anything about the money we paid the Spanish generals.'

What sort of money? 'Millions [of pounds].'

To Spanish ambassadors and politicians? 'To anyone who was any good.'

To Franco? 'Not from us.'

To Franco's brother (ambassador in Lisbon)? 'Well, his brother was a jolly man.'

So Lord Eccles was in commerce, anything from buying fifty-five thousand cases of Spanish oranges to bribing the grandees of Spain? 'The ministry of food didn't see that buying all the Spanish oranges wasn't just a question of price. They didn't see we had to throw extra money on the table because this was a move in the bribery war.'

Where did the money come from? 'The treasury.'

What did he put down on his expenses, 'Bribe to General X?' 'Oh, I can't go into that sort of thing. The arrangement was with the Bank of Portugal to make credits where we wanted them. I didn't handle the money. I said where it had to go.'

In Portugal, Eccles's main concern was to buy wolfram, which the Allies needed to harden steel. He got on very well with Salazar, who had been dictator since 1933, and indeed thought him a great man, who had rescued his country from disintegration. Salazar had never at that time travelled at all, not even as far as France, not even to visit the Portuguese colonies. But, untravelled as he was, he spoke of the United States as a country illuminated not by God but by electric light, a remark that so astonished Eccles that he put it in his foreign office telegram. Salazar also feared that Europe, after the war, might become an American satellite.

'He was,' said Eccles, 'very frightened of that. It was a prescient thing to say.' This was before America had entered the war, and before she realised her true power. Eccles, who was in Washington from March to June, 1941, says that was a time when America was a growing plant: every morning you looked out of the window and saw that it was taller than the night before.

In Washington, Eccles thought the state department a hopeless lot, and at the White House was amazed to see the press camped out in a ground floor room 'with whisky all over the place, and ham and eggs'. He told Harry Hopkins, Roosevelt's principal adviser, who replied that the reporters were a damn sight more important than members of Congress.

'Oh, I said, are they really? Then suddenly I said to him. ''But you see, you're a Roman empire. You're not a democracy at all.'' Augustus, as any classical scholar will tell you, paid his runners from Rome to Gaul more money than anybody else, because of course they were the only people who could transmit his orders. And here were these columnists, in the White House, working over the heads of Congress, for the president, and paid more than anybody else. He used them that way.'

But in spite of ham and eggs in the White House, Eccles had a sanguine view of the power of the United States, and believed that after the war America and Britain would 'rule jointly the wide world'. A sounding phrase, that?

'We still thought we were powerful, and the US even more powerful. So, who else was going to be powerful by the time we'd finished the war? No one.'

But ruling the wide world? 'We failed to live up to what we'd earned. I thought at least we'd lead Europe. They all wanted us to. The Labour Party let us down with a bump – they were much more interested in nationalisation, and giving India her freedom.'

While Eccles was negotiating in Madrid, Lisbon, and Washington, his wife Sybil – whose letters make up nearly half the book – was looking after their three children and the farm in Wiltshire, and writing about fetching the pig home, and about taking down signposts to puzzle German spies.

She did once receive silk stockings in an envelope marked OHMS, but it was rather a contrast of living styles between them, wasn't it?

Lord Eccles did not quite agree. 'Her father [Lord Dawson, physician to the King] was one of the most celebrated men of the age. Prime ministers, foreign secretaries – she knew them all by their Christian names. I wouldn't have got anything like as much rope to play with if she hadn't perpetually seduced them at home, a bit.'

Who? 'Halifax [foreign secretary before he went to Washington as ambassador] for a start. Then the foreign office officials. And the military.'

This worldly view of his wife did not seem to me to accord with Lord Eccles's stated view that women were lucky to have their lives shaped by their children. He said that women were lucky: they could do something men could not do, bear children. He quoted from the scene in Flecker's play, *Hassan*, where the women, watching their men go off to Samarkand, say, 'They have their dreams, and do not think of us.' But why, asked Lord Eccles, *did* men have their dreams? It was because they couldn't bear children. If they could, they wouldn't have the same dreams.

He had, he said, always been pro-women. That, I said, was evident. For instance, his account of Angel Peterson, the ambassador's wife in Madrid, flushed from playing with her children, was strongly erotic.

'Well, I always think of women in a slightly erotic way, yes.'

But he had written *to his wife* about Angel; and also about the girl whose black dress blew over her head; and also about the most beautiful creature in Spain being wildly in love with him; and also about the woman, who, having danced for him, said there was only one thing more she could do to cheer him up, at which her husband, who was there, said if she did he would kill her.

'Funny fellow,' said Lord Eccles.

He then made a distinction, he said a Shakespearean distinction, between constancy and chastity.

Then: 'Some of the most beautiful women in Europe had a go at me after the war. Really wonderful, I mean the top people. And I enjoy that, the little encounter. But when it comes to saying, "Do I want to see you at breakfast, do I want to go on holiday with you, the answer was no, because I've only got one woman".'

So he was saying he had been constant but not chaste? 'That's right. Neither Antony nor Cleopatra was chaste, by any means, but they were constant, and that is worth a lot. I believe that, you see, not by theory but by experience.'

Early in 1942 he gave up the most beautiful creature in Spain because, he says, he was a Presbyterian and it was giving him terrible guilt problems, and also because he'd had a hell of a row with his wife when he was home on leave just before that.

In Scotland?

This is stated in the book, and the matter is there for everyone to read between the lines, but it was the one thing Lord Eccles would not talk about. But he prints at length his wife's letter of 30 May 1942, in which she says his letters have lost their power to seduce and bewitch her, and asks why she should think he loves her any more. He says this came out of the blue and was by far the worst blow he had ever known.

Why did she write it then?

He thought she had gone away for the weekend with someone, was having an affair, but how was he to know?

But I said, he had written an emollient reply, not seeming hurt at all? 'I thought that was the best way to deal with it, and it worked. I was quite a negotiator by that time.'

A bit calculated, that? 'Well, I can only say I thought, absolute hell, I'm not going to lose that girl; she's the best girl in the world. If I'd said, "You can't be faithful while your husband's abroad", that sort of thing, it would only have made it worse.'

So there it was, Antony and Cleopatra, and he was choosing between power and love; he decided to come home, and must have wangled it? 'Yes, I did. Had to work very hard to get myself back home. The book does I hope show the grip I had on the Portuguese and the Spanish was fairly considerable. And then to say to the government, I'm throwing that away because I want any old job in London; in the war it was quite difficult.'

Here Lord Eccles returned to the idea of his book as both history and novel. The historian could never tell how his people felt, or whom they cared about, but the art of the novelist was to say, 'I can show you the workings of the watch. I'll open the back and you can have a look.'

The watch having been opened, I asked Lord Eccles about his hope that the post-war society would attain something halfway between the brigandage of capitalism and the paralysis of socialism. 'I've been a capitalist and made quite a lot of money, and thought what a rotten idea the whole thing was, but that it doesn't matter, if you pick up the money it's OK. But I didn't like it. I could see it was no good.'

Yes? The most interesting theory about this, said Lord Eccles, was Pétain's. He referred to a letter of 27 January 1940 in which he describes a lunch in Madrid with the Duke of Alba, a duchess, a countess, and Pétain, who was then French ambassador to Spain. Pétain had a plan for the peace. First he quoted Washington's speech on his retirement from public life to be a country gentleman; then he said the main supports of political prosperity were morality and religion; and then he said that absolute property ('shiver from Alba') could not exist, and nor could absolute equality. He said he wanted one armed force for the whole block, too, and then he and Eccles parted with a warm embrace.

At this point Lord Eccles said he too had had a plan in those days – a lot about sharing the world's goods between the rich and the poor.

A sort of north-south plan? And was he still inclined to it? 'I think I would be, if there was anybody who could do it. But you have a banking system which lends lots of money to these people who then waste it, and do nothing any good with it, and it really breaks your heart.'

So – flying boats to Lisbon, jewels, lovers, finery, intrigue, Utopias for after the war, and a shiver from the Duke of Alba. That's history, but, as to the novel, David Eccles, having in 1942 wangled his way back home again, did not find his wife, as he had feared, a stranger. 'One look, and the old enchantment renewed its spell.'

He had returned not exactly to obscurity but to a seat in the Commons. Twenty-one years later he became the last but one hereditary viscount ever to be created.

And compared to a viscountcy, I suggested, a life peerage, which is what he could expect today, would be a miserable thing? 'Well, if you feel about your land and your son, it is.'

And that was the essence of a peerage? 'It seems so to me.'

Lady Eccles died in 1977. Did he now feel, as she once wrote to him, that the war years had been a life beyond his dreams? 'It wasn't anything absolutely, you know, like looking back and saying, "This was the day I scored a century in a Test match; or something".'

—January 1983

TEDDY KOLLEK
Moderation and Megalomania

Teddy Kollek has just celebrated twenty years as mayor of Jerusalem. It is the City of David and the Wailing Wall, the city where Christ was crucified, the city where Mahomet ascended to Heaven. It is a city which might very likely be the cause and centre of any new Arab-Israeli war. It is some city, and a dangerous city.

But it is not just because he is mayor of Jerusalem that you go to see Mr Kollek. It is because in his lifetime he has seen the downfall of the Austro-Hungarian empire, the holocaust, the establishment of the State of Israel, and everything since, and because his perspective is wider and his experience longer than that of the present leaders of Israel. And it is because he is a Zionist who is not afraid to lament what he sees as the megalomania of Israel's recent past, in which he sees great danger.

Now, from 1949 Israel held only western Jerusalem; the new part. Since the Six Day War of 1967 they have held the whole city, having annexed the eastern and most holy parts. Mr Kollek is a firm believer in the art of the possible. He talks *Realpolitik* and, I asked him, hadn't he just said that he believed there would never be any agreement on Jerusalem between Israel and Jordan? Never? Didn't that sound like despair?

'No,' he said, and the word as he pronounced it sounded like a moan, as it might have been indeed, because he went on to say that, you see, he didn't think the Jordanians could accept any agreement that didn't include dividing Israel. And once they had this, they would never be able to hold it unless they also took Haifa and Acre and Jaffa and everything. Unless, in other words, they took the whole of the present State of Israel. That is what I understood him to mean.

I take this exchange out of its context, which I shall come to later. It was during a long talk in his office at Jerusalem City Hall, which looks very English provincial and was indeed put up during the British mandate by A. C. Holliday, ARIBA, and opened on 2 September 1930 by Sir Stewart Spencer Davis, Officer Administering the Government.

145

Inside, in glass cases, are mementos of Mayor Kollek's many overseas visits – a medal from the City of London, the keys of Dallas and Cincinnati, and a memento of the hundredth anniversary of the Atlantic City boardwalk. In a corner of his office perch two vast teddy bears and a koala bear. And behind the desk sits Mr Kollek, who has seen it all.

He is now seventy-four. He was brought up in an upper middle-class family in Vienna when it was the capital of the Austro-Hungarian empire. He helped found an early kibbutz. He raised money in America, by means lawful and unlawful, for the Zionist cause. He became minister in Washington for the new State of Israel. For thirteen years he was director general of the Israeli prime minister's office. Then he was persuaded to run for mayor, which he saw at the time as standing for i/c garbage disposal. He is a liberal European, and an Askenazi in a city most of whose inhabitants are none of those things.

It all goes back into what seems pre-history. One of his first childhood memories is of the funeral of the Emperor Franz Joseph in 1916. This, as it happens, is also one of the first childhood memories of Bruno Kreisky, formerly chancellor of Austria, a politician with whom, I supposed, Mr Kollek would hardly have seen eye to eye, since he had, among other things, received Yasser Arafat of the PLO.

'There is a difference, you see. I am tolerant and he is not.' They had been contemporaries and it was mere chance that he had become a Zionist while Kreisky had gone into the socialist movement. He remembers how in the first elections after the collapse of the Austrian monarchy there were posters in Polish, Hungarian, Slovenian, Czech, and he didn't know what else. Today you could find this variety only in the names in the telephone book. The cultural differences had disappeared. There had soon afterwards come a time when everyone talked about a united Europe when the separate European languages would disappear and only Esperanto would survive.

That was how Kreisky had grown up and that was why he had an aversion to Jewish nationalism. He thought him a very fine gentleman but wished he had been more careful in his contacts with terrorists and the PLO. Maybe, he thought, Kreisky was leaning backwards because of his Jewish complex: he could understand that.

Mr Kollek was in England before the war, looked up Sherlock Holmes's address at 221b Baker Street, and admired the imperturbability of the British. 'But later events have changed that a little, with the change from the self-confidence of a great empire. Or don't you agree?'

I was afraid I did agree. Mr Kollek then talked about the courage of Londoners in the Blitz. The sensation he best remembered was that of walking on broken glass on the pavements the next morning, the grating feeling under the feet.

But in spite of that admiration, he had thought that in the end the romantic English were always going to prefer the Arabs of the desert to the Jews? Not necessarily from the beginning, he said, and named old English friends, some of them relations of Balfour – of the Balfour Declaration which expressed HMG's sympathy with the idea of a national home for the Jews. Then there was Victor Cazalet, who died in the same plane crash as the actor Leslie Howard.

'Many friends,' he said. 'But in the end it was as you say.'

The romanticism of Lawrence of Arabia? Mr Kollek partly agreed, but yet, he said, Lawrence was basically a Zionist and had believed in the cooperation of Arabs and Jews. Mr Kollek said he frequently quoted a passage from Lawrence's *Seven Pillars*. After Feisal I had declared himself an Arab king in Damascus, there was a man who set out to ride a camel to that city. This man had one ambition, to become head of the veterinary service in the Arab kingdom and was hurrying to Damascus to stake out his claim. The camel had a sore, which grew and grew, but the rider thought only about the veterinary service and not about the sore, and the camel died the day before they got to Damascus. 'This is I think a very appropriate story. I'm afraid it's getting slightly appropriate for us as well. There is no direct relationship between what you say and what you do.'

He was talking about hypocrisy? 'Fantasy.'

We were to return to fantasy later, but first, having in mind Mr Kollek's early reputation for getting suitcases of money delivered to Brooklyn piers to pay for arms for Israel, I asked if in those days he hadn't been a fixer. 'I still am.'

And in 1939, when he was twenty-one, he went as a representative of the Jewish Agency to negotiate with Eichmann in Vienna, to persuade him to let Jews out. He had entry permits for England. 'He was sitting opposite me, as I am sitting opposite you. He was a normal SS official, nothing out of the ordinary, objectionable as all Nazis were, but not a great monster.' Many years later, when he was at the prime minister's office, Mr Kollek arranged the trial of Eichmann when he was found, arrested, brought to Israel, and hanged.

I asked Mr Kollek if on 14 May 1948, when he heard David Ben-Gurion proclaim the State of Israel, he had believed in his heart that it would survive. 'I believed we might pull it off. Nobody was certain. It is still in serious danger from all sides, partly from inside. The question is against what do you measure it – your own ideas and ideals, or in comparison to other states created at that time or since. Compared with the others we have done extremely well.'

As director general to Ben-Gurion, whom he clearly loved, Mr Kollek was in effect the principal civil servant of the state, and was often told, 'Just do it', and this at a time when Ben-Gurion's prestige was so great that you could gently achieve a great deal. Mr Kollek recalls a conversation, after Ben-Gurion went, in which Isaiah Berlin was arguing that the country should relax a little, and should not go on demanding heroism from people all the time. Mr Kollek disagreed with this. He now says he is not sure whether he had meant that heroism was still needed, or rather that Israel needed a few more years of the strength of Ben-Gurion at the centre. 'I think I should have said we should permanently have a very strong centre, because our people come from so many cultures and without a centre we might be torn apart.'

Had he felt that, particularly after the 1967 war, the Israelis had developed a sense almost of omnipotence? 'Yes. I felt we were a little self-inflated: no, very much self-inflated; and maybe a bit megalomaniac in many ways.'

That was a strong word? Mr Kollek gave an example. He said the Hebrew University had to be built on Mount Scopus. This is the hill that overlooks Jerusalem from the north-east, where Roman legions, crusaders, and the British in 1917, all camped before taking the city, and which from 1949 to 1967 was cut off from the Israeli part of the city. But he said they should have built a modest and not a megalomaniac building, something on a human scale.

It sounded as if he was talking about the sort of monumental post offices and government buildings that Mussolini put up all over Italy. 'Well, it wasn't only the building thing. In many ways we believed that our strength was greater than it was. You see, the man I believe was the epitome of megalomania was Mr Begin. I'm not arguing now whether he was right or wrong. I'm arguing about what he tried to do, measured against his strength, and here I'm influenced by something that may have been a very strong influence.'

What? 'During the Blitz Mr Ben-Gurion happened to be in London and, as he had very little to do, and as he always wanted to read Plato in the original, he studied Greek. The only two things I got from that were two words from the Delphic oracle – do you read Greek? – which meant, "Everything in measure". Mr Ben-Gurion in 1956, when the war in Sinai became inevitable, before the campaign, said he would never want to keep Gaza, because he wouldn't know what to do with 350,000 Arabs.'

Yes? 'Mr Begin tried later, in a Bismarckian way, to change the political situation in the Middle East, which you might have been able to do a hundred years before, but not in the time of quick communications, television, and great power interference. In 1870 yes, but Israel in 1970 couldn't conquer a great territory, incorporate a million Arabs, and build – and he gave up after a little while – build a canal from the Mediterranean to the Dead Sea. Now let's assume these things were justified – which I don't think they were – but there was no modesty about it. There was no clear appreciation of what your strength was.'

We were plainly back to fantasy, and Mr Kollek was all for reducing fantasy to moderation? 'Yes, and we lost that feeling of moderation. Ben-Gurion took great risks. He declared the state in 1948 and pulled it off. But because he had a feeling of moderation he was able to pull off the things that he did.'

Did he think it fair to make any comparison between his job and that of Mayor Koch of New York, which had an equally diverse population and must be the biggest Jewish city in the world? He said the basic difference was that in America there was the principle of the melting pot. Hispanics might speak Spanish, and their children might be taught in Spanish at a school, but in the next generation they would speak English. This is contentious, since American Hispanics show every sign of continuing to prefer Spanish, and insisting on it, but Mr Kollek is on stronger ground when he points out that earlier immigrants in New York, like the Italians and the Jews, were assimilated, and that Jewish children now often speak only a few words of Yiddish with their grandmothers. But in Jerusalem the Armenians, Abyssinians, Arabs, and Jews kept themselves apart and spoke their own languages, as they had done for 1500 years. If you had walked into the Old City a hundred years ago you would have found the same separate quarters.

What about the extremism of the religious Jews? He said he took it for granted. But they were going round smashing bus shelters just because they carried advertisements showing women? Mr Kollek said he had the advantage of old age and a long history. In the early 1960s the then minister of transport seriously wanted to build a long tunnel from the Mandelbaum Gate to the edge of the city, to stop the religious Jews stoning buses, but he had argued against the cost and things had quietened down. It wasn't, he said, the extremism as such that worried him as much as the ghetto mentality it showed. But though the religious, strictly orthodox Jews represented almost a quarter of the Jews in the city, they were a very small proportion of Jewry in the world.

But didn't it seem strange that a modern state had an airline which didn't fly on the Sabbath? 'Absolutely, absolutely. But this is also one of the inheritances that Mr Begin left us. He wanted to be a great leader, maybe almost a prophet, and he was willing to pay a price for it. It will take many years to overcome those years of his government.'

Well, the examples of theocratic states were pretty awful, weren't they – Calvin's Geneva or present-day Iran? He said you didn't have to go as far as that. Take Saudi Arabia. And it wasn't so long ago that it had been illegal to teach Darwinism in parts of the United States. 'If you believe in liberalism and humanism you have to fight all your life. You can't take rationalism for granted in this world.'

It was here that we came to Mr Kollek's view that Jordan would never agree a settlement either on Jerusalem or on the West Bank territory which Israel occupied in 1967. He believes the Arab states want not just the Old City back, or the West Bank, which includes such Biblical towns as Bethlehem, Hebron, and Jericho, but all Israel.

So what's to be done? 'What you can do is create a Jerusalem which at least is not obnoxious. Speak to the Arabs privately. They will forget after a while that you are a foreign journalist and stop making propaganda. We are the same way – we a little less, they more so. They will tell you that the situation is impossible, that they're occupied, but they will also tell you that it's a better city to live in now, and none of them will want to leave. The number of Arabs has doubled between 1967 and today, so it can't be so cruel here.'

But didn't the fact remain that Jordan wanted part of Jerusalem back and Israel would never give it? Mr Kollek here embarked on an essay on sovereignty illustrated with discursions into history. Israel had allowed Arabs in Jerusalem to remain Jordanian citizens and had thus given up a piece of sovereignty. When in 1935 the Saarland was given to Germany, after a plebiscite, all the inhabitants had to accept German citizenship. When the United States bought Alaska, Alaskans became Americans. He even went back to the Schleswig-Holstein question, that famous nineteenth century conundrum.

It was, he said, the tradition that people accepted the citizenship of the sovereign power. But Israel had given the Arabs the chance to remain Jordanian citizens. The Jordanian educational system had been kept, though some obnoxious things had been deleted from text-books, such as if you had ten Jews and killed six, how many Jews were left. Otherwise they were using the same textbooks as before. Jordanian doctors, pharmacists, and lawyers were allowed to practise. Jordanians living in Jerusalem were allowed to cross bridges into enemy territory. Sovereignty of a people did not need a geo-graphical line on a map. The world, and the Jordanians, would have to get used to this.

'But the trouble is,' said Mr Kollek, 'that so many friends of theirs, Europeans, give them hopes it will be different. It won't. They rely first of all on the United Nations, then on the Russians, then on the Americans, and then on Allah, and then on pestilence, and they haven't got rid of us by any of these means.'

Hadn't he written that, if Jerusalem were divided again, Israel could not survive intact? 'No. I said that it would be almost as great a blow as the Holocaust. You could have waited another ten years for the unification of Jerusalem, or another twenty years, but once united, if it were divided again it would be the severest blow to the Jewish people.'

Even in the Diaspora? 'Even in the Diaspora.'

And the faith of many would be crushed? 'Yes.'

They would cease to be Jews? 'No, nobody will ever cease to be a Jew once he's a Jew.'

Here Mr Kollek told me a story about his having once gone as a guest to a club in New York which he had not known to be restricted. He had asked his host, who was a liberal, how he could be a member of such a club. A club servant, overhearing his remarks that there were no Jewish members, came over and said, 'That's not true, sir. We have Mr Dillon.' Now Mr Dillon was a great investment banker and chairman of the Metropolitan Museum, but his grandfather had been a Jew who had become a gentile. Because of that grandfather, he was still, in the eyes of the club servant, a Jew.

—December 1985

THE DUKE OF EDINBURGH
The Unendangered Species

In a dead forest with not a live tree in sight, where there was once water but where there is now only desert, in the West African state of Mali, about seventy-five miles from Timbuktu, a breeze miraculously arose and I could have sworn I heard the Duke of Edinburgh say something about Noah's Ark.

I went and asked him. 'At least I'm glad you asked, rather than just take it off the wind,' he said. He then said Noah's flood had been a natural disaster, and now this drought was another disaster, and what could you do about a drought?

A day or two before I had visited two refugee camps in Mali where a lot of children are going to die. The famine is not remotely as bad in Mali as it is in Ethiopia and I don't want to suggest for one moment that it is, but many will die. In the face of Africa, stoicism is probably the only choice, but all the same I asked the Duke again if he thought nothing could be done. I had those children in mind.

He invited me to consider what would happen if more of the children in those camps survived, but with no more food to share between them. That is plainly sense, but I asked if it was not a bit cold-blooded. He asked whether I knew by how many people the population of India increased in a year. I did not know. He said it increased by fifteen million a year – twice the population of London. Very well, but we were in Africa.

That was in the morning. There was then a four-hour drive by Land Rover across the most ravaged bit of terrain I can remember seeing. I do not mean that it was as difficult to traverse as a mountain range, or as awesome as the great Australian desert, but it was across a plain where trees used to grow and fish used to be fished, but no more. Then we – another English reporter and I – made a two-hour flight by light plane, and arrived filthy, exhausted, and with one plane having turned back and with some baggage lost, and no certainty of a hotel room, at the Malian capital of Bamako.

152

We were standing quite filthy in a hotel lobby when HM Honorary Consul came up, explained that the Duke had arrived before us in his Andover of the Queen's flight, that his press conference was at that moment attended only by two or three Malians, and would we please come quickly? In exchange, he fixed us a room, so that was fine, and we were about to seek the Duke when the Malians departed, leaving no one. End of conference. Sorry, we said.

Once I was in my room, removing filthy bush clothes, the Consul rang again. If I could find the other Englishman, and if he, the Consul, could round up the Frenchmen who had come with us, please could we now meet the Duke in forty-five minutes? There is a certain deference to royalty which must be inherent in an Englishman, so I said certainly, delighted.

I changed into a decent suit, put on a cricket club tie, and went to the bar for a beer. There was the Duke also, the last man on earth I expected to find in the Timbuktu bar of that hotel. Since we had bumped into each other a dozen times already that day, I said good evening. 'No, not now,' he said, with the utmost irritation. I went and got a beer.

Then the press conference began, two Frenchmen, two Swiss reporters, two Swiss cameramen, and me. The Duke was by then most affable and asked where my English friend was. I explained that he sent his apologies, and was being sick. The Duke immediately sent his own doctor, which was kind.

I brought up the matter of Noah's flood and the present drought, which had been in my head all day. The Duke replied that some animal species were indeed simply dying out. But, I said, the principal species about which we were talking was Man, wasn't it? 'Speak for yourself,' he said.

Well now, the Duke was touring West Africa as president of the World Wildlife Fund, whose spokesman had stressed to me from Geneva that the Fund's concern was not only with animals but also with men and women. The spokesman made a great point of this. Furthermore, I had heard the Duke say to some French-speaking officials the day before that animals and human beings had to live together or die together. Furthermore, it stated clearly in the Duke's programme, 'Visit refugee camp', and I had indeed seen him, between the dead forest that morning and our conversation that evening, spend ten minutes looking round such a camp.

So I said, 'No, I don't speak only for myself. Cattle are dying, which is sad, but people are starving.' He replied that species were endangered all over the world.

'Yes, sir, but the camp you visited today was one I had seen before, and the species endangered there is man.'

'You cannot,' said the Duke, 'describe that species as endangered. There are thousands of millions of them.'

But I said, if half of those children were going to die under the age of five, they were endangered, weren't they? 'No, they're not. The population of this country is increasing by 3% per annum. Do a calculation and you will find it will double in the next twenty years. You can't say that's becoming extinct. Come on.'

So these people were not becoming extinct, I said, but surely they excited the pity of all of us. The Duke said lots of people were concerned. But wild species were becoming extinct. There were not many left of some species. Then he said, 'That's not to take away from the need to be humane and to look after people. But there are specialities in the world. Our speciality is the conservation of the natural environment.'

I repeated what the World Wildlife Fund had told me – that animals, plants and Man made up one ecology. The Duke suggested that the spokesman in Geneva had known me and told me what I wanted to hear. I said he had not known me at all, and I had not known him.

'In the end,' said the Duke, 'the conservation of nature is for its own sake. To be absolutely honest, it's not for the sake of Man at all. But in order to make it more palatable to a lot of people, you have to say, you know, we've got to coexist, and it'll be in the interests of our grandchildren and so on. Why do people protest about whaling? How many people in this world are ever going to see a whale? And yet they march up and down protesting against whale hunting. Why? You tell me.'

I said that in my experience they were mostly professional protesters. At this point you couldn't honestly say that relations between us were cordial, but they were never as acerbic as this transcription would seem to show. I have never known a man get irritated so easily, and I'm damned if I'd have liked to have served as a sub-lieutenant in any ship of his. But his mood can change rapidly to sweet, moderate charm.

Anyway, the French then entered the conversation, and the Duke explained to them that you can compare the effects of the drought to those of a volcano that had exploded. But more people died after man-made disasters like civil wars. Disasters, like wars, were mostly made by men. The French having finished for the moment, the Duke turned to me and said, 'You still aren't happy?'

I said I had thought about what he had said that morning. I had told him half the children in that camp would die under the age of five, and he had said yes, but had then asked what would happen if fewer died. 'Say 25%?' he suggested. 'Something like that,' I said. And then I reminded him that I had asked if that wasn't all a bit cold-blooded, or at any rate if the facts were cold-blooded.

The Duke then said, in exasperation, 'I will stop talking to you about the frightful facts of life. I will tell you what you want. I would like to give my shirt to those people if it would help them. Would that make you feel any happier?'

I said it was not that I wanted to feel any happier. It was that I wanted to understand him. I did feel (though I didn't say and now think I should have said) that there was nothing to choose between our views of the matter, so what was all the controversy about. Was he, I asked, saying that there was nothing, or very little, that one could do about a drought? 'No,' he said, 'there's nothing I can do about it. You do something about it.'

I said my capacity to do anything was infinitely smaller than his. He said, 'The World Wildlife Fund is not established to look after refugees. It simply isn't for that purpose. Now, my daughter, with the Save The Children Fund, she occupies herself with . . . If I was president of Oxfam or something, then I'd be concerned about this thing in an institutional way. I'm concerned about it in a personal way. You've got to stick to your last.'

'OK,' I said. The Duke laughed.

There followed two or three more questions from the French journalists. Then, at the end, I said that Mr Bush, Vice-President of the United States, happened to be coming to this same spot the next day. Indeed, we were using a room next to the White House press centre for our talk at that moment. Bamako was a distant place, and they were due to miss each other by about two hours. Were there any plans for them to meet at all?

'I saw him in Washington last year. You ask him: he'll give you the answers you want.' I suggested that one did not ask questions with the answers necessarily already in one's mind.

'I know the answers you don't want,' said the Duke.

'That,' I said, 'is highly unfair.' The Duke laughed and went out in a mighty good mood. Next morning he left before Mr Bush arrived.

That was on Saturday. Yesterday the Duke was in Senegal, which is quite another country in every way. At an embassy reception in Dakar he came up to me. We were both cooler. 'Been thinking about that 50%,' he said. 'Better if there were only 5% pregnancies and all the children lived.'

—March 1985

This is the only piece in the book which is not strictly a formal interview, because others were there. I include it because the other four present in Bamako were either French or Swiss, showed more interest in getting off to dinner than in talking to the Duke, and hardly asked him a thing.

THE KAISER'S DAUGHTER
Last Waltz with the Czar

I mean no discourtesy when I say that the first surprise was to learn that she was still alive; but Princess Viktoria Luise, the Kaiser's daughter, daughter of the last of the reigning Hohenzollerns, is not only alive but vigorous. She lives in a small house in Brunswick, at Stresemanstrasse 5, among pictures of Frederick the Great, of her father Wilhelm II, and of her own wedding day. She is now eighty-four. She went skiing until she was eighty. She proposed a toast to peace, and we drank it in pink champagne.

She was born in 1892, Princess of Prussia, Orange, Hildesheim, and of fourteen other territories; and, besides, Duchess of Saxony, Holstein, Schleswig and of twenty other territories. Today she is a citizen of the Federal Republic of Germany, though on her passport she is described firmly as Princess of Prussia and Duchess of Brunswick.

The last title came to her on her marriage to Ernst August, Duke of Brunswick, and her wedding picture is among the first she shows a visitor. I asked why the men in the scene were carrying flaming torches. 'It was the dance of torches in the evening,' she said. 'I danced with my husband, and then with my father, and then with the King of England, and then with the Emperor of Russia.' That was in 1913, the year before the deluge, and the last time those emperors and kings ever met.

The picture of which she is perhaps most proud shows her on horseback, in 1911, when as a girl of eighteen she was installed as colonel in chief of the Death's Head Hussars. It is a martial picture. Had she wanted to be a boy? 'Yes, yes, yes, yes. I was so delighted when I got my regiment. I had six brothers, and of course I was a half-boy.' She always liked to wear the Scottish kilt, because a man might wear that too.

When she was a girl, the Kaiser would tell them stories, and laugh, and slap his knees. In public he was not allowed to laugh. At the unveiling of one statue the drape at first stuck, and then fell and enveloped the mayor, who crawled around on the ground like a tortoise. The Kaiser kept his face, but afterwards exploded with laughter. Once he broke a chair under him at a banquet and bore it for as long as he could, until, when he rose to make a speech, he remarked that they might bring him another because the chair he had been sitting on had now only three legs.

Then the war. In 1914 the Kaiser had felt betrayed. He believed, said the Princess, that the King of England could prevent the war. This was the saddest and wildest misapprehension: how could he have believed that? 'He believed in the friendship of his cousin.'

Several times, here and there in the conversation, the Princess said how much her father loved England. In 1912, when he had first taken her to England, to open the Victoria memorial (the great golden thing in front of Buckingham Palace), he brought her on deck as they approached the English coast and told her that for him the sense of England was always the smell of English hay. 'When we came for the first time,' she said, 'it was winter, so there was no hay.'

The war dragged on, dragging Europe down with it. In Germany there was privation, in Russia revolution. The Czar, with whom she had danced, and all his family, were murdered at Ekaterinburg. How had she felt then? 'That it could happen to us all. As well. After a lost war, we all had the feeling the communists were coming up, and the whole country was nearly starved. They had nothing to eat.'

In 1918 the Kaiser abdicated in chaos and bitterness. The Princess thinks the abdication was inevitable but blames it principally on Woodrow Wilson. 'The abdication was the only way to get an understanding with America, don't you see? Because they tried to impress upon the population that the Kaiser was at fault.'

The Kaiser went to exile in Holland, never to return. The Princess lived in Austria and Germany and, in the 1930s, visited England. There she met the future Queen of England as a little girl coming in breathlessly from a dancing lesson and exclaiming, 'Mummy, it's wonderful,' and, at Chequers, Ramsay MacDonald, who wanted to know about Hitler. He thought Hitler was a simple man and told the Princess, 'I'm a simple man, too.'

And what did the Princess reply? 'I said if Hitler's for peace and not war we're all for him.'

It was after this visit that Hitler, through Ribbentrop, made the modest proposal that the Princess and her husband should arrange a marriage between their daughter Fredericke and the Prince of Wales, later Edward VIII, later the Duke of Windsor.

And what was her reply to Hitler? – 'No. We don't push our children.' Thus spake the Hohenzollerns. Besides, said the Princess, the Prince of Wales had other ideas at the time, or so she believed. It must be one of the more piquant ironies of a century disastrous for European dynasties that in 1912, on that first visit to England, Princess Viktoria Luise herself had been whispered in the press as a future bride of that same, much younger, Prince of Wales.

Was it true that throughout his exile the Kaiser hoped for the restoration of the monarchy? 'I believe yes. That in his heart, and he was a very religious man, he thought, ''If God wills that I come back, I will come back.'' '

He believed in the Divine Rights of Kings? 'In the Divine Right of the Emperor.' And did she so believe herself a princess of Prussia, through the will of God? – 'Yes.' Nowadays monarchies were different. There were constitutional monarchies. 'The young Spain' – and she referred to Juan Carlos, King of Spain, simply as Spain, in the way that the king of France might be called, in a Jacobean play, France – 'has been educated for kingship by Franco.'

By the will of the Caudillo, as it were, rather than the will of God. Sophia, grand-daughter of Viktoria Luise, is Juan Carlos's queen.

Throughout the interview the Princess's German publisher remained, and often helped her to find a word or a phrase. She explained that although, having had an English nanny, she had learned English before even German, she had forgotten much of it.

At one point, when the Princess spoke of peace, I said Germany had twice this century plunged Europe into war: she denied this was so with the first. Well then, Hitler had been a madman? 'Yes,' she said. 'At last. By his successes he lost his senses.' But had she known of his slaughter of the Jews? Dachau, after all, was about eight miles north of Munich just off the main road, and had been there since before the war. She said she had not known until the last. In the war she had lived in a castle in the Harz mountains, but had not known until after the war that there was a concentration camp behind those mountains. She would swear it.

Her friend the publisher then told a story, which he had from a nephew of the Princess's, who was an eye-witness, about the Kaiser and the Nazis. It happened that in November 1938 the Kaiser's sons were with him in Holland in order to draw up a new settlement of the family property. While they were together the news came of the Kristallnacht in which the synagogues of the German Jews had been burned. The Kaiser was distressed, and shouted at August Wilhelm, the only one of his sons who had joined the Nazis, that if he did not leave the party he would throw him out of the family. The eldest son reasoned with his father, saying that if his brother did this he would be murdered. The Kaiser relented, but still refused ever again to appear in public with August Wilhelm. That day the Kaiser cried.

In 1939 there was war. In 1941, still in Holland though by then in German-occupied Holland, the Kaiser died. Princess Viktoria Luise was with him and says that his last wish was that Germany and England should be friends. Four years later the second German war of the century ended with Germany not merely defeated but this time destroyed. Most of what used to be Prussia was parcelled out between Poland, Russia, and what became East Germany.

The Princess wants to see a reunited Germany, and in her heart cannot accept Willy Brandt's *Ostpolitik*, which formally recognised the existence of two separate German states. In a country which was now in the east her father had a hunting box. She remembers a church. The people were very loyal. 'And shall we,' she asks, 'now give them all up?'

But it would need a war to recover them? It must be done little by little, said the Princess; at which her publisher, mentioning that the Princess was not a politician, took the opportunity to produce a locket, found only that morning, which was a gift of Queen Victoria to the Princess as a child. The Princess had forgotten it. It opens to reveal a portrait of Albert, the Prince Consort.

We had been drinking tea, but now pink champagne arrived and we drank to peace, of which the Princess spoke much. I said the Princess had lost everything. She took this to mean a lost Prussia, and began to talk once again of never giving up hope. But I had meant her own loss, not only of rank but of material possessions. The publisher grasped this and explained to her, 'Living in such a house. No servants.'

'That is correct,' she said, but her family had always been religious and she prayed. I understood her to say that she prayed that, among other things, the young might have a faith of their own, and not have to go for ideas to Indian mysticism as so many did. Then she told me the story of the allegorical painting. It was at the time of the Boxer Rebellion, she thought in 1901. It was to do with the holy rights of Europe.

The Kaiser had painted this? 'Yes, yes, yes. It was a beautiful allegory. Woman, in all sorts of armour.' There were the women of Europe arm in arm – German, Austrian, French, and Russian; her father had not kept the Russian out.

And the English? 'Yes. And in the clouds, there was the face of the East, China, a Buddha. Here stood all Europe, looking up to that face. I never forget it, because I had to run through the room of my mother, and pass this picture, when I went to see my father. I always looked at the picture and thought, "My God, I only hope never never never."

'Underneath was an inscription which said something like, "Europe take care of your holy rights".'

Did she have that fear of the East now? She did, and felt the English did not know how near it was. Russia was now on the other side, on the eastern side. Before, there had been Russia and Prussia between East and West. The Prussian peoples had been perhaps the sentinels for Europe. Now she feared Russia and China.

We walked out together from the Princess's sitting-room into an ante-room. There is a doll's house, given to her by a long-dead Queen of Holland. There is a portrait of her late husband, who died in 1953: she keeps it surrounded with flowers. There was again the picture of herself as colonel of the Death's Head Hussars. She said her mount that day was called Trilby, a wonderful horse.

Then, again, the wedding picture. As she danced with the Czar, and as he talked to her, in English as he did with his own family, what did he say? 'He had wonderful eyes, very earnest, and very lovable. We danced and he embraced me, and he said, "I hope you will be just as happy as I." And I'll never forget that.' They were the last words he ever spoke to her.

—May 1977

CHURCHILL'S DAUGHTER
'OK, I had a World-Shaking Father'

Lady Soames, the youngest daughter of Winston Churchill, knelt on her sitting-room floor and we looked through photographs of her father and of the family. We came to one of Churchill in the early 1930s. She said: 'I don't, you know, think anybody's really reflected enough on how little presage there was in a way of the glorious years to come, if you like to look at it like that. Here he was, in pretty low water, at odds with his party, no real backing in the country. One of the things that I loved Papa for so much, apart from the many things, was his quality of undauntedness; because he was undaunted. And it wasn't like someone who just rushes like a bull at a gate. He knew. He felt down. He minded the reverses. But this amazing sort of determination to get up and get at it again, you know, to pursue what he believed. He could have said, "Oh well, dash it, I'll write books and paint", you know?'

The photographs were from *A Churchill Family Album*, a picture anthology selected by Lady Soames from family collections and now published as a book. Some of the photographs were taken long before she was born. Others show her father as she knew him when she was a girl as Mary Churchill. Others, more recent, show the family after her marriage to Christopher Soames, who became her father's PPS, then a cabinet minister, then ambassador to Paris, then the last governor of Rhodesia.

The book's frontispiece shows her mother and father at home at Chartwell in 1933, sitting in a sunlit room.

'Large orange cat,' she said. 'And my bantams.'

What? 'My bantams. They strayed around all over the place. They discovered that the dining-room had crumbs and they used to come in, just stroll in. I also had goats, and I remember one occasion when two kids rushed into the dining-room, but they were evicted rather hastily.'

Two of the first pictures are of Winston Churchill's mother, born Jennie Jerome of Brooklyn, and I said how American she looked, that bold, open, un-English self-confidence that would come today from Vassar and lots of money.

162

'Well, it didn't strike me, actually. The Jerome sisters didn't have American accents because they were all brought up in Paris, because Mrs Jerome decided to establish herself in Paris. I think it was something to do with Jenny Lind having taken up with Mr Jerome. So he made and lost fortunes in New York, and paid visits to Paris. I think he had a whole little theatre in New York where Jenny Lind used to sing. I think she was his mistress for some time. He was very musical.'

Then more pictures of Jennie Jerome who, after Lord Randolph Churchill's death, remarried twice. 'She did go it, didn't she? Isn't it fascinating that twice she married men twenty years younger? Go it, old girl.'

At one point Lady Soames reproduces in her book a magazine cutting, dated 1900, which describes her father as having had a touch of mysticism. Had she ever felt that?

'No, I don't think that I did. I mean, my father, I wouldn't put him on a list of my ten biggest introverts, do you see what I mean? On the other hand he wasn't a brash extrovert. My father was very sensitive in ways some people don't think he was. He understood depression, for instance. You know, his 'black dog'. It never un-manned him, but he knew about it, although he wouldn't have gone into it in the terms that psychiatrists could go into it now.'

Had she ever seen black dog in her father? 'Do you know, I really didn't. I think black dog had been exorcised to his kennel before I became aware of that sort of thing. I have to be very careful, you see, not to attribute to myself thoughts about my parents that I didn't think at the time. OK, I had a world-shaking father, but I hadn't really hoisted it in; how could I? It was only much later.'

Well, when had she realised her father was who he was? 'I was always educated at a little day school. Certainly by the time I was thirteen I was reading newspapers, and I think what began to hoist it in was other children's attitudes to me, because obviously they'd been told by their parents. You know they must have heard Papa being discussed, not necessarily to his advantage, but as a ''warmonger''.'

So her first real memories were of her father in the wilderness of the 1930s, not, say, as chancellor in the 'twenties? 'Certainly the 'thirties. I was born in 'twenty-two, so I was ten in 1932. I wouldn't have been able to understand the problems of India, but I knew there was a great wurra-wurra going on about it. The first public cause I felt passionately, in a primitive fashion, was the rise of Hitler, the threat of Germany, the turpitude of the government in not waking up and getting itself going.' That she said, was obviously her parents' view, but she did have a classics mistress who, when she was fifteen or sixteen, made her read Vera Brittain's *Testament of Youth*, and she also read *All Quiet on the Western Front*.

She was much younger than her brothers and sisters, eight years younger than Sarah, eleven years younger than Randolph, and thirteen years younger than Diana. 'But, they in their turn and I in mine, we were all admitted to dining-room meals much sooner I think than a lot of children of our class and age. We really went almost straight from the nursery to the big dining-room meals. I heard all this marvellous talk. It certainly sailed right over my head, but then gradually, from wondering whether there was going to be enough to have a second helping of cutlets, I started listening, and it was such fun, too, with people like Duff Cooper and Papa having mock battles of words, and awful explosions sometimes. I was fed a rich diet, which I think has a great effect on one, like music.'

From the age of six or seven she had been admitted to the big table, or, if there wasn't room, she and her nanny used to be put at the *katzchentisch*, the cats' table, in the corner. 'Quite early on, you know, there were the lovely moments when Papa would start reciting either the "Battle Hymn of the Republic", or Shakespeare.'

Why the 'Battle Hymn of the Republic', and did he *sing* it? 'More I think he would chant it out, and we would all do the Glory, Glory, Hallelujah. My father was very knowledgeable about the American Civil War. He could tell you all the names and acts of the generals. Now I'll get it wrong – was it Grant or Lee who could have been commander-in-chief of either the Confederate or Union Army? And Papa saying, "Think of that man's choice!" I can't tell you how thrilling he made moments of history. He was very funny, too – this combination of splendour and complete knockabout turns, Edwardian music hall songs that used to come out. There was a wonderful Edwardian comedian called the White Kaffir who used to sing the most extraordinary songs. You could rocket from Shakespeare back to music hall songs.'

At dinner? 'Oh, yes. Over coffee and brandy. Something would spark it off. Then "How Horatius Kept the Bridge", off we used to go into that.'

'How can a man die better ...?' I began, and Lady Soames supplied the next three or four lines. 'Whoosh,' she said. 'He used to go through all of it. Lovely.'

She would remember the abdication of Edward VIII? 'That I remember largely as marked by heated arguments between my

164

parents, because my mother thought Papa was taking completely the wrong line. My mother had in some ways a much shrewder political appreciation than my father. Very interesting. Well, my mother was very puritan and upright. She disapproved of the carry-on. I remember her saying, ''Winston, the people of this country, the humble people of this country, the middle classes of this country, the Empire (we still called it the Empire in those days), they will not accept Mrs Simpson as Queen Consort, not nohow.'' And he would argue that people were much more understanding these days, and that here [in the King] was a splendid, attractive character who had so many gifts in him, and I remember my mother looked very steely, because she didn't think that much to him. And she saw that my father could easily have broken himself on it politically, because I think it was the only time in the House of Commons he was absolutely shouted down. And he was absolutely crushed by the sort of contemptuous disdain of the shouting down.'

Crushed? 'Well, not crushed for ever. But it was a real put-down. And afterwards, it was rather touching, my parents were both at the coronation of King George [VI] and Queen Elizabeth. And within the service there is a moving and beautiful little ceremony for the Queen Consort, praying for Grace for her in the tasks she must perform, and Papa nudged Mummy and said, ''You were quite right. The other one would never have done.'' But he had felt that he [Edward] was being hustled, and my father had this great sense of chivalry, and friendship, and loyalty.'

I asked Lady Soames about the point in the book where she remarks that someone said of her father that he was easily satisfied, with the best. 'I think it must have been F.E. Smith who said that. I don't know, but I remember us roaring with laughter when someone said ''Oh, Winston, your tastes are extremely simple: you are easily satisfied with the very best.'' '

Well, it had been said that between the wars Churchill was rather broke, but surely he must have had his salary as an MP, for what that was worth; and for the earlier years his salary as a minister; and always his large income from writing? 'I tell you what. I find this very difficult to explain. Shall I put it like this? They *felt* pushed. In real terms they weren't pushed. I didn't realise this of course, because the land flowed with milk and honey. My father wasn't harassed about money. He was always ebullient. But my mother had been brought up poorly off and was horrified by bills not being paid, and by the knowledge that he had not really any capital. Then he got a legacy from a distant relation and with that they bought Chartwell, but right from the first my mother said, "We'll always be pushed here." I remember a letter of my father to my mother, dated in the early 'thirties I think, saying, "Darling, you don't need to worry about the October housebooks, I've sold two articles." I don't know, God knows, it was to the *News of the World* or something. Well, I call that, that is not a household that is running on a firmly based economy.'

Not a household like the Duke of Marlborough's? 'No, exactly... There was never any sort of penury. There was occasionally, "Now we must economise", and terrible rows about turning the lights off, and, you know, we'll only have cream once a week or something. It used to last exactly ten days.'

But, Lady Soames said, her father had lost a sizeable whack in the American stock market crash of 1929, and, returning from America and being met by Clementine on the station platform, had impetuously told her there and then. That winter most of Chartwell was shut up, and she remembers living in a small house in the grounds which Churchill had largely built himself.

Built himself? Lady Soames said that her father had built with his own hands the wall round the kitchen garden at Chartwell, taking seven years to do it.

Yes, but a wall was not a house. 'No, no, they had builders and bricklayers. But he used to do quite large bits. Of course he wouldn't have done whatever holds the entire house up. That would have been dicy. I remember him on hands and knees on a great sort of sack, you know, splodging away with cement, smoothing things over.'

Turning to a picture taken early in the century, I wondered if it was generally known any more that Churchill had been a member of the great Liberal government of 1905. 'No, isn't it extraordinary. If he hadn't done anything else in his life he'd have been remembered as part of that great reforming government. Someone said the other day that other than Lloyd George he had introduced more great reforming acts than any other minister. His Sweated Trades Act – everyone has forgotten about that; we take it all for granted, naturally. Why not?'

I said I recalled seeing a cartoon in Arthur Scargill's offices at the Yorkshire headquarters of the National Union of Mineworkers which recalled Tonypandy. 'It's passed into folk history. People will say, "Your father caused the soldiers to fire upon the miners." Totally untrue. Policemen with rolled-up mackintoshes. We think we have industrial trouble now. Look at 1910-11 – dock strikes, rail strikes, lock-ins, lock-outs. Much more bitter than now.'

Now one of the pictures in the book shows a portrait of Churchill done by Sir William Orpen in 1915, just after the disaster of the Dardanelles. The caption says that Clementine did not at first like the picture, thinking it showed too painfully the personal torment her husband had suffered, but later came to think it the best portrait ever painted of him.

'I know exactly what you're going to ask, yes.'

Well, was there any parallel between this portrait, and the much later one by Graham Sutherland, presented to Churchill in 1954 by both Houses of Parliament, which he and Lady Churchill disliked so much that it was destroyed?

'I asked my mother about that. She had come to think that it (the Orpen portrait) was a true statement of what Papa was thinking at the time; so did she not think she could have changed her mind about the Sutherland one? She was absolutely adamant that she wouldn't have done. But again, funnily enough, the whole Sutherland picture saga is almost impossible to agree about. Because I don't really understand how they got so het up about it. My mother had no need to tell me, but she did tell me most things, and it was destroyed very soon after it was presented, I mean within a year, and I didn't know about it until ten years later, just after Papa's death. I've never understood it, but a scunner they took to it; they certainly did.'

Then, on one page, three pictures – one of Churchill in absorbed conversation with F.E. Smith, one of Churchill with F.E. Smith's wife, and one of Churchill with his cousin Sunny (ninth Duke of) Marlborough. Churchill is wearing spats.

'I love the clothes,' said Lady Soames. 'I love spats.'

And co-respondent shoes? 'And co-respondent shoes. I love it. I love that with F.E. They're really at it, aren't they, hammer and tongs. I always think it's sad that two of my father's greatest friends, Sunny Marlborough and F.E. Smith, both died younger than him; they faded out so early in a way, but then of course he lived so long.'

Then a group picture at Chartwell showing Tom, the Mitford sisters' only brother, killed in the war; Randolph Churchill, very good-looking; and, among others, Charlie Chaplin, whom Churchill had earlier met in Hollywood.

'Charlie, I think, came twice to Chartwell. They got on rather well. And he was a very, very diverting, charming man. I remember him in the front hall, just before he left; quite suddenly he became Napoleon. He put on a hat, I think a trilby, this way on, you see, and he suddenly was Napoleon. The other thing he did was, he suddenly fell flat on his face. He did a stage fall, and he did it just to amuse us. I was absolutely staggered. It was great fun.'

Another visitor was Lawrence of Arabia who used to come on a motor bike dressed as Aircraftsman Shaw. 'He was absolutely charismatic. What I do remember, very, very clearly – and you can see how this would affect a child; I was twelve or thirteen – is that he'd arrive on his motor bike in his aircraftsman's uniform, and once Papa said to him, "Do remember you're a Prince of Arabia", or something. And one night he came, he arrived on his motor bike, and he came down in those marvellous robes of a Prince of Arabia. I remember as a child. Can you imagine?'

Looking rather like Peter O'Toole? 'Looking exactly like Peter O'Toole. When I saw the Lawrence film I thought it brilliant to have got those extraordinary eyes. I don't remember him saying anything very interesting, but I do remember this wonderful transition, which rather stunned me with pleasure and surprise.'

Then those war-time speeches. 'The Battle of France is over: I expect that the Battle of Britain is about to begin.'

Lady Soames said, 'I certainly heard the one about the So Few – the So Many, the So Few. But what I do remember is that extraordinary summer when we all behaved in a sort of normal way, but we talked about the invasion as if it were a sort of slightly tiresome thing that was going to happen and sort of spoil the crops, you know. I found in my diary the other day where I've written down, "Papa says that the invasion, if it's going to take place, will certainly be in the next two or three days." This is why I like these photographs which were taken at Chequers when we were expecting the invasion. This was five minutes in the sunshine. Of course one never really hoisted the awful things that would have happened, but we'd had fairly sharp object lessons in what we might have expected, from Poland, so we can't have thought it was going to be a teddy bears' picnic.'

And then the Fall of France, when Churchill was flying off to meet the French government in different places; and when France would not hold firm, he was shattered, and wept.

I asked about de Gaulle, whom Lady Soames must have met when she was at the embassy in Paris in 1968-72 and, much earlier, when he came to England in 1940. 'There is a story,' she said. 'I hate telling apocryphal stories. I think this is true in fact, that my father had seen de Gaulle, and though he didn't realise of course the actual role de Gaulle had played, he'd seen de Gaulle at meetings. And Papa apparently passed de Gaulle in a doorway, and said "Vous êtes l'homme du destin." He sensed, he couldn't have known, he sensed, that this was someone who wasn't going to give in quite so easily, wasn't going to lie down.'

The maid came in to tell Lady Soames there was a telephone call from her sister's house. She returned and said she must go to her sister immediately. Next day the death of Sarah Churchill (Sarah, Lady Audley) was announced. Lady Soames is thus the last surviving child of Winston Churchill.

—October 1982

THE ENTERTAINERS

CLINT EASTWOOD
The Man with the Palaeon Cortex

To Claridges, that notorious hotel of the wild West End, to see Clint Eastwood, lean, 6ft 4in hero of Westerns, anti-hero of Dirty Harry cop movies. Now and again in his films he says a few words, and everyone listens. Most often he keeps his silence, and everyone listens to that too.

In his suite he sat back real easy, though with his back – no doubt by instinct – to the wall, and his hands hanging loosely by his hips, and I asked him about a brief scene in *The Outlaw Josey Wales* when, after God knows what hardship and slaughter, he just touches with cupped hands the hair of his waiflike leading lady.

An Eastwood silence followed. Then he said, 'I just think the gesture is – it's his – it's a – it's a – expressive way of affection. It's just like there's no reason why a big man has to be any less tender than a small man, or a truck driver any less than an accountant, because, sometimes, men who are fairly sure of themselves don't mind showing tenderness.'

To do justice to Mr Eastwood's way of speaking you need a kind of musical notation. The timing counts for a lot. And when he says Yes (and he is very good at one word answers) it won't do to transcribe it as Yes, but Yeah won't do either. It's almost Yep, but with the 'p' barely sounded. Uh huh is, however, a fair transcription of one of his most characteristic remarks.

I began by saying that Eastwood was a very English name, and asking how far he could trace his family back. Never done it, he said; perhaps afraid of what he'd find out; all he knew was his father was English-Scots, and his mother Irish.

What about his young days? There was a scene in a film of his called *Honkytonk Man* where the hero, played by himself, says that his early days were all right, no, they were the happiest of his life, even though they were spent in emigrant shacks, drifting round with Okies, refugees from the Oklahoma dustbowl: hadn't his own early life been something like that?

'Well, I didn't live in quite so bleak a situation as this fella did. He was kinda drifting around, a starving musician, song writer.'

But hard times? 'They were some hard times. I had enough to eat.
I was very young though. I didn't – my parents were those who had
to worry about it all. I know my mother once told me that they, she
and my father, gave up eating on some occasions. But most times I
remember them getting by OK.' They were in California. His father
got a job at a gas station where Sunset Boulevard meets Highway 1
down by the ocean. He still has a picture of his father there, in a
pump jockey outfit. As for himself, well, he says, smiling his distant
High Plains smile, he never was much out of work until he became
an actor. Before that he always managed to scrounge up something.
But no, he didn't remember these bad times with any bitterness,
because he was not much of a man for the past. It just wasn't too good
a time. Then Mr Eastwood said nothing at all and slowly ate an
apple. This economy of word and gesture is congenial to an Englishman like me, but I did remind him, after a while, that there was
silence. (Laughter.) The laughter came from an audience consisting
of a studio executive, a studio publicity girl, and a reporter from the
New York Times wangled in by Columbia-EMI-Warner to sit and
listen.

While Mr Eastwood was in his apple-eating and therefore slightly
laconic phase, I mentioned to him John Wayne, actor (Eastwood:
'He played some Westerns also'), and then we turned briefly to the
Cherokee Strip, which had belonged to the Indians, was then bought
by the US government, and in 1893 was the scene of a land race,
when would-be settlers lined up at the start and then rode hell for
leather to stake a claim. It's a sequence out of a hundred Westerns,
only in that particular race Mr Eastwood thinks his great-great-
grandfather took part. A lot of the riders, he said, would get a piece
of land, and stake it out, and sell it right away. They were in it for the
ride, and for the profit, and not all of them for the land. He didn't
know what his great-great-grandfather was in it for.

This brought us back again to *Honkytonk Man*, where in one
sequence an old man surveys the scene of that race, and sees it has
now all turned to a dustbowl. I think it is time to describe this film,
which I have mentioned before. It is not a Western. It is set in the
1930s, when this singer, a man in his forties but near the end of
everything, is driving east, back to Nashville, Tennessee, where he
has an invitation to audition at the Grand Old Opry. The man is a
natural singer, but breaks down coughing in the middle of his
audition. He has come all that way just to fail. But some recording
company people hear him, and offer him a flat twenty dollars a song
to record for them, which he does for two days, between coughing

bouts, and then dies. But he has at least left his records behind. It is a classic American tragedy.

'Thank you,' said Mr Eastwood. It was only the second of his twenty-eight films in which he died, and, as he puts it, the film died with him. It was not one of his box-office hits. The fans prefer him to live. He too was moved by the film as he made it. 'Yep. It's like he's waited just too long. He's a consumptive, and it's catching up to him.'

This was a film which he both starred in and directed, and I asked how much of a free hand he had with it.

'Complete.'

Nobody from the studio had suggested it might be more commercial if he put in such and such a scene? (Silence.) 'Several people made the suggestion that he maybe didn't have to die at the end.'

My God.

We talked a bit about his latest release, a sexual thriller called *Tightrope*, a film which needed a Hitchcock to direct it, but didn't get one. Mr Eastwood plays a cop (not Dirty Harry) who is himself familiar with the girls of New Orleans cathouses, and finds himself investigating a series of murders of these girls. It is complex. At some points it is conceivable that the cop himself may be the murderer. What's interesting about this film, when you talk to Mr Eastwood, is how emphatically he condemns the sexual predilections of the character he plays as decadent. He is not, after all, emphatic about much. It is not his style.

But surely it was fantasy, I said: and, if it were decadent, at least stylishly decadent? Mr Eastwood would have none of this. 'He's sort of willing to accept whatever the style of the moment is, with the girls. He allows himself to get into a decadent situation, but I don't think he's pleased with himself. He's weak that way.'

My guess is – and it is a guess on the sole evidence of a few films and an hour's conversation – that Mr Eastwood is a puritan, with all the sexual intensity that implies, as is abundantly demonstrated in the caress of the girl's hair with which I began this piece. It was at this point in the interview that he talked about tenderness, and from that we went to instinct, and he became absorbed in a consideration of the spirit and the brain. It happened this way. I said I believed he had once said that everyone had to have an edge, and that his edge was instinct. He thought he might have been paraphrasing something from the film of *Josey Wales*, but anyway he guessed if he did have a strong point, instinct was it.

And if you started analysing instinct, it would be gone? 'Yes. It's something – gut, or soul, or heart, or whatever it is, wherever you want to place it, wherever it comes from.' And then he said he supposed it was the brain, and was leaning forward, cupping his hands again, this time holding in them an imaginary brain. Laughter from the audience. He was absorbed and took no notice.

'There are several sections to the brain,' he said. 'There's the palaeon cortex and the neo cortex. Ancient man was just a palaeon cortex. And then the brain evolved and it became neo cortex, which gave him the power of analysis, and pondering different things. But still the palaeon cortex of the brain exists, and that's where animal instinct lies.'

And he was strong in palaeon cortex? 'I probably didn't get any of the other.' He was smiling that withdrawn High Plains smile again.

Then he said people who were politically aligned, Left or Right, people who were dogmatic and hard-core, tended to be boring. They became obsessed, couldn't talk about anything else, and were sure that anyone who disagreed with them was a fool. They could only talk to their own kind. We then got on to violent demonstrators, of whom he has been reported to disapprove. 'It seems like in the quest for peace people can get so rambunctious that they become killers. And it's like people in the quest for religion. In the name of God they slaughtered – but which God is right, mine or yours? You're pro-life, you're a pro-lifeist, but you bomb an abortion clinic, and risk killing somebody? How pro-life is that?'

We changed tack, and I reminded him that Norman Mailer had once said he (Eastwood) had the face of a man who could be a murderer or a saint. 'He wrote it. I don't analyse my face. Maybe that quality has worked for me somewhere down the line.'

Was it true that, as a director, he tended to use fewer takes than most others? 'Yep, I think so. When I see the take I like, I print it and walk away.'

I said I once watched Charlie Chaplin, years ago, directing *The Countess from Hong Kong*. As a young man, Chaplin must have made hundreds of films in one take, or two takes, but with *The Countess* he was taking ten. 'Yep. Maybe he didn't know where he was going to go next. Maybe that wasn't his prime moment in life. I don't think it was. I saw the film. Who knows what happens? A person's living all this time, he's done all these films, he's got to the point where people would speculate he's some sort of a genius. And right away — what better word to ruin a person? In the early days he had to move; he probably liked the spontaneity. I'm always trying to make it in one take.'

Now I came to the question I had waited to ask. In *Josey Wales* there comes a moment where Mr Eastwood is cornered by four hoodlums, and invited to surrender his guns, taking them out of their holsters, real easy, and presenting them butt first. He does this, but as one hoodlum makes to take them, the guns are whipped round by a miraculous sleight of hand, the hoodlums are dead, and Josey rides again.

'Right.'

Could he really do that?

'Uh huh.'

But I wanted to know, as a matter of simple mechanical curiosity, whether for that shot he did need ten takes, and dropped the guns nine times out of ten, or whether he could do it straight off.

Mr Eastwood looked at me real cool. 'Years of playing in *Rawhide* [Laughter], day in day out, six days a week, you're constantly – you constantly – and after a while you get so you can kinda . . .'

He said no more. The explanation was complete.

And was he in fact a decent pistol shot? 'Okay.'

I gestured across the room, suggesting a target. 'We wouldn't want to take him out,' said Mr Eastwood, mistakenly assuming, I believe, that I was setting up the *New York Times* man. (More laughter.)

No, I said, that clock face. 'Sure. You bet.'

It was a small, Frenchy clock, about twenty-five feet away, and it would have been a very good pistol shot. 'You bet.'

He could do it with a .44 Magnum? 'Oh, easy with that. It might take out the mirror behind, and make it uncomfortable for the man in the next room. [Laughter.] Take the face right off that clock.'

As I was leaving, Mr Eastwood said he hoped his eating of that apple, which had admittedly been a crisp one, hadn't showed up too much on my tape. At the door, he offered me my pick from a basket of fruit that had just been delivered for him. I took a very crisp apple, and, though it would no doubt have been precious to the Clint Eastwood fans still waiting in the snow outside the wild West End hotel, I kept it and ate it on the way home, real slow.

—January 1985

In April 1986 Mr Eastwood was elected by a landslide to be mayor of Carmel (pop.5000) a small coastal town south of San Francisco where

177

neon signs, traffic lights, snack bars, and ice cream cones are forbidden as unecological. The job pays two hundred dollars a month. Mr Eastwood said he would be taking a two-year holiday from film-making. He also said he had no further political ambitions, but his supporters saw him as a second Reagan.

GERMAINE GREER
Buck's Fizz and Polymorphous Perversity

Germaine Greer is offended by the cover of her new book, *Sex and Destiny*. She loathes it. It takes the form of a woman with wide-open, straddled, lengthened legs so that the whole figure resembles a gigantic wishbone. She says it was even worse at first, because the figure had long hair, a slightly come-hither expression, and large round breasts. She told her publishers it was sadistic, and not on.

'Sadistic?' they asked. And she replied, 'How do you make a wish on a wishbone?' And they replied (and here Miss Greer telling the story imitated the lisping voice of a child), 'You bweak it.'

So the design was slightly modified so that the figure *might* be taken to be androgynous. Then, she says, the publishers took refuge in total inaction, told her the salesmen liked it, and so on, and so there it is. She loathes it.

We met for lunch at Brown's hotel in Mayfair. Miss Greer is striking, in a way that no photograph will convey, and in a way that her writing does not convey either. She will have to forgive me for saying she has the instant animal attraction I remember well in Billy Graham, only she is more rapid. And she is polymorphous. Polymorphous is a word she likes to use, though not about herself. In an hour and a half with her I saw at least two forms of Greer. When we talked about this and that, or about her family, she was a shining companion. When she got on to her book she used words like 'disinformation', and assumed quite another shape.

Well, we had met in the hotel lounge, she had given that awful and quite meaningless cover its just deserts, and after a while I suggested we should go into lunch and she should bring her drink with her.

'I'll swallow it,' she said, drinking down her Buck's Fizz, 'and bring it in that way.'

We ordered from a vast French menu. She evidently speaks an accentless French, which she demonstrated by speaking it to the waiter. The waiter then asked me if there was a room number.

Miss Greer, very fizzy: 'Wouldn't it be fun if there was a room number? Do we look like we're sharing a room?' I asked her about her father, who was a newspaper advertising manager in Melbourne. And her mother's father, she said, was an Italian salesman, the best salesman in his area, who sold Kia Ora. Here she broke into fluent Australian: 'Kia Ora Tomato Sauce. Kia Ora Pineapple Pieces.' His mother had so many children she didn't know their names. Well, one evening he had a heart attack in his car. His wife, Alida, hadn't spoken to him for forty years. So he sat unconscious in the car, for two days, with his face against the steering wheel.

Dead? 'Dying.' He was taken to hospital and his wife, Miss Greer's grandmother, was asked if she didn't want to go and say goodbye. 'I haven't spoken to him for forty years,' she said, 'and I see no reason for starting now.' Miss Greer said unforgivingness ran in the family.

And her mother's grandmother, she said, was a beautiful Danish woman with a mass of honey-coloured hair who was a lady-in-waiting or a maid or something in one of the Kaiser's households, in Hamburg. Miss Greer thinks she was an adventuress. Anyway, this honey-coloured woman emigrated from Hamburg to Australia, followed by her two men, one a Prussian and the other a Dane. She is supposed to have married first one and then, on his death, the other, but in fact had two husbands at the same time, and they settled in Bendigo, which is a gold town, and ran the Golden Swan hotel, which is now the YWCA. There was also an Irishman, who was kicked in the head by a horse at the Bendigo races and had a silver plate in his head, and the story was that the honey-coloured woman's daughter (who became the unforgiving Alida) was the daughter neither of the Prussian nor of the Dane, but of the Irishman. 'Which as far as I'm concerned,' says Miss Greer, 'is just as it should be.'

One of Miss Greer's later ancestors became Australian minister of munitions in the First World War, and wanted to write the family history, but Alida, who was more fly, burned the lot in a panic, lest, says Miss Greer, 'he should deliver it into the hands of the cormorant public.'

It was Miss Greer's childhood ambition to go to university, to be an intellectual, and to leave Australia. By the time she was twelve she spoke three foreign languages – German, French, and Italian. She had learned some German and French at school, and talked with Germans on the beach and with a German boy on the train. When she was eleven she met her first Italians, at school. She played with them, and within a year was speaking Italian. The first good-looking people she saw were these immigrants. She saw women with their hair knotted and their ears pierced and wearing black dresses, and thought Gee, they were terrific; they made her mother look like an off-duty barmaid.

Miss Greer, just about here, began to say we knew Britain had supplied mustard gas to Iraq, at which I, wishing to get away from something of which we both knew nothing, asked her instead about the high days of feminism in the 1960s. Was it true that she had worn the springs from old diaphragms round her wrists, as decorative jewellery?

She said it was in 1960, and it was to upset people.

In 1960 she was, what, twenty, twenty-one? 'Uh huh. Didn't have many worn-out diaphragms? Correct. But I had one or two. Didn't do it very long. They weren't very attractive to wear, and I didn't have enough money to have them gold-plated or anything.'

But the background to this, she said, must be understood. She and her friends were Sydney libertarians, anarchists. Nobody had authority over any other person.

A mish-mash of nineteenth century Russian anarchism? 'Not a mish-mash. It was the real McCoy.' Anyway, whenever there was an abortion to be got, it was the one plea for money that had to be honoured regardless of whether you had any connection with the pregnancy. Because this was expensive, they were anxious to keep the number of pregnancies down, and therefore they taught people to use a diaphragm.

The Marie Stopes of Sydney? 'No, we weren't allowed to preach. We were not allowed to tell anybody what to do, and I still don't tell anybody what to do. I'm sick of being blamed by people for what they did. No, but they don't usually blame me; they praise me. But I didn't want anyone to leave their husbands, did I?'

What had she meant when, in *The Female Eunuch*, published in 1971, she had said the cunt must come into its own? 'What I didn't mean was that it must be sanitised . . .'

Not sanitised for our protection? 'Exactly, I didn't mean it was to be sanitised and made perpetually available, troops for the use of. If I said the cunt must come into its own, I thought it must begin to express its own sets of priorities, instead of capitulating to somebody else's set of priorities.' She thought that, today, even fewer women than in the 1960s were doing what they really wanted to do to make the best use of their mental and physical powers. More and more women were swopping one kind of oppression for the men's kind of oppression, and actually increasing the oppression of both parties.

Women, she said, were working at monotonous, taxing, and immobilising jobs, and being grateful for it.

But so were men as well? 'I would not deny it. But women do it cheaper, and that's a problem for both sexes.'

We jumped somehow to romantic love, and Miss Greer, amused, asked what women would do now that they have rediscovered that they really like romance. I see the difficulty. To take the highest of romance, does she not write in her book that to modern man (by which I take her to mean modern woman as well) Tristan and Isolde seem simply neurotic, since anxiety inhibits orgasm, and orgasm is seen as everybody's right and bounden duty? She plainly believes nothing of the sort herself, and I asked her if she were not moved by *Tristan and Isolde*.

'I only like the *liebestod*,' she said.

That's when the man is dead. Miss Greer at times can't resist being plain perverse, as when she throws in, amused again, that some works of D.H. Lawrence are, wouldn't I agree, seminal?

She had said unforgivingness ran in her family: was she herself unforgiving? She said she could forgive treachery but not disappointment. As I discovered, I was about to disappoint her. It happened this way. I had misunderstood her to be in favour of a return to chastity, at which she declared she was sick and tired of disinformation and this time would nip it in the bud. She was not in favour of chastity for its own sake: the question was whether there wasn't some virtue in restraint, in particular if such restraint enhanced sexuality itself.

'Look,' she said, 'the point of the book is that it's an attempt to disrupt our certainty that our Western way of life is the pinnacle of human achievement.' There were places in the world where restraint was part of the structure of society, and she'd seen bringers of the Western way of sex arrive in Bombay wagging condoms, and shouting and screaming, 'Come on, come on, what you should be having is more orgasms, more sex.'

Then she said she did not, actually, give a shit about us.

Us? 'The rich,' she said, indicating the restaurant. 'The people who are sitting in hotels like this, eating this food, the people who live in this country.'

She then said, out of the blue, that she did not think her book was as hermetic as some people seemed to think.

Hermetic? 'Yes, incomprehensible. It's not a series of riddles.'

Now I had not said the book was incomprehensible, but since I could see no single theme I had been taking a topic here and there and putting it to her. I said that this business of the bringers of Western sex descending on India was something she seemed to find evil: her word, evil.

She said she would read the passage out to me *slowly*, It came at the end of a chapter called 'Polymorphous Perversity'. She said she was disappointed with me because it was just like talking to someone from the *Daily Express*.

Yes?

She read out the first sentence of the passage, and then, after saying it had lots of words in it which I might not understand, read it again, and then read seven sentences in all, with commentaries of her own between them. I have to summarise. The last seven sentences of the chapter proceed by what she calls Aristotelian logic to demonstrate that the Western preferences and beliefs described are a kind of mental chaos, and therefore evil.

The waiter had left us alone for a while. I had been so intent on Miss Greer's Aristotelian logic that I had not noticed her glass was empty. She seized the wine bottle and filled both our glasses. I suppose my very noticing of this is an admission of an instinctive chauvinist prejudice that men are the pourers of wines and the dreamers of dreams.

Anyway, I was surprised at her use of the word *evil*, and, taking another tack, asked if there were not a sense of disgust which ran through the whole book: the expense of spirit in a waste of shame, and all that?

Miss Greer said it was possible for a man to debauch his own wife. If she had a man who brought home a vibrator, she'd throw him out with it.

Yes, I said; she did have a certain vigour.

Then she talked about a woman who was looking for tenderness and closeness in a relationship – 'relationship', she repeated, in a mocking American accent – 'and found instead that she was simply being fucked.'

But that wouldn't be particularly good for the man either?

'Depends. My husband, he suddenly started talking to me as if I were a whore.'

What happened? 'I left him. It was just a game, you understand, and I'm sure I took it much too seriously, but I sure didn't like it.'

(That was a long time ago. Miss Greer married in 1968, it lasted only three weeks, and a divorce followed in 1973.)

We talked about libido, which she defined as the desire to know, the love of the world and the going out to *meet it, energy, élan vital*; not lechery, which was the final remains of the libido of exhausted people.

We then sat over coffee, chatting about congenial things like *The Spectator*, of which she said she recently declined the editorship; then, all amiability again, and unforgivingness forgotten, we got up from the table, and she went into the hotel lounge to meet her next interviewer.

—March 1984

NORMAN MAILER
The Perfect TV Commercial

'Reagan,' said Norman Mailer, 'he's a bunkum man. I think he's even unaware what a conman he is because I don't think he understands economics. He's an actor. He's good enough to do soap operas, which is what he's doing. I'm sure he's a perfectly pleasant man, as far as that goes. Marie Antoinette was doubtless a very pleasant lady. But he believes America's a magical place, and that everything will turn out all right. That's what they used to tell us in B-movies fifty years ago.'

Then Mr Mailer went back to his own life and times in Brooklyn in the 'thirties, when his father, who was an accountant, a little man, five foot two or three, used to come home in the evenings and his kids used to go down and meet him and ask, 'Did you find work today, Dad?' He would shake his head quietly, and Mr Mailer still remembers the look in his father's eyes. That was real, but then there were the B-movies where everything always turned out right.

'Ronald Reagan, he made those movies. He grew up with them. He believes in them. That's what he's selling America now. And America's always been the religion for most people in America. You know, America's the true church. He's the high priest of that church. The trouble is, it's not a church that's taking care of anything.'

Mr Mailer is a most amiable man to meet, a decent chap. He has given a thousand interviews and must be sick of it all, but never showed this for a moment. He is described, in one of the quotes on his book jackets, as a bum, but he is a bum who tends to wear pin-stripe suits made by Jones, Chalk, and Dawson of Sackville Street. He says his third wife, Lady Jeanne Campbell, took him there years ago and they've made for him ever since.

As to his being a bum, that had been written by a female American film critic, the Queen of American film critics (and American critics take themselves seriously, much more seriously than English ones). He had said she was a woman you wouldn't make a pass at no matter how drunk you were, and she replied in kind.

Anyway, we had started lunch with a few words about Germaine

Greer, because we were at Brown's and the last time I lunched there was with her, and she is a woman at whom a Mailer hero would definitely make a pass.

'Very odd lady,' he said. 'I always like her more or less than I think I'm going to. I think she almost can't stand people arriving at a given state of feeling towards her. You know, if she feels they hate her, she's going to undo that. If they love her, woe to them.'

I recalled that when *The Naked And The Dead* was published here in 1948 the *Sunday Times* said it was not a book a man could leave lying around lest it should fall into the hands of his womenfolk, and he said he loved the word 'womenfolk' in that sentence. We had come a long way since then. The change in language was often the best way to measure a change of history.

We got to Mrs Thatcher, and the Brighton bomb, and Mr Mailer said she was the stuff of which great figures are made. If she had a bit of heart and a bit of wit she would truly be a great woman. He followed her (for the *Mail on Sunday*) during the 1983 election, and had to admire her. She was the best politician he ever saw on the stump. But in another way she scared the hell out of him. 'You know,' he said, 'the real prospect for England, in a funny way, if this keeps up, is to become two countries. To have two fifths of the country, up north, seething perpetually, totally dissatisfied – how can that end up? They're going to get angrier.'

One of my abiding memories of Mr Mailer is hearing him say, sometime in the mid-'sixties, that it was only a question of time before the first act of fornication was shown on television, and that the question would then be, could we look our wives in the eye afterwards? I had always taken this as meaning that in Mr Mailer, who is Jewish, there lurked some part of a Calvinist conscience.

'Well,' he said, 'what I meant by that was, were they screwing better on stage than you're screwing your wife.'

I said I had obviously misunderstood him.

'The trouble with my remarks is that they're too damned double-edged.'

I had thought him beset with conscience.

'I get beset with conscience, but not on that occasion. I was thinking, if you take your wife along and you see a sexual athlete tooling a woman on the stage, how do you stack up afterwards.'

Couldn't you just say to yourself, well, the man on stage was a professional? When I watched cricket at Lord's I didn't mind that players were better than I was. 'Well, I'm not English. I'm American. We see all things as possible. We don't allow anyone to be better than ourselves.'

But here I think Mr Mailer's own recollection perhaps did him less than justice, because when I referred later to the cuttings files I saw he was reported as having asked, 'Would we feel tender to our wives afterwards?' And that is a different thing.

We briefly skirted the cruel American concepts of equality and of the right to the pursuit of happiness, both disastrous to those who believe in them, exchanged a few remarks about sexual obsession, and then came to one of Mr Mailer's tests of character – the big man who could knock people about but doesn't. He embarked on a yarn about his friend Tom who had once been inter-collegiate light heavyweight boxing champion at Georgetown. Well, they were in a bar, and Tom had his girl with him. A man came in and started pestering her and she made distress signals to Tom. Tom gently remonstrated with him. 'All right, outside,' said the man. They went outside.

'I was there,' said Mr Mailer. 'The fight lasted about two punches. So what did Tom do? He's bending over the fellow who's waking up, and he says, "Fellow, don't feel bad about this. You were out-matched. I used to be very good at this." That's my idea of a gentle-man.' (Much laughter.)

On, then, to the matter of Changing the Consciousness of the Times. Twenty-five years ago Mr Mailer said he wished to write a book to effect such a change. Had he been serious? He said he had been. Was he still? He was; on a good day he thought he might already have done it, on a bad day that he had not. But if it had been achieved it was not with one book but with many, bit by bit.

Well, what books had in the past made such a change? *Sister Carrie*? He thought not: that had changed the literary consciousness of the times, but that was a smaller feat, also accomplished by men like Bellow, Cheever, Updike, Styron, and Gore Vidal. But Mr Mailer thought that, to a degree, and through the body of his work, he could make the larger claim. How? 'I think what I've done for the con-sciousness of the times, if you insist that I speak for myself, is that I've given it an awareness of how awful the engines of aesthetic destruction have become. I've been the one who's been crying out against modern architecture for twenty-five years.'

Here he condemned airports that looked like universities that looked like prisons, and went on to condemn plastics as something that debased the real standard of living – 'which is how much sensuous pleasure we take in the moment to moment of our days.' Take garden parties, he said, where you were served drinks in plastic glasses. He didn't know if that happened in England but it did all the time in America. As drinking men we would both know what that did to the fun of the occasion, dulling the senses, deadening the spirit.

So he wanted the real thing? He would like his women to dress, say, in cotton, silk, or wool? He said he would, and spoke some feeling words about women who walked round encased in two prisons, the first of airless, synthetic fabrics, the second of deodorants to hide the consequent reek of sweat. He had been doing his best, one quarter effective anyway, to fulminate against the onrush of technological nonsense.

The novels of Mr Mailer's which gave me pleasure are the early ones, *The Naked And The Dead* and *The Deer Park*, and I was discourteous enough to say so. He said those hadn't changed any consciousness, but *Ancient Evenings*, the one before last, set in ancient Egypt, might have done.

But *Ancient Evenings* didn't get read, did it? 'It certainly didn't give immediate consumer satisfaction,' he said, laughing aloud at these words and then telling me where they came from. He said there was this Cadillac salesman who was running down European cars, saying they were giving you all the wrong things, like acceleration, and handling, and braking, whereas what people wanted was immediate consumer satisfaction, by which he seemed to mean automatic locking and so on.

Then Mr Mailer told me the motor car story which, if it did not have a faint tinge of Hemingway about it, would be pure essence of Mailer. He drives a BMW 535. Well, one icy winter's night he took an exit off a superhighway, and he took the exit at forty, maybe fifty, too fast, and then he saw that there was a hairpin bend on the exit road, and trees behind, and there was ice on that bend.

So he braked as hard as he could, and then took his foot off the brake before the car hit the ice. 'I knew then it was up to the car more than to me, and that thing went round without getting into a spin, and it made the turn and came out. And I turned to my wife and said, ''Honey, thank God for the good old BMW'', and we both burst into laughter because it was the perfect television commercial of all time, you know. But it's true, if I'd been in a piece of Detroit machinery I'd still be up in those trees.'

—October 1984

CATHLEEN NESBITT
Separate Beds

Cathleen Nesbitt celebrated her ninetieth birthday yesterday. She made her first appearance on the London stage in 1910. She met Sarah Bernhardt. Name any English or American actor or actress of the last seventy years, and she has worked with them. She knew the Lunts before they knew each other. She still takes all the work she is offered. This summer and autumn she played at the Chichester Festival. When we met at her flat in London a few days ago she had just returned from the retake of some television thing about which she declined to talk, saying she didn't want to be libellous.

As a little girl she went round the world on the tramp steamer of which her father was captain. She remembers herself, aged eight or nine, sitting with her back against the warm funnel reading *Little Women*. She always had her head in a book, and was never seasick. By the age of ten she was a well-travelled girl. She remembers seeing Constantinople by moonlight. When she first saw Paris she thought: 'How like Buenos Aires.'

Back home at school in Belfast she shared the history prize of twenty pounds with Helen Waddell, who was to become a celebrated medievalist, and took herself off to Paris to learn French. Later she became an au pair at Lisieux. Her arrival there, in the dark, sounds like something out of *Villette*. Back in London at drama school, she suddenly felt one day that she had authority as an actress. She was playing the part of a French children's nurse. She *knew* she looked as a French nurse should. Even now, she says, when she has been at it for seventy years, if she feels she is absolutely right for a part it gives her a confidence which communicates itself.

She certainly had confidence, though she was shy. In 1911 the Abbey Players came to the Court (now the Royal Court) in London, and needed understudies for an American tour. With the rashness of the very shy, Miss Nesbitt approached Lady Gregory, saying; 'I am an actress.' She recited one stanza of 'The Lake Isle of Innisfree' to Yeats, who said wearily, 'Enough', and she had the job, and made her first visit to America.

Once again back in London she played Perdita in Granville-Barker's production of *The Winter's Tale*. Henry Ainley tried to seduce her while his mistress was having a baby. Harold Macmillan saw her Perdita and later told her how enchanted he was. Rupert Brooke saw it several times, asked to be introduced to her, and was at a party given by Eddie Marsh, later Sir Edward and a friend of Churchill and of Maugham. So began their affair.

Brooke was not the languishing romantic that his reputation has made him. 'Oh, good God, no,' says Miss Nesbitt. 'He walked miles and taught me to walk miles.' At weekends they always took a train somewhere, then walked, and sometimes stayed overnight at a hotel. Mrs Belloc-Lowndes once saw them together in a railway carriage and felt a wave of magnetic attraction between them. Miss Nesbitt understands this. Today, in a tube or a bus, she sometimes watches people, and, if they're not conscious they're being watched, can feel what they are thinking about or hear what they are saying to themselves in their minds.

Brooke read her Donne and Shakespeare. She remembers Shakespeare's terrible sonnet beginning: 'The expense of spirit in a waste of shame/Is lust in action . . .' Brooke had written a poem called 'Lust', which the publishers retitled 'Libido'. In the copy he gave her, and in all his presentation copies, he crossed out Libido and wrote Lust in his own hand above it.

They always had separate hotel rooms. 'That would seem so strange today. He would come in and talk to me, and sometimes talk away, and lay down his head and go to sleep. But he would always go back to his own room. So we were never lovers together in the modern sense of the word. I suppose in today's climate we'd be living together from the word go.' As it was, she was getting over Henry Ainley, and Brooke was recovering from an unhappy affair with a girl at Cambridge, who had lived with him, who had suffered a miscarriage, and with whom he had fallen out of love. So they were both thinking that this time they wanted to be certain.

There were long absences during their acquaintance. They met in December 1912. The following May he went across America and to Tahiti, where she thinks he was in love with an island girl. Something in his letters told her this; she knew that he had found something warm and comforting. When he returned in May of 1914, the war was upon them, and soon he was dead.

'And then I suddenly felt, "Oh, it's so awful. He's gone, and there's no issue. And if I'd had a child by him . . ." ' They last met at Yarmouth, when he came to see her on tour. They were very close then, and she thinks that if his leave had been longer they would really have been lovers.

Did he want children? 'Yes.'

Did Miss Nesbitt still feel she ought to have had a child by him? – 'Still, I sometimes do. Particularly when I used to go and stay with Mrs Brooke, his mother who's godmother to my son [by her later marriage]. When I brought the baby there to spend weekends, I'd feel a little pang. If only I'd had more sense ...'

After Brooke's death she went again to America, in the middle of the war. A Russian called Boris, who sold tickets for a travelling company, told her she had the face of a lioness cub and asked if it was true that she was still a virgin. She was then about twenty-nine. She thinks the Russians are amazing people. She told him she was. He was astounded, and very gently said goodbye.

Late in 1920 she accepted Charles Morgan's invitation to play Cleopatra in the Oxford University Dramatic Society's production of *Antony and Cleopatra*. Her Antony was Capt. C.B. Ramage, President of the Union, who proposed to her and was accepted at the dance the night after the play. 'I'd only met him in the time we rehearsed. He was very good-looking. He'd a beautiful voice. ... I suppose playing Antony and Cleopatra together we got closer than if we'd known each other as just people who met in the street.'

Ramage became a Liberal MP in 1923, and then, says Miss Nesbitt, there was an election and something called the Zinoviev Letter, and he lost his seat. He never won another. They had a son and a daughter. They separated in the late 1940s.

Throughout the 1920s and '30s, and throughout the war, Miss Nesbitt's career went well. In 1949 it flowered when she played in *The Cocktail Party* in Edinburgh, London, and then in America. She settled in New York, going out to Los Angeles every now and again to do a film or some television. It was only in 1969 that she returned to live in England again. She can't remember how many films she has been in. She would have said seven or eight, including *So Long at the Fair, Three Coins in the Fountain,* and *Separate Tables.* But the other day an American told her she had appeared in thirty-seven. 'Pictures I'd completely forgotten. One with Maurice Chevalier. Films with – what was that girl's name? – Margaret Lockwood.'

In all that time she got on with nearly everyone, which is a miracle for an actress. Marlon Brando (with whom she played in *Desirée*) was a darling, with charming manners. 'And there's an actor called Nicol Williams, always known as a wild man. I played with him in New York and found him enchanting. He's very talented. He played Uncle Vanya terribly well, and afterwards he sang to a steel band. Nothing he can't do.'

She and Bryan Forbes were talking one day, and saying what nice people actors and actresses were, on the whole. She said she could think of only one she had actively disliked, and he said so could he. They both wrote the name on bits of paper, and it turned out to be the same name, that of the late Nancy Price. 'And I must say,' said Miss Nesbitt, 'she was the worst bitch.' In 1938 Miss Price was producing and also acting the mother-in-law in *Thérèse Raquin*. The posters said: 'Nancy Price in *Thérèse Raquin*', and the names of the other actors, including Miss Nesbitt, came below. One day Miss Nesbitt arrived at the theatre to discover that all the bills had been changed, and the name of the play altered to *Thou Shalt Not Kill*.

Why? – 'She thought it made me too important, since I was playing the part of Thérèse, that the play should be called *Thérèse Raquin*. Must have cost her the earth to change all those bills.'

Miss Nesbitt still goes to Los Angeles whenever she is asked. In her flat she has an Emmy, a television Oscar, which is in two bits because she dropped it. It was for a Hollywood version of *The Aspern Papers*, an absurd nonsense, she says. They changed the name to *The Masque of Love* and set it in Los Angeles, and she made herself up to look like Clara Bow and doesn't think they noticed. There could not, she says, have been much competition, because it won an Emmy.

And now she is ninety. She says everyone seems to think that ninety is very important. 'In Bertrand Russell's phrase, at least I have the gift of survival. When he was in his early seventies people thought he was a silly old gentleman, but when he lived into his nineties, veneration crept in. And so it is, one finds. People in the theatre, which is a great democracy of age and everything else, do rather bow down and open doors for me, and things which they never did before.'

But one's friends all died. 'I was talking to Rebecca West today, and we were both saying how many of them had died. I mean – Gladys Cooper, Edith Evans, Sybil Thorndike. And then you suddenly think back, and all the people you knew when you were young, they've all gone.'

But did she feel the loss of friends with the same passion as she had when she was young? – 'I personally find I can take things, both good things and bad things, with less passion really. Because I remember I was surprised. A very good friend, Zena Dare, I met her in the King's Road one day and we made a date to get together the following week, and two nights after I was listening to the six o'clock news and they said Zena Dare had died. And if that had happened thirty or forty years ago, I think it would have taken weeks before I got over it, but as it is, it gave me a shock, and I thought: "Oh God, we were going to see each other", but ...'

—November 1978

MICHAEL CAINE
The Romantic Englishman

Michael Caine, having exiled himself to Hollywood for six years and become not just a British star but an internationally bankable name, has bought himself a house near Henley and is soon coming home.

Yes, but when he left hadn't he said, 'Please don't change; keep everything as it is,' and hadn't everything changed? 'Oh God, yes. Out of all recognition. Except the weather and the English countryside. I very much make my own life, so I come back to the English countryside, and that's where I spend my time. I used to live in Brixton, yes I did, Stockwell Park Walk, behind the Odeon, when I was married for the first time. I worked in a laundry. England has changed in the places I came from, but not in the places that I want to come back to.'

We were talking in a pub next to the studios in Cricklewood where he is filming in *The Whistle Blower*. He acts the part of an ordinary, patriotic man whose son works at GCHQ Cheltenham. When the son dies in dubious circumstances, Caine starts lifting stones and discovers underneath the seamy world of the secret service. The producer is Geoff Reeve, who made that memorable film *The Shooting Party*.

In the pub, someone dumped a plate of hot pie in front of Mr Caine. Yes, he said, the working-class places he came from had changed. He was born in St Olave's hospital, Rotherhithe, which had since been changed first into a lunatic asylum and now into film production offices. And Mayfair – when he left it was full of rich Americans but now was full of rich Arabs. The English had always changed one set of rich foreigners for another set of rich foreigners. But Henley, that hadn't changed in three hundred years.

Just behind Mr Caine's seat was a glass case containing a large stuffed bird. That, he said, was a pheasant. During the war he was evacuated to Norfolk, and lived in the squire's house, below stairs.

Eating leftover pheasant? 'That's where I got the taste for all that stuff. I used to drink the wine. I used to finish off the cigars. They'd leave a long cigar end. I got all my ideas of the country, and that's what I'm doing now. Obviously, if you were a psychologist, you'd say, I see where his frame of mind has got to. I'm basically returning to my childhood in a different position. I'm the squire. And I think my entire life has been spent trying to get back to the squire. That's what I think I'm doing.'

And he remembered also the happy days of his childhood in the East End, with his mother cooking, waiting for his father to come home from the fish market where he worked as a porter. He tries to recreate that for his own family, and now he's the host, because he's the only one with any money.

My own plate of pie arrived. Caine looked at it. 'Well, it's edible,' he said, and we talked about Korea, where he did his National Service in the infantry. He remembers it as a war of trenches and no-man's-land, like the 1914 war. On patrol you always kept your finger inside the trigger guard, because if you took it out and something happened, you'd be so scared and your hand would be shaking so much you wouldn't be able to get it back. People never thought of things like that. In the movies, wars were always well thought out by the director. In real life it was confusion, abject terror, and laughs, hysterical laughter. One particular night he thought he was going to die. He remembers what his thoughts were – that they were going to pay dearly for it, and he would take as many as he could with him. He always reacted like that to any form of attack.

Back from Korea he became an actor, got bit parts on the stage and in films, and married his first wife, an actress, and then, in his twenties, he went off for six months to Paris. Why? 'That's when my father died. And my marriage broke up, and I was out of work. So I took the insurance money on my father, and went to France.' He chose France because it was nearest, and there was a train from Victoria every night. The fare was seven quid. He only went for a week, but kept on staying, taking odd jobs, working in bars or washing up. When he came back his agent had a part for him, and though things weren't smooth, they weren't so rough.

But by the age of twenty-nine he had been acting for nearly ten years and only had half-a-crown in his pocket. Then came *Zulu*, which made his name and paid him four thousand pounds. He was still two thousand pounds in debt, but then he made films like *The Ipcress File* and *Alfie*. 'So I was very lucky. It's very difficult when you're a young actor. We're all going to have our failures, but suppose you have your first five failures when you start?'

Mr Caine has always wanted to meet Kim Philby. He was once

going to play him in a film but the finance suddenly and mysteriously dried up and he never knew why.

Suppose they met. What would he want to know? 'I want to know *why* deep down. And does he think the system he's living under is better? I remember Armand Hammer [the oil man] saying that he was sitting next to Lenin just after the Revolution, and Lenin said, "Do you think it will work?" And he said No. And Lenin said, "Neither do I." And that's one of the few things Lenin was right about. None of it works.'

Mr Caine then gave reasons why Russia, with resources almost equal to the United States, didn't work. He is deeply and instinctively suspicious of socialism of any kind. I reminded him that just before he emigrated he had expressed his fear that a British electorate would vote in a government which they might then find themselves unable to vote out.

'Ha ha. They did it. They voted for Maggie Thatcher.'

Yes, but . . . ? Mr Caine said yes, he had meant a government of the Left, and the Left was then getting extremely Left. When you lived in America you realised how much socialism there was in England, and how massive it was, though it might be benign. In America, any English socialist would be regarded as a communist, even Mr Kinnock. Mr Scargill would have been assassinated.

He thinks the old feudalism has been replaced by a new feudalism, that of the paternalist state, to whom people look for everything. 'You go into a council house. You say, "That wall's been peeling since I was last here three months ago." And people look at you and say "Yes, They won't come and do it." It never occurs to them to buy a pot of paint and do it for themselves. I agree with the NHS, and pensions, and looking after the disabled, all these things, but when you get to fully-grown, fit men, that's where my foot comes down with a firm thud, because I actually think that the paternalism of the government has now been woven into the minds and thinking of people.'

Making them helpless, did he mean? 'Yes. I come straight from America to here, and I watch and I listen, and people say the most extraordinary things. "When are *They* going to get me a job?" Who are we talking about? God . . .? "*They* have got to do something." What would do something for you is, you get up at half-past eight in the morning, and you go out and make a product at a price the world wants.'

What? 'Cars.'

But surely nobody wants British cars? 'They buy Rolls-Royces and Jaguars, because they are made properly.'

Wasn't he saying, in effect, what Mr Tebbit has been misreported as saying – 'Get on Your Bike?' 'Well, I suppose I am in a way, because the apathy here, the lethargy, is quite incredible.' We had, said Mr Caine, exported our good people. In America, you ran into any number of people who were doing well there, having been educated at this country's expense.

Himself among them? 'It includes me, yes. Or, it doesn't any more, because I work here too. What I am saying is, you can't run a system where you export your best people. I mean, if I was going to be sick, or out of work, I'd be running back here, because it's an easy touch. I certainly wouldn't be sick or out of work in America. This is the easy touch here. Which may sound wonderful, but as Ronald Reagan said – when they asked for higher social security in the United States, he went on television and said, "Ladies and Gentlemen, your fellow Americans cannot afford to give you a raise".'

At this I did object that it might be fine for Mr Caine to hold such views, since he was abundantly capable of looking after himself, and he took that point. But it's also only fair to point out that, though the American views he expresses certainly coincide with his own, he is reporting the real views of the great majority of Americans who, with their own instinctive get-up-and-go, and instinctive belief in the efficacy of self-interest, cannot for the life of them understand the British dependence on an ever-present state.

'It is impossible,' says Mr Caine, 'to explain to Americans, as I'm always being asked, "How come you build state-subsidised housing for the poor, with garages? Why would a man who can afford a car want a state-subsidised house?" '

This is a question which is plainly near to Mr Caine's heart since in the 1970s, when he had a flat in Mayfair, and was paying vast rates, and 83% income tax, and 98% on investment income, and was, as he says, helping to build garages for those who were too poor to buy their own house, he wasn't, himself, even allowed to park in the road outside his own flat.

Mr Caine did not love his own exile. The first year, when he could not by law return to England for one day or one minute, was murder. He paid his American taxes, where the top rate is 50%, and says there is no way he could have gone to Switzerland and lived in misery on a mountain in order to pay only 7%. And though he succeeded well, and made the bankable international name he wanted, he was still afraid that he might be the first European millionaire refugee to emigrate to America and come back broke.

He thinks it reasonable to have left when he had to pay 98%, but will be happy to pay the present top rate of 60. But his principal reason for coming back is that his daughter Natasha, by his second wife Shakira, is now twelve, and he wants her to have an English education. At the moment she goes to a convent school in Beverly Hills, where the nuns wear mini-skirts. Mini-skirts? Well, he says, skirts look shorter on a nun. It's a good education, very strict, but children in Hollywood grow up tough. He is looking for a private English day school where Natasha can be educated to the hilt.

So now, he says, his new house is being done up and he is on his way back to England.

To be a squire? 'Yes, to be a squire.'

Did he behave like a squire? 'I hate hunting. I hate horses. I live a very reclusive life actually. I know one or two people in the village and they come and see me. The vicar and I are great friends. I don't want to be a squire. I don't even believe in squires, but what I'm doing is living the way squires used to live. With the gardeners, and staff. I haven't got a pony and trap though.'

—February 1986

ED KOCH
The Hi! and Mighty

Ed Koch, Mayor of New York, the ultimate politician, had been mentioning his vitality, energy, leadership, and intellectual honesty, and was about to launch into an anecdote about bubonic plague, when he broke off and said, 'Look, I don't want to sound arrogant, so if you'll leave the arrogance out when you write this I'd appreciate it.'

So, OK. I'll play fair by stating that in private Ed Koch is not arrogant. He just believes what he says. The man has been nominated by both the Democratic and Republican Parties for a second term as mayor. There's no way, God willing, that he can lose the mayoral election, and Koch believes and says that God is great. We were talking after a day in which he had been campaigning at a pace no English politician would even try, and indeed we'd been talking on and off throughout the day, between his street-corner speeches. It was a day in which he'd been asked three times when he was going to run for president, which he had three times denied, each time with suitable conviction.

The long day started at a flea market at Stuyvesant Town, near what looks like a vast block of GLC flats. He kissed a black baby, congratulated its mother, reached out to shake every hand in sight, and proceeded at a brisk walk yelling, 'Hi!' Then uptown to march about three miles in a German-American parade up Fifth Avenue past the homes of the very rich, all the time throwing his hands high in the air and yelling, 'Hi!' and 'How'm I doing?' at the top of his voice.

He is a man of the people – even of the rich. He marches in shirt sleeves partly because that's his working uniform and partly because a jacket isn't comfortable if you want to throw your arms in the air every ten seconds. Then, when he goes on to Shea Stadium, in Queens, he and his entourage travel in three nondescript cars – no limousines for him – and with no visible police escort, only two discreet bodyguards. At Shea, before he pitches the first ball in the afternoon game for the Mets against the Cardinals, he sits down to a salad lunch and talks about liberalism.

'I have,' he says, 'been mugged by realities.'
What?

Look, he said, he'd always been for reform, always a liberal. He'd campaigned for Adlai Stevenson and George McGovern. He was still a liberal. But now he had gradually come to see that the people who had opposed him twenty years ago had been right.

'I've been mugged by reality.' How? 'Suddenly you look about you and you see people are frightened, people are assaulted.' The pendulum had swung too far, so now he wanted more cops, quicker trials, and longer gaol sentences.

He'd tell me the best story. He was at a meeting of senior citizens and an elderly lady asked him about mugging. ' "Ladies and gentlemen," says I to them, "a judge I know was just mugged this week, and do you know what he did? He called a press conference, and told the reporters that this mugging of his would in no way affect his future decisions in such matters." And do you know what happened? An old lady got up at the back of the room and said, "Then mug him again." '

Why was Mr Koch running as both Democrat and Republican? He was bound to win as a simple Democrat anyway. He gave the routine answer that, at this moment in history, he needs Republican support and Republican money from Washington and from Albany, the state capital. This doesn't quite wash, since neither Washington nor Albany will love New York City any more no matter how many nominations the mayor has. I asked if it wasn't a bit like dual nationality, and he said no, and went on to talk about Fiorello LaGuardia [Mayor, 1934-41], who though a Republican had been supported by labour unions and had been 'the most admired mayor of the modern era, by me and by everyone who talks about mayors'. Mr Koch wants to be admired. He admits to vanity.

At that moment, a waiter appeared bringing champagne from 'a gentleman at another table'. Honest Ed Koch declined, but when pressed said, 'OK, what year?', and had glasses poured for his aides and for me, but not for himself.

What did he remember of the bad days of the Depression, when in 1931 his father, who was a Polish immigrant furrier, went broke? 'I was poor. I didn't know I was poor, because we were all poor.' It was Koch Brothers. His father and his father's brother and their families all lived in a two-bedroom apartment in Newark. Nights, the young Koch worked a hat-check concession. He remembered all right.

Yet, from these beginnings, and after being in Democratic politics for years, he could still get on well with so stringent and witty a reactionary as Mr Buckley? He said he certainly could. 'Regretfully, some other people I know, if you're not in agreement with them, think you're a devil incarnate. The liberals, and I am one and don't ever want to run away from that, are more intolerant of differences of opinion than conservatives. They will forgive you your aberrations. The liberals will not.'

The talk then turned to Prince Charles, whom Koch had lunch with in June. 'Decent guy,' he said. 'But I was thinking to myself, why did I have to ride in the open car with him? [Laughter.] But he cancelled that, not me. Not in person, but it was their [the British] cancellation.'

So they brought out the armour-plated Cadillac, and everything was fine. The only trouble was that the mayor later told everyone what the Prince had said over lunch. 'So,' said Koch, 'I was told later that I'd violated some protocol, that you're not allowed to repeat what a prince says to you. Well, I don't hang around with princes.'

To come back to that morning, what about the people who had asked him when he was going to run for president? 'Never. I took an oath, before the Western Wall in Jerusalem, never to run for anything but mayor.'

Was he so much a practising Jew that the oath would bind him? 'I'm not an orthodox Jew, but nothing is holier than an oath before the Western Wall.' The Wailing Wall? 'The Western Wall. Let's put it this way. We were wailing when we didn't own it.'

So he had taken an oath in good faith. Might he not, also in good faith, find good reasons to change his mind? Apart from the oath, he said, other offices – senator, vice-president – didn't interest him.

So then we went out into the stadium, where Koch kissed two babies, shook hands with a priest, autographed a baseball for a nun, stood with his hand over his heart and sang the words of the 'Star-Spangled Banner', tossed the first ball, and then set off miles across town to Main Street and Roosevelt Avenue, Flushing, where he dived into Sokal's Deli. A plastic soap box was produced – the same object later appeared in other places, being carried around for the purpose – and Koch stood on it and addressed the customers.

'Everyone raise their right hand.' Everyone did.

'I solemnly swear. Say it.' They repeated the words after him.

'That I'm going to run to the polls.' They repeated this too.

'And vote for Ed Koch.' They swore that too.

Having thus secured the promise of thirty-five votes, and explaining as he went that he used to make them say, 'So help me God', but now thought that was going a bit too far, Koch was on his way to a street corner at Forest Hills, and then to a block party at Jackson Heights, Queens, a district which has come down in the world. There he was asked about the subways, said he was trying, and neatly side-stepped to the Brooklyn Bridge, which is showing some, but fewer, signs of falling apart. Rome, he remarked, had not been built in a day, and New York would not be rebuilt in a year. This being accepted by everyone as reassurance, off Koch swept again, but this time to Gracie Mansion, a lovely classical house of 1797 which is the mayor's official residence. He came out on to the veranda in shirt-sleeves, poured from a two-litre bottle one glass of warm plonk, which he freshened with ice cubes and gave to me, and then sat back and looked down the lawns to the East River.

Could New York, I asked, be rebuilt at all? Was it rebuildable? Sure, he said. Maybe not the way he'd like to see it, but sure.

I recalled a letter to the *New York Times* in which a reader had lamented the loss of the subways to criminals and to neglect, and the loss of the parks in which many people will not now walk, and reminded him of the cartoons in the *New York Post* of collapsing buses and collapsing subways, which were funny because in essence they were true.

'Am I saying it's not true?' He was not. He was saying that, true as it was, the city was rebuildable, and if he were a demagogue he would be saying it would all be put right more quickly. No, he wouldn't, I said: not if he wanted anyone to believe him. 'Hum,' he said. 'I'm not a demagogue either.'

It was then that he talked about vitality, his ability to work forty-eight hours at a stretch And then catch fifteen minutes sleep on a car ride. He could sleep anywhere. He could sleep on a board. 'I am also honest intellectually, and that's *rara avis* in politics, to be honest. I won't say I'm the only one, but it is not the coin of the realm.'

Then, after his request to leave the arrogance out, he got to bubonic plague. The definition of a plague, he said, was that if you didn't have any, and then you had one, that was a plague, but any-way the story was that the health department called him up one after-noon and said there was plague in town.

'Bubonic plague? I mean, that's the *Middle Ages*, right? Well, this guy from Arizona, this nut, saw a dead squirrel, picked it up and threw it at his wife. Either he got a flea off the animal, or the god-damned thing bit him with its dead teeth, nobody knows. So I said, OK, now, what happens if . . .' And the city doctors told him that bubonic plague was not catching. It was only if it travelled to the lungs and became pneumonic plague that it was catching.

'So,' said Koch, telling a story his aides and bodyguards had obviously heard before, 'so I said, this is easy, I can do this on one foot.' He called a press conference. 'I said listen, am I lucky. We have a case of bubonic plague. Jesus, imagine if it were *pneumonic*. All right?' (Much laughter.)

'It's true. I wasn't conning anybody. I said bubonic plague. It's dangerous to the guy that has it, but he can't spread it. I told everybody. There was no panic. Now can you imagine if rumours spread that the city was keeping quiet the fact that it had bubonic plague in town? People would leave. Isn't that so?'

And then the bridges would fall down under them as they fled? 'OK. Right. But explain to the people. Don't con them. Don't lie.'

We talked briefly about his often expressed view that the British should get the hell out of Northern Ireland. He said he believed it, so he said it. He was no diplomat. Did he say aloud everything he believed? 'Regretfully on occasions, yes.' Did he ever lie? 'Oh, I'm sure I have, but not that I can remember, and that is the truth. And never politically. It has to be very rare that I'll even obfuscate.'

On principle, or . . .? 'Well, both. On principle, and secondly it's always found out, and then you look like a schmuck. I mean, I do have credibility.'

Then we left for Central Park, where he was to open an open-air concert by Simon and Garfunkel. On the way in the car, he recalled parades where he had been booed. 'In my own head,' he said, 'I'm saying that I'm at Yankee Stadium (as a player) and though they're booing me they're really cheering me. Because I know the people at Yankee Stadium. They're booing simply because that's the tradition. So I psych myself up.'

But was that intellectually honest? 'What I'm telling you is that most of those people in that parade really liked me. I know that they're booing me but they don't really mean it. New York is a little street theatre. It's not made up. It's part of my personality.'

Then the traffic got so dense that the Queen of England would have had to walk. Koch, and his aides got out and, holding on to each other so as not to be separated, pushed through the dense crowds of young people in the park up to the site of the concert on the Great Lawn of Central Park.

There – such is the power of democracy and pop music – he cheerfully hung around for forty minutes while a couple of pop stars got ready. Then, when he was at last called upon to do his bit, the second most conspicuous holder of elected office in the United States, and possibly the second most powerful elected official after the president, walked on stage unannounced and simply said to a crowd estimated at four hundred thousand, 'Ladies and gentlemen, Simon and Garfunkel.'

That was all. That's *Realpolitik*.

—November 1981

202

JOAN SUTHERLAND
The MGM Lioness

Joan Sutherland is briefly in London to give a thirtieth anniversary gala concert at Covent Garden. The anniversary is that of her own first appearance at the opera house in October 1952. We met in the Duke of Bedford's retiring-room at the opera house, very grand. She came in, after morning rehearsals, happy and full of the news that she is going to become a grandmother next spring, and we talked about this and her early memories of her mother.

As a young child she was brought up at Point Piper near Sydney, in a house overlooking the greatest natural harbour in the world. 'Where a thousand ships of the line could lie at anchor,' she said. 'Wasn't it Captain Cook said that?' From the house it was 111 steps down to the beach to have a swim, and 111 steps back again, and they sometimes thought it was just as well to take a cold bath in the house and avoid the climb.

At the age of six she had a pink portable gramophone, and records, of Caruso, Galli-Curci, and Melba.

And listened to them?

'Oh yes, because my mother sang. I sort of grew up under my mother's feet at the piano. From about the age of three I used to sit there. I was a pest. I think when I used to imitate her, she used to say, "Not quite like that, don't make that throaty sound." I think she was of the ilk of Stignani: without being presumptuous, I know she was. She was seventy-four when she died and she could still sustain the most wonderful line from the bottom to the top of the voice and back again.'

Her mother never did sing professionally. I remembered Pavarotti saying that his father, given the opportunity, could have made a career. Dame Joan said she thought that was true. Her own son Adam, who is now twenty-six, could sing, but had no desire to, and was working as a hotel manager in Australia. 'And if my mother had sung, perhaps I wouldn't have sung. I would have wanted to do something else. I'm going to be a grandmother, so maybe Adam's child, male or female, may sing. It may skip a generation.'

Joan Sutherland was born in 1926. I asked if she remembered the slump of the 1930s, which is as bitter a memory in Australia as in any part of Wales. 'We were talking about it in the car this morning. My father was in trouble really, though he didn't let on, in debt because the people who owed him money couldn't pay him. Although we lived in a hot climate we didn't have a refrigerator. We didn't have a car.'

She remembers the war. Japanese midget subs penetrated the harbour but most of their bombs were duds anyway, and the good old joke in those days was that things 'Made in Japan' never worked. Her uncle was an ARP warden, but they didn't take it seriously, and ...

At this point lunch was brought in and placed on a Regency sofa table, which, happening to be Regency brand-new, had a high and unnatural shine. One of its flaps also had a slope to it.

'Oh my godfather's,' cried Sutherland in that magnificent voice, and for a second we both watched a bottle gathering momentum across the table, sliding upright, about to dive over the edge. It was caught barely in time.

'Oh, yes,' she continued. 'The war. My brother was in Malaysia, captured, missing for quite some years. We realised it was serious when we saw so many Americans about. And we were all knitting Balaclavas which seemed ludicrous out there, but it was for the Russian campaign. We were untouched, except, when you think about it, there were so few men about the city. From nineteen to forty the men were missing. It was sort of strange.'

She learned shorthand-typing because singing was too precarious. She went in for competitions at the Sydney Eisteddfod and in the Mobil Quest, run by a petrol company, and in 1951 sang her first operatic role in *Judith*, at the Sydney Conservatorium. Thereafter she told her boss she was going to leave to take her chance at singing. He said just as well, or he'd have sacked her since she was taking so much time off singing in Queensland and wherever. She left with his blessing and came to London. She married Richard Bonynge, a fellow Australian, and they lived in a fifth floor flat in Notting Hill with a piano bought for fourteen pounds.

'Flat you couldn't call it,' she says. 'Digs.'

Thirty years ago she joined Covent Garden, where she sang smallish parts for years. But the cuttings show that for one night she did, after only two months with the company, sing Amelia in *Un ballo in maschera*, by any standards a splendid part. She remembers they had two Germans and a South American singing the role, and all were suddenly indisposed.

'It was Christmas,' she says. 'Now, whether they really were indisposed, or whether it was Christmas, anyway I got an SOS. I hadn't done it from memory. I said, "But if I go on and make a mess of it, you'll kick me out." And then I said to myself, "Well, if I *don't* go on and make a mess of it they'll still kick me out."'

So she did it.

And that was when she was on about £10 a week? 'Not *about*. £10 it was.'

She made her name, as the world knows, in the title role of Donizetti's *Lucia di Lammermoor* in 1959. It was the first production that had ever been staged at Covent Garden with her in mind. It was the first role she had ever sung in Italian. Certainly she knew that Melba had sung Lucia at Covent Garden in 1888, though she doesn't think they had that precedent in mind, and she didn't think Melba had too much of a success.

No?

'Times have changed. I mean, things are so different even in the years that I've been singing. I mean, prima donnas would say . . . Or even, in Patti's case, she used to send her maid, who would say, "Madame Patti stands here and then Madame Patti goes there," and the rest of the cast could go to hell.'

Did she sometimes wish she could send her maid? 'No, I like to know what's going on around me.'

Most of Dame Joan's performances are now conducted by her husband, but in earlier days there were other conductors; and there were conductors and conductors. Now, Serafin, wasn't he once so delighted with her for some reason that he gave her sixpence, that being all he had to hand to give her? 'He did. He put his hand in his pocket [here she mimed a man searching in a waistcoat pocket], and took out a sixpence, and said, "That's for your E flat." It was in the old chorus-room upstairs.'

Had she still got the sixpence? 'No, I think at that stage I must have needed it for something, probably to go towards the baby's milk or something. And now that baby's wife is going to give birth, I can't believe all those years have gone.'

That was Serafin. What about Maestro Santi in Venice, about 1962? 'Let it be known,' she said, 'that I'm not the only person to have a disagreement with that gentleman.'

Well, I said, La Fenice had put out a statement about the disagreement between conductor and singer over tempi, and then said, and this was no doubt in translation from the original Italian, that she had left with 'furious mumbling words in English, made incomprehensible by an Australian inflexion'. What were these famous furious words?

'I probably was calling him a silly old four letter word or some-thing. I do know that just before that the chorus had walked off the stage.'

Next Monday, she said, she'd be in New York, at the Met.

What for? 'For *Lucia*.'

What, after the concert in London on Sunday? 'That's something that kills off the singers, that dreadful jet plane. In the old days Richard and I would go by ship, four days, a nice little laze on the ship, play Scrabble or cards, or read some book, or Noël Coward would be on the ship. Now you get on one of those hideous planes and get there as fast as you can, and I think it's what kills off the voices today. The young people, they're finished before you've even got a chance to hear them.'

She and Noël Coward were great friends. They lived next door in Switzerland. She thinks he was Massenet-ish in some of his com-positions, and has recorded some of his songs. Not 'Mad Dogs and Englishmen', though. He never would let her do the humorous songs.

We ate our chicken salads and talked about this and that. She loved *The Ring*, but wished directors would stop being inventive and do it the way Wagner wanted. And she had seen a production of Rossini's *Semiramide* where the designer thought it should all look like an Assyrian frieze. Well, that was all very well, but all the men ended up walking round with what looked like fibreglass mantelpieces on their shoulders. Horrendous to spend so much money on such rubbish.

We talked about her *Merry Widow* in Sydney and then Mr Bonynge arrived. Covent Garden backstage is a maze, and it had taken him ages. 'Ah,' she said, 'you didn't live in the hole for years the way I did, you see.'

Did they, I asked, know Patrick White, Australian novelist, Nobel prizewinner?

Mr Bonynge: 'Sure do.'

Sutherland: 'Naughty old devil. He's a bitter old fellow, with no reason at all.'

At this, the remains of lunch – bits of salad and chicken bones and all – began to slide again, and this time would not be stopped. We picked up the bits from the floor.

Well, I said, Mr White had written about a dinner party at Kirribilli in his autobiography, and aggrievedly recorded her as having assured him she'd never read a word he'd written. (This is in a book in which Mr White also takes the opportunity to rubbish the Queen, the Duke of Edinburgh, a former governor-general of Australia, and his friend Sidney Nolan.)

'I *tried* to read his books,' said Dame Joan. 'It was infuriating trying to get to sleep at nights, reading the books, so I mean . . . '

Mr Bonynge: 'She told him she loved *Thornbirds*. That was what did it.'

Dame Joan: 'It wasn't that I was putting down his own writing at all.'

Mr Bonynge: 'Just being your truthful self.'

Dame Joan: 'What did he expect, after a performance? What had I done? *Norma?*'

I said I should love to have seen Mr White's face.

Mr Bonynge: 'His face was a picture. [To his wife.] It would have been far more of a picture if you'd told him you'd sat up till four o'clock in the morning reading it.'

We talked about Australia and Europe. They now live in Switzerland, but now wouldn't want to spend twelve months a year there, or in Australia, or anywhere else.

So Joan Sutherland will sing her concert on Sunday – Verdi, Bellini, Rossini, and other things. Then off to the Met to rehearse Lucia. Next year she returns to Covent Garden to do *Esclarmonde*, a little known Massenet, and then, some time after that, a final *Lucia* at Covent Garden.

She looks like her portraits. She looks, as her husband puts it, like the MGM lion. And next May she'll be a grandmother.

Mr Bonynge: 'She's not bearing up too badly, is she? Next year, she's doing *La Fille du Régiment*, at the Met, and she's decided to rename it La Grandmère du Régiment.' (Laughter.)

—November 1982

FRANKIE HOWERD
Delusion, Love, and Work

'Smoked pungent beans?' pronounced Frankie Howerd, reading aloud from the menu. 'Transylvanian stuffed cabbage? Gipsy quick dish? Fascinating, I must say. Minced goose? Never heard of minced goose before. I'm going to try that goose. Can't come here and eat fried liver.'

Mr Howerd is a great stand-up comic. Undoubtedly the exotic words on the Gay Hussar's menu in Soho are congenial to his manner of delivery, but if you suggested he could ad-lib a comedy routine just by reading the menu – as it has been said of others that they could raise a laugh by reading the London phone book – he would reply with resigned impatience that he never ad-libs, and that his scripts are all carefully worked on and rehearsed. I never met a man who used the word 'work' so often.

Since, for me, his most memorable work was on the wireless in 'Variety Bandbox', I asked why he didn't even mention that show in his *Who's Who* entry. He said first that he had never read it, and then, 'I'm in twice, actually. I'm very proud.' So he is. If you look up *Howerd, Frankie* you are referred to *Howard, Francis Alex*, which happens to be next to *Howard, Elizabeth Jane*. When he started on the halls, after the war, there were too many Howards in people's minds, Trevor Howard, Leslie Howard, so he changed the *a* to *e* thinking that at least people seeing the name on a theatre poster might think it was a misprint, and at least notice the name.

'But people still write to me as Howard,' he says. 'Oh they do indeed. They do. Especially if they want free shows. Charities write to me as Mr Howard. This is the essence of tactlessness.'

The goose arrived. 'When I was young,' said Mr Howerd, 'I was more delusional than I am now.' Growing up before the war in south London, he was given a part in a church dramatic society show at the age of thirteen, in a play called *Tilly of Bloomsbury*. There he was coached by a kind lady who helped him overcome his stutter, and one of the churchwardens told him he would become an actor.

What did he see in his delusions? 'Views of what could be. A kind of dream. Great big theatre, I could see that. Then to work in the theatre. Then I'd be a star, and be famous.' He went for a scholarship at RADA, where they gave him some Shakespeare to read, which was disastrous. 'So I thought: all right, if I can't be an actor I'll be a comedian. I'll settle for that thing.'

He became an insurance clerk, but says he was very properly sacked for incompetence. Then in the army, in the war, he applied for ENSA, but they asked him if he was a professional, and he had to say he was not, and they turned him down again. It was only after the war, when he was waiting to be demobbed in Germany, that they were so desperate they sent round a circular saying anybody who could do anything, please report, and then he did get into an army concert party. When he was demobbed, his commanding officer, Major Richard Stone, who was later to become Benny Hill's agent, gave him a piece of paper saying, 'To whom it may concern: I think this gentleman should be given a chance.'

'Where are you working?' asked the agents to whom he showed this letter.

'I'm not working. I wouldn't be here if I were.'

'Sorry,' they said.

Then he did get work, at first on the halls, and then in radio, which could then make a man as famous as television or a record in the Top Twenty can today. At the age of twenty-nine he was a household name. This prosperity lasted for many years, but then the music halls disappeared and radio was overtaken by television. Suddenly he was no longer booked at all. He calls the years from 1959 to 1962 a period of darkness.

'I was terrified. I was very upset. I'd devoted my life to it. I had to give myself a talking-to, and say, "Look, maybe this is what you've got to face up to, and not go on hoping and hoping. And that's it. That's it." '

He looked for a pub in south London, thinking that being a publican was the next thing to show business. One he looked at was in the Old Kent Road. He passed it the other day.

Had he thought, seeing that pub, 'There but for the Grace of God go I?' 'No. That would be rather patronising, I think. I might have been very happy there. You never know.'

He said he was terrified, that he was ambitious but not confident, that it was a time of darkness, so I asked Mr Howerd why the most insecure people seemed to choose the most insecure professions. 'Well, I quite agree with that. When I was younger I was so nervous that people asked me why I didn't give it up. It never occurred to me.

But the survival rate isn't high. But you see, I don't go for all this business of the broken-hearted clown. Because I think a broken-hearted clown would be a damn sight more broken-hearted if he wasn't a clown.'

I mentioned Osborne's play *The Entertainer*, and the comedian Archie Rice, and asked if it seemed authentic to him. 'I certainly didn't think it was me, for a start.'

I should have had the sense to leave it there, but mentioned another play, Trevor Griffiths's *Comedians*. 'Look,' said Mr Howerd, 'all these plays have *backgrounds*, of technical experience or work, which are authentic. Within that background you've got these particular people being written about, but you can't say everybody, even a comedian, is that sort of person. You can't say that every doctor is the same. They're individuals. People who are given the freedom to do what they want are fortunate. I've been given opportunities, some taken, some bungled. I've walked a lot of tightropes, because of my nature. My temperament is an actor's, with its certain weaknesses, and certain fortitudes. As a doctor told me once, doctors need patients as much as patients need doctors. The point I'm trying to make is, actors need to act, doctors need to doct.'

After his dark years Mr Howerd began to work again, in 1963, first with the musical *A Funny Thing Happened on the Way to the Forum*, and then in the BBC series *Up Pompeii*. Fame returned. Now he has written a book called *Trumps*, which I had expected would be autobiographical but which turned out to be a series of funny stories. But at one point he does write, after a dozen anecdotes on love and marriage, that in love there are no winners. He calls this one of the Rules of Howerd. I asked him about this.

'Well,' he said, 'in love there shouldn't be.'

Ah. I had misunderstood him to be saying that in love there were only losers. He had not meant that at all?

'Love is an emotion you can't *use*. If you love someone very much you're very vulnerable. You aren't a winner: you lose control of the situation. If you love your work, if you love doing something.'

But surely we had been talking about people? 'It's all the same thing. It's love. You are therefore to some extent at the mercy of it. Love is an emotion in which you lose your ego. If you do that, you don't win.'

We were firmly back to work. 'You see, if I may say so, actors never talk about performing. They never talk about acting. They talk about working. "Where are you working?" In the old music hall days it was the Book. "My book's full." "I've got a week out." "I haven't got a week in the book."'

210

Did he ever get the feeling, after a long series, that he would never be so good again? 'No, I mean, I never had the feeling that I was good in the first place. You may think this over-modest. But I think it's the truth. I said that when I was very young I wanted to be famous, in my dreams, but that's not quite the same thing as doing it and saying "Aren't I marvellous", because I never thought that.'

Comedy, he said, was difficult. 'If you're going on the stage, in the dark, and things are going badly, there's no doubt about it. You know. You've got intelligence. And you don't need intelligence either. You've got ears. Comedy, you can't computerise it. People tend to cry at the same things, but we don't laugh at the same things. Tragedy's tragedy. But comedy: some people like it sophisticated, even intellectual. Some like visual humour. A lot of people have said to me, "You're terrible." I accept that. All one hopes is that one will have enough people liking one to give one a living.'

And there were vogues. 'Some people are discovered more after they've died. They can become vogues after they die. It happens to comedians. Max Miller's had a revogue in recent years.'

About here, I told a joke of my own, stolen from a New York acquaintance years ago, about the American stand-up comic and the psychiatrist. In America, comics are paid even more than psychiatrists. Well, there was this stand-up comic who went to see a psychiatrist. 'Lie down,' said the psychiatrist, 'and tell me all about it.' The comic did, and now the psychiatrist is doing his act in Philadelphia.

Mr Howerd even laughed a bit, but he would not be drawn into psychiatry, psychology, or anything so earnest. 'You talk about stand-up comics,' he said. 'I think people who do solo work of any sort are obviously more vulnerable. Francis Chichester sailing on his own round the world.'

Francis Howerd then went on to talk about ad-libbing, which he never does. He almost never departs from his script and breaks into something else. Like starting to play Beethoven in the middle of Chopin, he said. There were some comedians, very few, who would work a club audience, provoking a heckler and then ad-libbing, but that was not for him. For him, people heckling out of the dark would be an aggression. It would be like McEnroe playing tennis, and people moving round just as he was serving. Some comedians thrived on ad-libbing; most didn't.

I said many politicians did, and that Mr Heath in particular used to come to life when he left his prepared script and ad-libbed. 'Yes,

211

quite. But that's not the same thing, if I may say so, as being a lovable comedian.'

Then work again. One should take one's work, but not oneself seriously. One should, he said, be a master craftsman, which indeed, he said, he was not . . .

Surely he was? And if he wasn't, why not? 'Well then, that's because I didn't have the innate enough delusion to begin with. Or shall we say my talent didn't reach up to my delusion; put it that way.'

Mr Howerd has just been working in Gilbert and Sullivan's *Trial by Jury*, for a television film. At first he found it difficult to learn the songs.

'I've been used to doing sentences with a certain rhythm which is very much me. Like, "Oh, this woman came, well, depends what you mean by, Ah, now it's strange you should say that." You see, I have my own kind of rhythm. To learn the words of songs is much more difficult. I could learn reams of patter if it were written in the way I speak. The only way I got well known in the first place was my own way of doing, mangling, the English language.'

But he had learned to do the Gilbert and Sullivan by taking home tapes of the orchestra and singing to the music for two hours a day. It was like ballet dancing; you did your exercises every day. You rehearsed and rehearsed, and worked and worked and worked.

In front of a mirror? 'No mirrors. I don't want to be disturbed.'

—September 1982